CITY FOR THE 21st CENTURY?

Other titles available from The Policy Press include:

CITY FOR THE 21ST CENTURY?

Globalisation, planning and urban change

Martin Boddy, Christine Lambert
and Dawn Snape

First published in Great Britain in 1997 by

The Policy Press
University of Bristol
Rodney Lodge
Grange Road
Bristol BS8 4EA

Telephone +44 (0)117 973 8797
Fax +44 (0) 117 973 7308
e-mail: tpp@bris.ac.uk
Website: http://www.bris.ac.uk/Publications/TPP

British Library Cataloguing in Publication Data
A catalogue record for this book is available from the British Library

ISBN 1 86134 048 6

Martin Boddy is Professor of Urban and Regional Studies at the School for Policy Studies, University of Bristol. **Christine Lambert** is Reader in Planning in the Faculty of the Built Environment, University of the West of England. **Dawn Snape** is a Research Director at Social and Community Planning Research, London.

Front cover: the Brunel Centre and Murray John Tower. Photograph supplied by kind permission of Jim Lowe.
Back cover: the Renault Building in West Swindon, designed by Norman Foster and constructed by Ove Arup Group. Slide supplied by kind permission of Ove Arup Partnership, London.

Cover design: Qube, Bristol.

The Policy Press works to counter discrimination on grounds of gender, race, disability, age and sexuality.

Printed in Great Britain by Hobbs the Printers Ltd, Southampton.

Contents

List of tables and figures

Tables

Figures

Preface

City for the 21st century? was commissioned jointly by the Economic and Social Research Council (ESRC) and Thamesdown Borough Council. Professor Howard Newby, chair of the ESRC at the time, and David Kent, then chief executive of the Borough Council, saw this as a fitting way both to mark the establishment of the new Swindon Borough Council which became a single-tier local authority in April 1997, and to mark the presence of the ESRC itself in Swindon, having relocated from London in 1988. The study was intended in part as a follow-up to the earlier book by Michael Harloe, *Swindon: a town in transition*, published in 1975. This originated when he was employed by the Borough Council between 1967 and 1969 as one of the team of officers preparing a feasibility study for the second postwar phase of town expansion. This earlier book provided an authoritative account of the first phase of Swindon's planned expansion in the first 25 years of the postwar period. It also provided a key contribution, more generally, to the study of planning and social policy over this period. One aim of this present study was to bring the account up to date, covering the 25 years since Michael Harloe's earlier work. At one level, therefore, *City for the 21st century?* provides an account of the economic, physical and social development of Swindon itself. It also aims to examine and to contribute to our understanding of broader processes of economic and social change operating at local, national and global scales and of the role in this of planning and the policy process.

Swindon has, itself, been the focus for a series of major research projects funded by the ESRC. The scale and pace of growth and change locally and its key location in the heart of the M4 growth corridor have been such that Swindon has been selected as a case study for a succession of large-scale national research projects. It must be among the most studied places in the whole of the UK. In the mid-1980s, Harloe himself, as an academic researcher at the University of Essex, teamed up with Keith Bassett, Martin Boddy and John Lovering at the University of Bristol, to work on an ESRC-funded case study of Swindon as part of the national 'Changing Urban and Regional System Initiative'. Projects which have focused on Swindon included survey work and case studies carried out in Swindon as part of the national ESRC 'Social Change and Economic Life Initiative' by Martin Boddy and John Lovering, together with Jonathon Gershuny and Michael Rose, then at the University of Bristol. Swindon was one of six localities included in this major national initiative including research teams from across Great Britain. Survey work conducted in Swindon as part of this national study was featured in a range of publications including Rubery and Wilkinson (1994), Anderson et al (1994), Gallie et al (1994a; 1994b), MacEwan Scott et al (1994) and Penn et al (1994). Other projects have included a study of 'Socio-economic Restructuring and Changing Patterns of Long Distance Commuting in the M4 Corridor' as part of the ESRC 'Transport Initiative', carried out by Martin Boddy together with Andrew Leyshon and Nigel Thrift of the Department of Geography, University of Bristol and a study of 'Training Needs and Training Provision' as part of the ESRC 'Adult Training Initiative', carried out by Martin Boddy, Kevin Doogan and John Lovering.

City for the 21st century? builds on this earlier work.[1] Unpublished working papers by Keith Bassett and Michael Harloe produced for the 'Changing Urban and Regional System' (CURS) project in particular provided valuable material for Chapters Four and Six (Basset, 1987; Harloe, 1987a; 1987b). Interviews conducted by various members of the CURS project team with local people in Swindon in 1986 are also quoted in Chapter Seven. *City for the 21st century?* also reflects a considerable volume of original research carried out by the authors in the course of 1996 and 1997.[2] This included analysis of a wide range of data[3] and documentary material. David Gordon of the School for Policy Studies, University of Bristol, carried out original research on indicators of poverty and deprivation, reported in Chapter Seven. Research by the authors also included over 50 interviews recorded with senior managers of the major local employers, elected members and officers of the Borough Council past and present, officers of Wiltshire County Council, and representatives of a wide range of other private, public and voluntary sector organisations in Swindon.[4]

We would like to thank all those whom we interviewed for this study and who provided a great wealth of material – interviews were conducted on a non-attributable basis and in order to preserve confidentiality individuals are not acknowledged here. We have listened carefully to all we were told even if not all those with whom we talked will agree with every conclusion we have drawn. We would like to thank those officers and staff of the Borough Council who not only gave of their time but also responded to our many requests for documents and information. We must also thank all those who live or work in Swindon and who have provided so much material for social research in the postwar years. Those whom we have met have been almost without exception proud of Swindon and its achievements over the years. It is a fascinating and remarkable place. We owe a formal debt of thanks to the ESRC and to Swindon Borough Council for their funding and for their support throughout our work. We would like to thank the two anonymous referees who read and provided valuable comments on the initial manuscript of the book. Finally, we are very grateful to David Worth at the School for Policy Studies, University of Bristol, for producing the maps and figures for the book, and to the staff of The Policy Press for their patience and professionalism.

Notes

[1] The book draws on work carried out under the following ESRC grants: 'Changing Urban and Regional System Initiative', grant number D04250015, 1985-87; 'Social Change and Economic Life Initiative', grant number G13250014, 1986-87; 'Transport Initiative', grant number WD08250013, 1988-89; 'Adult Training Initiative', grant number, C11250012, 1988-90.

[2] It also reflects original research undertaken for the purpose of this book funded by the ESRC under award number 0909600148 and by the former Thamesdown Borough Council.

[3] Unless otherwise noted, data presented in tables throughout the text were accessed via the National Online Management Information System (NOMIS), University of Durham.

[4] Verbatim quotes from interviews are italicised in the text. Quotations from documentary sources are inset in normal type and referenced. All interviews were recorded and transcribed.

one

Globalisation, planning and urban change

Urban change and the development of individual towns and cities nationally and internationally have been profoundly affected over the last 20 to 25 years by a combination of factors, economic, social, technological and political, operating at national and global scales. These factors have impacted at the local level and have provided the context for local change. Particular local areas are not simply, however, the passive beneficiaries or victims of these broader processes of change. Processes operating at the local level combine with and shape these broader processes. Understanding this combination of processes operating at local, national and global scales is essential if we are to make sense of change on the ground in particular places and to understand the broader processes of change themselves.

This, essentially, is the aim of this particular study – to examine the ways in which this broad set of factors operating at national and global scales have combined with policy and action on the ground at the local level. The vehicle for this is a detailed study of Swindon at the heart of the UK's M4 growth corridor (Figure 1.1). The scale and pace of growth and development in this particular locality, economic and social as well as physical, make it ideal for this purpose. So, too, does the extent to which it has become increasingly integrated with the national and global economy and the extent to which its growth and development have related to that of London as both national capital and global city. Initially, therefore, this chapter summarises key factors in terms of globalisation and economic change, planning and the

Figure 1.1: Swindon's strategic location

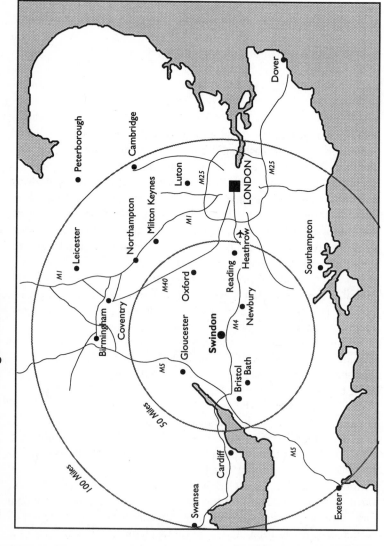

urban system and the main issues which these raise. It then goes on to outline the study itself and the structure of the book as a whole.

Economic performance

The UK economy as a whole has, since the mid-1970s, experienced successive periods of recession and recovery, whether measured in terms of output, employment, unemployment or other economic indicators. Unemployment, nationally, broke through successive historic thresholds, to reach more than 3 million by 1986 and did not fall below the 3 million mark before 1993 (government figures for unemployed claimants). Recovery then saw the total drop to just below 1.6 million by mid-1997. On the other hand, the last 25 years or so overall has been a period of economic growth and employment growth nationally. Particular turning points can, to some extent, be linked either to shifts in domestic policy or to specific shocks from outside of the domestic economy. With the UK economy increasingly tied in to the international and global economy and financial systems, however, the overall pattern of recession and recovery in the domestic economy has, to a major extent, been driven by factors common to national economies in Europe, North America and beyond.

Globalisation

This same period has also seen what some have characterised as the increasing globalisation of economic activity, financial systems and corporate enterprise (Ohmae, 1990). There has been considerable debate over the extent to which these represent truly global processes as against what might be more accurately described as processes of change operating at an international or multinational level (Hirst and Thompson, 1996; Held, 1995). The extent to which globalisation has, in fact, become increasingly dominant over time; and the extent to which the rise of multinational corporations and global financial flows has, in turn, diminished the role of nation states has also been questioned. It is clear, however, that globalisation, to the extent that it stands for major shifts in economic systems and economic organisation at the international level, has had major impacts on particular territories, whether national, regional or local. What also seems clear is the increasing interdependence between processes operating at these different scales. Understanding this interdependence is therefore of increasing importance (Amin and Thrift, 1994).

At an economic level there has been an increasing flow of foreign direct investment, particularly between North America, Europe and Japan (Dickens, 1992; Stallings, 1995). Capital investment has been increasingly mobile seeking out appropriate locations for different elements of overall corporate activities and linking these by air travel and air freight, electronic communications and cheap bulk transport including containerisation. This has resulted in an increasingly complex division of activities between different parts of the globe – an increasingly complex 'international division of labour'. At the same time, a succession of national economies have undergone an accelerated process of industrialisation (South East Asia in particular). Countries such as Indonesia, Malaysia, Thailand and parts of China have been following close on the tail of the more mature 'tiger economies' of Hong Kong, Singapore, Taiwan and South Korea. To these should be added the core urban areas of several of the Latin American countries, with the emergence of newly industrialising areas of Eastern Europe also a possibility (Hall, 1995). This reflects the growing globalisation of technology and information combined with the pursuit of low-wage production sites. It also, however, reflects the rapidly increasing technological and skill levels of those newly industrialising countries. This has resulted in increasing competition for the older industrial areas, including Europe and the UK. It has further added to the international division of labour. It has also added more complex patterns of foreign direct investment both within South East Asia, for example, and from the more developed countries of the region such as South Korea into Europe and North America.

Markets and corporate structures have also become increasingly international or global in scope and increasingly competitive (Stallings, 1995). This has been reinforced both by the creation of wider economic blocs including the European Community, North American Free Trade Organisation and, in South East Asia, the East Asian Newly Industrialising Countries

(EANICS) and the Association of South East Asian Neighbour (ASEAN) countries and also, more generally, by the reduction in trade barriers via a succession of agreements on trade and tariffs. In this context, the UK has increasingly been seen by overseas investors as a platform from which to access European Community markets. Seen from the perspective of specific national economies or localities, globalisation has freed up some elements of economic activity from traditional geographical ties making it increasingly footloose. At one level this has increased the volume of potentially mobile investment. On the other hand, it has generated increasing competition between places as the range of alternatives open to corporate investors has multiplied. Differences between places have in some ways become more critical in the competition for inwards investment.

Industrial change

The high point for the UK as a whole in terms of employment in manufacturing industry came in the mid-1960s. Since that time the national economy has been fundamentally transformed. Major decline in traditional manufacturing sectors has been juxtaposed with massive expansion across a broad range of service industries. In 1971, manufacturing accounted for over 38% of all jobs in the British economy and considerably more in terms of output. By 1993 this was down to only 18%. Service sector employment, on the other hand, grew from 46% in 1971 to 75% by 1993 – three out of every four jobs. There has been massive growth in employment in financial and business services, in media, telecommunications and information-based activities. There has also, over this time period, been dramatic employment growth in the provision of services to individuals and households including health, education, leisure and entertainment. Much of what remains of manufacturing activity, moreover, has itself been transformed, with the emergence of new industrial sectors based on high technology, new materials and new production processes. Driving this transformation in industrial structure have been major shifts in patterns of international investment and competitiveness in different product markets, major shifts in market demand, and far reaching technological change impacting on both products and processes and on the transfer of people, goods and information.

This has been characterised as a shift from an industrial (meaning manufacturing) to a 'post-industrial' society. Fundamental to this has been the increasing importance of information, information processing and exchange as the basis of economic activity, to the extent that commentators have identified the emergence of the 'informational economy' (Castells, 1991; Hall, 1995) or 'network society' (Castells, 1996).

New production systems and new industrial spaces

Also integral to this transformation in industrial structure, it has been argued, has been the decline of economic organisation and production systems based on mass production and the rise of new forms of flexible production system. This, it is suggested, has seen a shift from the 'Fordism' of the archetypal car assembly line, to what has variously been termed 'post-Fordism', 'flexible production' or 'flexible specialisation' (Amin, 1994). Fordist production systems were characterised by large, capital intensive enterprises incorporating successive stages of the production process in an essentially vertically integrated system marked by top-down, hierarchical control and production of standardised goods for mass markets. Flexible production systems, on the other hand, are characterised by interlinked networks of complementary producers and smaller scale batch production for more differentiated and specialist markets. Elements of mass production remain. Flexible production systems, however, increasingly, it has been argued, dominate economic production as a whole. Meanwhile, larger corporations have tended to restructure themselves internally along the lines of such flexible production systems.

Interlinked complexes of flexible producers have, in turn, been seen as the basis for the emergence of dynamic new industrial districts (Scott, 1988; Storper and Scott, 1989). Typically cited examples include Silicon Valley and the Boston Route 128 areas of the USA based on high technology, craft-based production in the Emilia-Romagna district of Italy, and the Baden Württemberg district of Germany, among others. The development of high technology industry in Britain's M4 growth corridor and science-based industrial development around Cambridge have also been cited as examples, although clearly very different in scale to Silicon Valley, for example. The growth of institutional supports and broader social structures, including both governmental and non-governmental institutions, has been seen as important to the success of such regional production complexes. This, in turn, has given rise to the idea of the 'embedded firm', dependent for its success on a wide range of economic and social linkages within its immediate milieu (Grahber, 1993).

There is considerable debate and disagreement as to the nature of these contrasting production systems and the extent to which this supposed shift has permeated economic production overall (Sayer and Walker, 1992). Much of the detail remains disputed and grander models and portrayals of epochal shifts have increasingly been qualified. Models of flexible production systems may capture some elements of change in production in certain sectors of production under particular circumstances but fall a long way short of dominating production overall. The same argument can be levelled against the notion of 'new industrial districts' which can better be seen as particular forms of new production system rather than as any generally emerging form. The debate as a whole draws attention, however, to the important shifts in forms of production which have undoubtedly accompanied economic development over the last two to three decades.

Linked to debates over new forms of production system, new forms of flexible labour market have been seen as increasingly significant. The labour market has been seen as increasingly polarised (Atkinson, 1986; Pollert, 1988). Core workers, it is argued, enjoy job security, career progression and fringe benefits. Those in the expanding periphery or flexible fringe of the labour market suffer temporary contracts, insecurity, low pay, part-time and other variations of working hours contracts to meet the needs of employers. This represents one form of flexibility. Other parts of the labour market are, it is argued, characterised by the 'flexible worker', both multiskilled workers and generalists required to be flexible as to tasks undertaken in the workplace – in contrast to the rigid task specialisation and job demarcation typical of much of traditional manufacturing industry. Again, the extent to which this represents a general feature of the way in which labour markets have developed in the recent decades has been disputed, but the idea of labour market flexibility does capture important elements of employment change.

The changing urban system

The role and structure of cities themselves has been changing. At the peak of the urban hierarchy, cities such as London, which transact a substantial part of their business at a global scale (Hall, 1995, p 21), together with larger national capitals, have reinforced their roles as high level service centres. They have increasingly attracted international finance, legal and business services, together with media-based services, education and healthcare, tourism and entertainment. At the same time, from the 1950s in the USA and the 1960s onwards in Britain and mainland Europe, there has been a marked decentralisation, initially of population and, sub-sequently, of employment and economic activity. Deconcentration around the major global cities – including London – has been particularly marked.

In the case of the UK this initially took the form of suburbanisation, together with some reconcentration around secondary centres within the outer metropolitan area. Deconcen-tration was reinforced by planned decentralisation to the regions, and to the new and expanded towns. A more generalised process of 'de-urbanisation' developed from the 1970s onwards, driven as much by market forces as by any planned strategy. Containment policy, including green belts and more general planning constraint, tended simply to push development pressures further out from London and the South East, leapfrogging areas of constraint. The Census of Population shows that over the course of three decades, London itself, the major conurbations, larger cities and industrial areas of Wales and the North have tended to lose population and employment. The larger urban areas have generally declined most rapidly. Smaller urban areas, particularly those outside of the industrial areas and the South East, have gained both population and employment. The more rural areas – together with New Towns – have expanded most rapidly. This process of de-urbanisation, marked in the 1960s, accelerated in the 1980s and remained strong in the 1990s (Breheny, 1995, p 416).

Changing patterns of job opportunities and employment reflecting both relocation and new investment have been a key factor driving de-urbanisation. The housing market and the attraction of lower house prices in the 1970s and 1980s have also played a part and seem to go some way to explaining the process, particularly in relation to decentralisation around London itself.

An increasing preference for non-metropolitan areas in terms of quality of life may also have been a factor (Breheny, 1995). These patterns of change seem likely to continue. As Breheny concludes: "The evidence suggests that the process is as strong now in the UK as at any point in the postwar period, with accessible lowland and remoter rural areas receiving the greatest percentage and absolute levels of growth." (1995, p 424). In policy terms, as Breheny observes, policy at the local level is increasingly to resist further growth – a NIMBY or 'Not In My Back Yard' strategy. The capacity of localities to resist will depend in practice on the operation of the formal planning system. As Breheny observes, however, pressures for growth, both demographic and economic, are such that the evidence "casts serious doubt on the ability of central or local government to resist, still less reverse, counter-urbanisation trends" (1995, p 424).

The increased development pressure on major metropolitan areas in the 1980s and 1990s also generated new forms of urban development and expansion internationally, together with some evidence of reconcentration in secondary centres within the major metropolitan agglomerations themselves (Hall, 1995, p 27). New commercial sub-centres were established, as with London's Docklands in the case of the UK. There has also been growth in the form of new metropolitan sub-centres some distance beyond the major agglomerations, typically around major public transport interchanges, and there has been the development of what commentators such as Dillon et al (1989) and Garreau (1991) have termed 'edge cities'. These have been seen as multifunction developments oriented largely to road-based transportation and generally lacking any traditional high density urban core as such. Around the major metropolitan areas, these developments have tended to support axial development in specific growth corridors, the product in some cases of planned growth strategies (Hall, 1995, p 29).

Planning policy and practice

Against this background of de-urbanisation and the emergence of new urban forms, commitment to public sector management of urban and regional change via the planning system has been an enduring feature of British public policy. Key features of the early postwar planning system still persist – control of new development based on a comprehensive set of locally produced plans, urban containment and countryside protection via green belts and other protective designations. Regional assistance, on the other hand, has been very much scaled down and policies of managed decentralisation to new and expanded towns discontinued. This, in part, reflected the switch in policy emphasis towards inner cities and urban regeneration from the 1970s on. The essential structure of the planning system as set up in the late 1940s is still recognisable, however. The guiding principles, moreover, remain oriented to efficiency in terms of land use and infrastructure investment, the protection of landscape and amenity and to the control of tendencies to 'market failure' inherent in land and property markets.   The detailed operation of the system has undergone significant change, however, reflecting the changing economic and political context. This capacity for quite significant shifts in orientation and in implementation at a practical level have been increasingly evident since the early 1980s.

In a context of rapid economic development and urban growth in the 1950s and 1960s, physical development frequently outstripped the provisions of development plans.   Central government initiatives related to regional planning and the New and Expanded Towns programmes were in some ways more significant in planning terms over this period than the development planning system.   Responding to this, national planning reforms established a new system of structure plans and local plans intended to be more robust in the face of economic and urban change. Implemented following local government reorganisation in 1974, plans were to be drawn up by local government to provide a basis for both strategic and for more detailed local planning policy. Delays in practice in producing plans, coupled with low growth and lack of development pressure in many areas, however, limited the effectiveness or indeed relevance of plans in practice. The planning system itself then came under increasing pressure after 1979 from Thatcherite governments committed to a New Right agenda of deregulation and free enterprise. Enterprise Zones and Urban Development Corporations were set up in a number of urban areas, taking over control of planning and development from local government. Pressure was also brought to bear on local authorities, generally, to be more accommodating to the needs of the market. This was reinforced by the willingness of central government to override local policies of constraint contained within structure plans and to support appeals from developers against refusal of planning permission by local authorities. In this context, economic growth and a massive inflow of investment into property development in the mid-1980s laid the basis for a speculative boom in development, particularly in the South, facilitated by the government's deregulationist agenda. Boom was, however, soon followed by slump and a period of deep recession in the property market from which the sector was slow to recover.

In planning terms, moreover, the Thatcherite agenda of deregulation proved to be somewhat short-lived. By the 1990s the idea of active planning policy and the need for more orderly management of the development process was becoming more acceptable, particularly given disillusion with the fall-out of the 1980s boom and bust. This was reinforced by the growing political significance of environmental interests arguing for stronger countryside protection and the increased salience of the environmental agenda at global and national level, emphasising resource conservation and growth management. Under the provisions of the 1991 Planning and Compensation Act, the planning system of the 1990s is increasingly 'plan-led'. As a part of this, a comprehensive system of Regional Planning Guidance has also been introduced. There are tensions within the system, however, at a number of levels. In part these reflect reliance on voluntary agreement between local authorities, particularly between district and county-level authorities, whose interests in relation to sensitive questions of growth and its distribution may well conflict. The mid-1990s' reorganisation of local government reorganisation has also fragmented existing mechanisms for strategic planning in many areas, and interlocal conflicts over new development look set to increase. Added to this, there are no clear mechanisms for debating and agreeing the distribution of forecast growth in population and employment between regions. New household projections published by the Department of the Environment in 1995 forecast an additional 4.4 million households in England alone over the period 1991 to 2016. With growth pressures concentrated in southern England (counties to the west and north of the metropolitan area in particular), this is probably set to be the major planning issue in the early part of the next millennium.

Sustainable urban development

As indicated above, policies of containment and formal green belt policy were embodied in postwar planning legislation. Together with 'NIMBYism' and a growing resistance to the continuing encroachment of green field development, they have expressed a general concern to limit and control the spread of urban development. Growing concern over issues of global environmental change and sustainability, culminating in the Rio de Janeiro Earth Summit of 1992 and Local Agenda 21, however, placed broader issues of sustainable development firmly on the urban policy agenda and there is a new emphasis on 'sustainability' in national planning policy.   Definitions of sustainable urban development not only identify specific local issues and locally concentrated impacts but link local development to broader environmental concerns, including energy and resource consumption, waste management, CO_2 emissions and global warming. Basic principles of sustainability, in particular intergenerational equity, in turn, underlie these broader definitions.

In more prosperous countries such as the UK there have been some attempts to address these broader issues.   Attention has tended, however, to focus more narrowly on issues of traffic flows and congestion, modes of transportation, and on consumption of the countryside. This, in turn, has fed debates on size, density and problems of urban development appropriate in terms of sustainability.   Again, in relation to more prosperous cities in particular, the debate has extended the idea of sustainability beyond more immediate environmental or ecological concerns to include the urban environment itself, both physical and social, with recognition of the importance of urban culture and quality of life as integral to ideas of 'sustainable' urban development. Thus, for Haughton and Hunter:

> ... a sustainable city is one in which its people and businesses continuously endeavour to improve their natural, built and cultural environment at neighbourhood and regional levels, whilst working in ways which always support the goal of global sustainable development. (Haughton and Hunter, 1994, p 27)

Issues of sustainability have increasingly started to inform both formal planning mechanisms and planning policy and debate at the local level. There is a sense, however, in which traditional concerns over conservation and containment of development pressures have simply been recast in the language of sustainability without embracing the broader principles of sustainabilty linked to global environmental concerns or intergenerational equity. There are also doubts as to the capacity of the planning system to deliver 'sustainable development', however interpreted, due in part to the fragmented institutional context in which the system operates.

The policy context

There has been profound change, more generally, in the overall policy context in relation to urban and regional issues at a number of different levels. The election of the Thatcher government in 1979, committed to a far reaching neoliberal or New Right economic agenda, was clearly the major factor in the UK context. Particularly marked in the UK, it was a period, however, which saw similar moves across a wide range of nation states as politics and governance adjusted to the shifting economic, social and political terrain at national and international levels. It was a period which also saw a major sea-change in Labour Party policy and the subsequent election of 'New Labour' in 1997 with a massive majority provided the potential for continuing change in the policy environment, the consequences of which at a practical level remain to be seen.

In terms of economic policy, deregulation and marketisation in the Thatcher years and after had profound implications for many sectors of the economy. Consequent restructuring had major impacts in terms of investment and employment both positive and negative on many localities. Equally important was deregulation of the labour market and the effective undermining of union power, the latter aided by record levels of unemployment. Labour market flexibility was an explicit policy objective on the Conservative political agenda. The now familiar policy agenda also included privatisation, marketisation and deregulation throughout the former public utilities, public transportation and the rail system, now operated by profit-based, private enterprise within a national regulatory system. It also saw the introduction, in the health service in particular, of 'quasi-market' systems, designed in theory at least to introduce some of the benefits of market mechanisms to the allocation of resources within the public sector. These developments profoundly changed the basis for the provision of urban services. They also resulted in major restructuring and in some cases job losses within these areas of industry and service provision.

There has been an equally fundamental shift in the nature of local government. Successive Thatcher governments imposed a complex series of financial cuts and controls of increasing severity, strongly resisted and contested by many Labour authorities. These progressively tightened the screw on local government spending and financial autonomy in terms of local taxation, spending and service provision, and also investment in housing, local facilities and infrastructure. This left taxation and expenditure levels at the local level effectively controlled by central government. Central government's contribution to local expenditure was much reduced and overall levels of local spending generally were significantly cut back. Pursued in the name of economic policy and the need to control levels of taxation and public expenditure, this was clearly also a political offensive by successive Conservative governments against Labour-controlled local government.

Local authority powers and service provision were further cut back and constrained by a series of more specific policy measures. These included privatisation of local authority-run public transportation and changes in the management of schools. The 'Right to Buy' legislation forced local councils to sell public housing at discounted rates while limiting their capacity to reinvest the proceeds. Councils were also required to put out to tender a range of services including, for example, waste collection, building and maintenance services and the running of leisure facilities and management of public open space. Together with reforms in health and education, these measures taken together represented a major shift in the overall regime of social policy and the welfare state.

There was also significant innovation and change in terms of formal urban and regional policy. Central government support for the regions has been progressively curtailed over the last 20 to 25 years and concentrated on those areas with the most severe problems. European funding has become increasingly important including both the Regional and Social Funds and a range of other specific programmes such as the Konver Initiative for areas hit by defence cuts. Attempts to secure a share of European funding have thus been increasingly a feature of strategy at local and regional levels within Europe. Specific urban policy initiatives over this period included Enterprise Zones and Urban Development Corporations, as mentioned earlier. Inner-city policy in general has been increasingly prominent in policy terms, although limited in scale in terms of actual resources. It has also been recast on a number of occasions with the Single Regeneration Budget the latest innovation in the 1990s.

In terms of the policy process, competitive bidding among local authorities has increasingly been built in to the allocation of funds. Local government has also, to a greater extent, been required by central government to establish various forms of consultation mechanisms, partnership and joint working, particularly with private sector business interests but also with community-based interests, as a condition for bidding for central government and European funding and initiatives. This has been the case, for example, with the Single Regeneration Budget, the Lottery and Millennium Fund, European Social Fund and Konver. Partnership, policy networks and joint working have increasingly been seen as a means of securing policy effectiveness and as a basis for constructing broad-based support for a wide range of initiatives at the local level. As implemented by successive Conservative administrations, this was also, however, in part, an explicit attempt to enhance the power and influence of local business interests in particular and to curb what was seen as the concentration of power in local political elites. Training and Enterprise Councils (TECs) and later Business Links, dominated by local business interests, were also set up, taking over responsibility for government training schemes, enterprise support and related services. TECs, in particular, have come to represent a new locus of power and influence within many localities in relation to economic development, training and employment.

The study

This, then, is the background to the study itself, which is presented in the following chapters. It provides the context for understanding how broad factors operating at the national and global scale have combined with policy and action at the local level. The detailed study presented in the following chapters and focused in particular on Swindon, at the heart of the M4 growth corridor, provides the vehicle for this. As suggested earlier, the scale of growth of Swindon in the postwar period and the massive transformation of the locality in terms of economy and labour market, population and social structure as well as physical growth and expansion make it ideal for this purpose. It presents in many ways a starkly exaggerated picture of processes of change which have operated at national and international scales more generally over this period. It has also, itself, become increasingly tied in to these processes of change operating at national and global levels.

Built, historically, around the massive Great Western Railway engineering works, early postwar expansion initially reinforced the dominance of engineering-based manufacturing. Subsequent decades, however, saw the growth of a more diverse range of activities. It attracted major investment from an expanding roll-call of leading UK and overseas corporations, including major multinationals such as Intel, Burmah Castrol, Motorola and advanced US plastics manufacturer Raychem. Financial services company Allied Dunbar, Nationwide Building Society and National Power established head office and major administrative functions in Swindon. It also attracted national warehousing and distribution functions for WHSmith, Renault and the country's largest operator of book and record clubs, Book Club Associates. Japanese car manufacturer, Honda, has established a major car plant locally while Rover Group's car body plant, set up originally in the 1960s, remains a key employer owned, now, by BMW.

As noted earlier, growth pressures have generated particular patterns of urban development around major metropolitan centres. Swindon provides the ideal opportunity to examine the changing nature and implications of these wider growth processes around London and the South East through the postwar period. It also provides the opportunity to focus on the management of urban growth and expansion and to examine the changing role and structure of the national planning system over this same period. The concentration of these growth pressures and the scale of physical expansion in the Swindon locality throughout this period makes it particularly relevant for this purpose. Looking to the future, the late 1990s also saw government at the national level seeking to determine how projected household growth of 4.4

million is to be accommodated, with much of this pressure directed on counties to the west and north of London, including Wiltshire. Again, therefore, Swindon provides an excellent opportunity to examine the nationally significant tensions between the planning system at the regional and national level, and policy at the local level, in the context of major pressures for growth and development – the key issue which is likely, as noted above, to dominate the national planning agenda in the early years of the next millennium.

The major aim of the study is, therefore, to explore how processes of change, economic, technological, social and political have combined together on the ground. The aim is to examine how these processes of change operating at national and global scales have both impacted on and been shaped by policy and action at the local level and by the historic development of economic, social and physical structures in a particular local context. In terms of the structure of the book itself, **Chapter Two** provides an overview of the growth and development of Swindon in the context of economic and social change and the evolving policy framework and planning system at the national level from the 19th century to the late 1990s. **Chapter Three** focuses on economic and employment change over the last 25 years, relating change at the local scale to economic transformation at national and global levels. **Chapter Four** then examines economic strategy and industrial development focusing on the relationship between policy and action at the local level and the broader context of national policy. The next two chapters focus on planning and the development process. **Chapter Five** looks at planning and development issues in relation to industry and employment. **Chapter Six** then focuses on planning and development in relation to housing and on the overall process of town expansion and physical development. **Chapter Seven** examines Swindon's distinctive social development policy over successive periods of town expansion, going on to explore patterns of social change, integration and exclusion, culture and community since the late 1960s. **Chapter Eight,** finally, returns to broader issues outlined in this introductory chapter, drawing out conclusions and implications in the light of the study as a whole.

two

Overview

This chapter provides an overview of Swindon's growth and development from its early establishment around the massive Great Western Railway (GWR) railway engineering complex in the mid-19th century, through to the eve of the next millennium. It looks at the origins of town expansion in wartime planning and relocation. It provides an account of its initial postwar growth as an expanded town. It then provides an overview of the second phase of planned development which took place from the late 1960s and which was to see major physical expansion, population growth and inwards investment. This was a process which saw the total transformation of Swindon's economic and social structure and its emergence as a major growth centre, fully integrated with the services, high technology, and information-based economy of the prosperous south of England. It was also a process which brought an influx of inwards investment into the local economy from the USA, Europe and Japan, and saw Swindon increasingly tied in to the national economy, to London as both national capital and world city and to global economic forces.

Swindon and the Great Western Railway

In 1841, with a population of under 2,500, Swindon was chosen by Brunel as the site for the GWR's engineering works. Swindon's selection reflected its strategic position on the GWR network – the junction of two lines, a gradient requiring a change of locomotives and adjacent canals to supply both coal and water (Peck, 1983, pp

8-10). Location then, as later, was crucial to the development of
the town. The works expanded dramatically, producing
locomotives, rolling stock and other railway equipment to become
one of the largest industrial complexes in Europe employing, by
1892, over 10,000 people. Old Town and the New Swindon of
the rail works coalesced, physically. The Old Swindon Urban
District Council and New Swindon were unified and incorporated
in the same year as the Borough of Swindon, with G.J.
Churchward, Locomotive Superintendent of the rail works, as its
first Mayor (see Figure 2.1). By 1911, the town's population had
risen to more than 60,000 (see Figure 2.2), representing a
geographically isolated, working-class community transplanted
into the heart of rural Wiltshire, sharply differentiated in
economic, social and cultural terms from the surrounding area.

Employment in the rail works peaked in 1924 at around
14,400, although major expansion had run its course by the eve of
the First World War. The works totally dominated the town in
the interwar years and, though declining subsequently, remained a
major employer through to its final closure in 1986. Its
significance, however, went beyond its employment role, major
though this was. The rail works effectively shaped the town and
its subsequent development from the interwar years and beyond,
not only in economic but also in social, political and cultural
terms. Early plans for town expansion formulated in the latter
years of the Second World War and the early postwar years were
explicitly framed in response to the decline and threatened demise
of the rail works. Other industries were increasingly important in
the postwar years, but it was concern over the longer term future
of the rail works which drove the continued bid for diversification
and the attraction of new industries which continued through the
postwar decades. It was, moreover, the particular political and
social character of the town and of the Borough Council, forged in
the context of railway engineering, that led it to embrace the
opportunities for expansion offered in the postwar years with an
enthusiasm which stood in stark contrast to the rural interests of
surrounding Wiltshire.

Employment in the rail works first declined with the onset of
recession and falling demand in the late 1920s. Collapse of the
Welsh coal trade, which had been a major source of traffic, was a
key factor. In the longer term, however, it was the expansion of
road transport after the Second World War which undermined

Figure 2.1: Local authority boundaries, Swindon and Thamesdown (1900-1997)

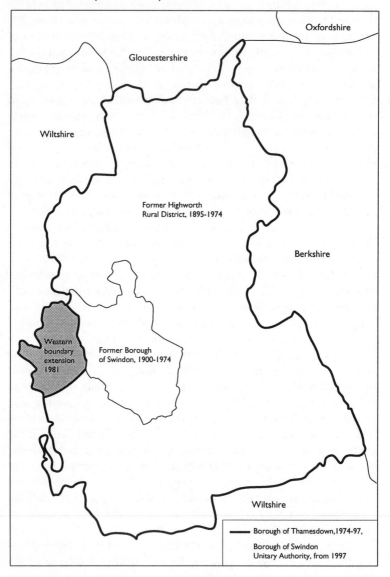

and eventually led to the demise of rail engineering employment locally. The works remained a major employer in the interwar years, although employment had fallen back to around 10,500 by 1939. Employment decline was not as severe, however, as in some single industry, working-class communities over this period; the expanding car industry at Oxford provided some job opportunities. Several new employers had also been attracted in during the interwar period, partly by the availability of female labour. Among these was Garrard Engineering, which initially made mechanical record players, and also W.D. and H.O. Wills cigarette factory and clothing companies, Compton Son and Webb and Cellular Clothing. Population growth, however, levelled off and declined slightly in the 1930s and on the eve of the Second World War, the town had the ominous characteristics of a single-industry town threatened by decline (Harloe, 1975, p 42).

Wartime production and an influx of war workers brought new industry and employment to the town, turning it into a major military–industrial complex. The population of Swindon and the two surrounding rural districts increased sharply, from around 88,000 in 1939 to 104,000 by 1941. Production at the rail works switched to military needs and factories were established locally, away from high bomb-risk areas closer to mainland Europe. These included Vickers Armstrong at South Marston Airfield, Armstrong Whitworth and Plessey. Military bases were also established close to the town and several, including RAF Lyneham, remain as major employers. This in itself generated considerable demands for housing and social provision. Together with prewar concern over economic decline and reliance on declining rail employment, this led the local authority to formulate plans in the latter years of the war to retain wartime employment and to establish early on a trading estate to attract new industries. Wartime production was thus an important basis for postwar modernisation and diversification. Wartime developments represented, in effect, the first of several phases of planned relocation of employment and population. In this, as in other respects, the needs of war demonstrated the capacity for government intervention and planning.

As early as 1943 the Borough was putting the case for administrative autonomy from the County as a County Borough, but although securing some concessions it was a case it was not in effect to win for more than 50 years. Importantly, as well, however, the Borough was formulating the case for planned expansion in the postwar period. These were set out in *Planning for Swindon* (Swindon Borough Council, 1945), which argued for economic expansion linked to the need to improve housing and the physical facilities and environment of the town. The case for industrial development was succinctly set out in a 'Memorandum on the Potentialities of Swindon for Industrial Development' (Swindon Borough Council, 1945a), published by the Borough in the same year, linked to the need for diversification to combat dependence on the GWR. This advanced the case for Swindon as a locus for postwar expansion, offering access and com- munications, skilled labour, factory space and the possible conversion of wartime factories to peacetime production, space for expansion and a commitment on the part of the local authority to provide housing and community facilities.

Leading officers of the Council were strongly in support and, with Labour in control of the Council for the first time in 1945, a policy of major expansion and diversification gained general support. Sixty-one per cent of Council members at the time were railwaymen, with close ties to the unions and deep roots in what was still a traditional occupational community. There was, how- ever, a broad-based coalition of interests in favour of expansion locally, including opposition 'Independent' Councillors repres- enting the shopkeepers and traders. The GWR, nationalised in 1947, acquiesced in plans for growth while Plessey and Vickers backed expansion as a means of overcoming labour shortages. Little occurred in practice in the initial postwar period other than a limited amount of local authority housing development, but these early moves by Swindon paved the way for future expansion.

Town expansion and London overspill

Policy developments at national level and new legislation in the form of the 1952 Town Development Act were to provide the opportunity to implement the strategy of planned expansion. The government's Board of Trade was, at the time, seeking to divert new investment to the newly designated Development Areas, through the use of Industrial Development Certificates (IDCs). A major component of national strategy was to relocate industry and jobs to the peripheral development areas in order to combat the effects of industrial decline and rising unemployment in the regions. In parallel, however, the government was also seeking to relieve growth pressures and to improve housing conditions in London and other major conurbations. The approach, formulated in the 1944 Abercrombie Plan and elaborated in 1951 in the County of London Development Plan, was to decentralise industry and employment to a range of new and expanded towns, mostly within 50-70 miles of London. As Harloe (1975, p 273) points out, far from being elements of some overall policy framework, these two components of nation strategy were, to an extent, contradictory and in competition with each other.

The New Towns programme, initiated in 1946, was, however, little help to Swindon, which was considered too big and too far from London to meet the policy aims of the first generation of New Towns. The ten London New Towns designated between 1946 (Stevenage) and 1949 (Bracknell) were all 20-30 miles from London. In 1952, however, the Conservative government's Town Development Act provided Swindon with its opportunity. This Act was intended to provide more rapid decentralisation from the congested conurbations and at lower cost than through building entirely new settlements. It was to operate by subsidising the expansion of smaller existing towns through formal overspill agreements. National policy objectives coincided with Swindon's desire to diversify its employment base and to improve the quality of the town and its amenities. The Borough responded enthusiastically to the possibilities offered under the new Act. Anticipating passage of the Bill itself it went ahead with land purchase and started early negotiations with the London Borough of Tottenham even before the legislation reached the statute book. This provided the basis for the initial phase of postwar expansion and, with the reluctant agreement of Wiltshire County Council, the Borough secured ministerial consent to expand its population to 92,000 within 20 years.

Planned postwar growth resulted initially in the rapid expansion of east Swindon, the first of a number of major phases of planned expansion. This initial phase was largely undertaken under the powers of the 1952 Town Development Act. Population overspill from London was a key component. Initially, in-migrants from London were housed on the town's Penhill Estate (see Figure 6.2, Chapter Six). This had, in fact, been started in 1951, before the official town development scheme, to meet pressing housing needs generated by postwar expansion. The Council acquired land, initially by compulsory purchase, to the east of the town, and further land was subsequently acquired by negotiation. The second of two compulsory purchase orders was originally rejected by the government as being outside of the scope of the 1936 Planning Act. The first of a series of set-piece struggles between the Council and interests opposed to its plans followed that were to mark the future development of the town in successive decades. This second compulsory purchase order, under the 1952 Town Development Act, was, as Harloe documents, fiercely opposed by rural interests locally. The case became a national issue, providing a focus for rural opposition to the takeover of land for housing in the postwar period. There were articles in the national press, Conservative MPs lobbied nationally on behalf of those opposed to expansion locally and the issue was raised in the Commons. Despite Ministry of Agriculture opposition in Whitehall, the order was eventually confirmed. The Council went on to acquire a further 1,000 acres by negotiation and to obtain planning permission against continuing opposition from the Ministry of Agriculture. Following completion of Penhill in 1955, development started on local authority housing at Walcot, followed in 1956 by Park South and then Park North. Walcot West and Lawns, also on land acquired by the local authority, were designated for private housing, separated physically, as Harloe (1975, p 77) observes, by a major spine road.

There had been steady growth in the interwar period with population growth of around 30,000 in the 50 years 1901-51. This, however, was to be the start of Swindon's major postwar expansion (see Figure 2.2). The town's population grew by almost 30,000 (43%) between 1951 and 1966.

For the most part, those moving to Swindon came from London under the official town development scheme, or as 'key workers' from elsewhere in the country. By 1966, 19,600 people from London had moved into local authority housing in Swindon and a further 5,600 key workers from elsewhere in the country (Harloe, 1975, p 76). A further 22,000 people were housed from the local waiting list. Many of these moved into new housing. The total number housed, however, included a large volume of re-lets as local authority tenants increasingly moved on into owner-occupied housing. Harloe estimates that from 1953 to 1966 around 47% of the total inflow of local authority tenants in

Swindon came from London under the provisions of the town development scheme. They were in housing need and registered their housing and employment requirements via one of the London local councils with the Industrial Selection Scheme. Where employers were unable to recruit via this means, they were allowed to advertise in London for key workers who, as such, were also eligible for local authority housing in Swindon. Another 30% of local authority tenants came as key workers from London via this route, and a further 21% as key workers from elsewhere in the country. Much of Swindon's population growth at this time related specifically to overspill policy. It was also directly linked via the Industrial Selection Scheme and Key Worker Scheme, to the management of employment growth and to meeting the specific needs of local employers. Development was financially beneficial from the Borough's point of view. Land was purchased in some cases by compulsory purchase at agricultural values. Central government paid special housing subsidies, and the returns on development provided a stream of funds for further land purchase.

Figure 2.2: Population growth, Swindon (1911-2011)[1]

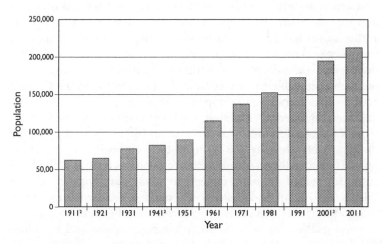

[1] Area of modern Swindon Borough
[2] Estimated
[3] Source: 1901-71, OPCS; 1981-2011, WCC estimates

By the late 1950s, there was renewed pressure for housing growth over and above that provided by the initial expansion within the Borough boundary, east of the town centre. Private developers were already buying up farm land adjacent to Walcot. The Council, however, was aiming to establish a comprehensive plan for this area (Harloe, 1975, p 170). The Council applied for planning permission on 400 acres of land beyond its eastern boundary, and it also asked the County to designate a much larger area for town development. The Council undertook a complex programme of land acquisition over the next few years. Designation of the whole area for town development was likely to raise issues of principle and lead to delay, so instead the Council took the more immediate route of deeming itself planning permission which, together with its substantial landholdings, gave it effective control of the area as a whole. Although planning permission represented a significant departure from the development plan, it was approved by the Minister without a public inquiry.

Unlike earlier development in east Swindon, this subsequent phase did not rely on a formal town development scheme or direct links with London overspill. In the event, development was delayed by recession and the credit squeeze of the early 1960s. The area was subsequently, however, developed for industry and housing as South and North Dorcan. Unlike other Labour authorities at the time, the Borough was not ideologically opposed to owner-occupied housing per se. While it remained at this time opposed to the sale of local authority housing, with demand for public housing able to be met from the existing stock, the Council actually undertook the development of housing for sale to owner-occupiers in Dorcan. Housing was commissioned by the Council from a private developer and offered for sale with local authority mortgages on advantageous terms to local authority tenants, those on the waiting list or those who would have qualified for local authority rented housing under the town development scheme (Harloe, 1975, pp 81-2). Purposely built to standards superior to those of adjacent speculative private housing in order to push up housing quality, the scheme proved highly popular and by 1969, 850 houses had been provided on the Covingham Estate in North Dorcan.

Development of the Dorcan area was based on the Council buying up land ahead of development, beyond its existing boundaries and in the face of speculative acquisition by private developers. This was a forerunner in many respects to the much larger scale development of West Swindon in the 1970s. Adopting an entrepreneurial approach, the Council was seeking to control and to secure comprehensive, planned development through a combination of land acquisition and ownership, securing planning permissions and, where necessary, of negotiation with private sector interests. There was, as noted earlier, flexibility in terms of housing tenure, including local authority building for sale. Land acquisition at less than full development value made development both viable and beneficial in financial terms and enabled the Council to ensure the quality of housing provision and amenities. This, as noted, was pursued in the absence of the specific designation of the area for town development. The Council had also built up a professional and highly effective development organisation, able to emulate the New Town development corporations and to pursue development while securing returns on development for the local community. On this same basis, the Council took an active role in town centre redevelopment, and this same experience was also to be applied to good effect in the western expansion.

By the early 1960s, overall growth in terms of population and employment had, however, begun to slow with the onset of recession. The rate of flow of in-migrants was drying and there was increased competition from New Towns nearer London. On top of this, the Board of Trade, keen to channel growth to the declining peripheral regions of the country, also began to take a tougher line on granting the IDCs necessary in order to locate manufacturing enterprises outside of designated Development Areas. New employers had been attracted to Swindon but, contrary to postwar hopes, only limited diversification away from general and electrical engineering and vehicles had been achieved. Pressed Steel (later Rover Group) had built a major car body plant in the town, continuing the emphasis on engineering employment, and Swindon remained an overwhelmingly working-class town, highly dependent on skilled male manual employment. Publication in 1964 of the government's major review of regional policy for the South East, *The South-East study* (Ministry of Housing and Local Government, 1964), and a shift in the strategic planning framework at national level was, however, to provide the basis for a second major wave of expansion which was to run from the late 1960s right through to the end of the century.

Strategic growth: a new city

'Swindon: City for the 21st Century' was later to become a slogan
for the Council and other interests locally in the late 1990s. The
idea of Swindon as a city had been conceived much earlier,
however, in a strategic planning context at regional and national
levels. The Borough Council was itself pushing for further
expansion from the early 1960s. As Harloe (1975, p 279) notes, it
had commissioned planning consultants in 1963 to prepare a plan
of how the town could be expanded to around 230,000 in
population (Vincent and Gorbing, 1963). This was overtaken by
the government's *The South-East study*, which covered the period
up to 1981 – this was one of a series of regional plans produced,
nationally, in the 1960s. Population growth forecast for the
region in this period was around 3.5 million, only 2.25 million of
which could be accommodated through normal development
plans. The remaining 1.25 million was to be accommodated in a
second generation of new and expanded towns, well beyond the
metropolitan area.

The report recommended major development in the Newbury,
Swindon, Didcot area to relieve pressure on London and on the
green belt. In the spring of 1965, consultants Llewelyn-Davies,
Weeks and Partners were commissioned to investigate the
proposals in more detail. Published in December the same year,
the report recommended that:

> ... planned development should take place in the
> Swindon area to absorb an increased population
> of 125,000 by 1981, rising to about 300,000 by
> the end of the century. Taking into account the
> present population of Swindon, and the
> immediate surrounding area, this will result in a
> total population in the new city of about 250,000
> by 1981, and perhaps over 400,000 by the end of
> the century. (Llewelyn-Davies et al, 1966, p 2)

A new city at or close to Newbury was rejected as being too near
to London for "massive new development". The study also
considered the possibility of absorbing the planned population
growth in "a diffused pattern of development" but noted the
"inability of such a pattern to meet the social and economic
objectives implicit in *The South-East study*, together with the

threat it would pose to amenities in the study area". This option was rejected in favour of "a location where a major single development or closely linked developments, could be achieved" (Llewelyn-Davies et al, 1966, p 1). Having considered the possible sites it concluded that "the only area that is available for development, on the scale envisaged in the terms of reference, without damage to the landscape and without loss of very high quality agricultural land, lies around Swindon". The report went on to note that:

> ... there are also overwhelmingly positive reasons for regarding Swindon as the best place for a new city. These include its key position on the M4, its position on the main railway to the west, scheduled for development under current British Railways plans, and its geographical position in relation to London and other surrounding towns and cities. (Llewelyn-Davies et al, 1966, p 2)

Areas to the east, north and west of the existing town were considered possible sites for major new development.

The then Minister of Housing and Local Government accepted in principle the consultants' recommendation that major development should take place in the Swindon area in preference to Newbury. As Levin (1976) makes clear, Swindon's enthusiastic response to the possibility of further expansion within the strategic planning framework was an important factor, in contrast with opposition from local authorities and local populations closer to London, particularly in Berkshire. So, too, was its track record in terms of successful expansion in the previous period. *The South-East study* had observed that: "Swindon is the outstanding example of a successful town development scheme." (Ministry of Housing and Local Government, 1964, p 74). Other reports at the time, by the Economic Planning Councils for the South East and South West also backed the proposals, although estimates of the likely future population varied considerably. The consultants' study suggested that the Greater London Council (GLC), Wiltshire County Council and Swindon Borough should consult together with a view to undertaking expansion again under the terms of the 1952 Town Development Act. Joint teams from the three councils subsequently undertook a study, *Swindon: a study for further expansion*, published in October 1968 (Swindon Borough Council et al, 1968). This report, known locally as the famous 'Silver Book' (after its cover) and referred to below by this title, was to provide, in effect, the overall planning framework for successive waves of expansion, initially to the east of Swindon and subsequently to the west and north.

The 1968 *Silver Book* study extended the planning horizon a further five years up to 1986. It saw population growth to 121,000 by 1966, 205,000 by 1981, 241,000 by 1986 and perhaps 296,000 by 2001. In addition to planned in-migration of 75,000 people, it saw population growth fuelled both by a high rate of natural increase in the young population of the town and by spontaneous in-migration alongside planned relocation, stimulated by the town's growth   It identified 13,000 acres available for development up to the year 2001, mainly to the west and north west of the town, which could accommodate an additional 175,000 people. In the event, because of concerns for the pressures that would be generated on the countryside and villages around Swindon by the speed and scale of the suggested growth, the Minister limited the planned expansion through migration from London to 75,000 by 1981, implying population growth to around 200,000 by 1981 and 250,000 by the millennium. This still implied commitment on the part of national government to massive expansion in the Swindon area and a major national role for Swindon alongside the expanding economy of the South of England.

The highly detailed study set out many of the principles which have subsequently informed both the physical and the social development of the town, as described in later chapters of this book. In this sense it was much more than a master plan in land-use planning terms – the physical plan and layout for the western expansion, for example, came subsequently. Rather, it embodied an overall philosophy and approach which was to inform this second major phase of development. It established the principle of 'urban villages' with a population of 5,000-8,000 combining into districts with 25,000-30,000 as the basis for physical development and provision of amenities.   It provided for a mix of local authority and owner-occupied housing, the latter including both local authority and privately built dwellings, in order to achieve a 'better social balance'.   Social development was a key concern, alongside economic development.   Based on the experience of earlier town expansion, continued attention to the integration of incoming families was recommended, with neighbourhood workers as a focus for reception and social development work. Health, education, welfare, sports and recreational provision were a priority. Their provision was focused around urban villages and district centres and plans also provided for the early and adequate provision of shops, post offices and similar services. The overall emphasis was thus on the planned and integrated development of housing, social provision and services, with explicit attention to social and community development.

Financial appraisal suggested that there were no reasons why the development as outlined in the study should not proceed, and indeed, it observed that "from the Borough's point of view there are compelling reasons why it should" (Swindon Borough Council et al, 1968, p 133). The new 1963 Local Government (Financial Provisions) Act allowed interest payments to be rolled up and deferred until development yielded a financial return. Land purchase under the Town Development Act together with government and GLC housing subsidies, would be financially advantageous, and the report noted that the development would provide the community "with a return on its investment". Indeed, the report explicitly forecast a significant reduction in the rates as a result of planned expansion compared with natural growth – a reduction of around 2s 0d in old money compared with a rise of around 5d in the pound.

Swindon Council set out to realise the possibilities for expansion offered by the strategic planning context of this period, taking an active role in the development process. Initial development under the *Silver Book* proposals was in east Swindon, with Eldene and Liden in South Dorcan, designed on the urban village principle set out in the *Silver Book*. With the completion of South Dorcan, major development switched to West Swindon, identified in the *Silver Book* as the major focus for future growth. Described in more detail in Chapters Five and Six, in the western expansion the Borough Council bought up land ahead of needs, developed industrial estates and sites for office and commercial development and private housing. It also invested heavily in social and community facilities in line with the recommendations of the 1968 study (see Chapter Seven). Revisions to the Town Development Act in 1968 importantly provided for per capita amenity grants for social provision, including community centres and play areas on new estates. The western expansion (now 'West

Swindon'), with a planned population of around 30,000 was the main focus for development. Here the local authority played a leading role as landowner and developer, in partnership with or alongside the private sector.

The South-East study, the 1966 follow-up study by Llewelyn-Davies et al, and the *Silver Book*, reflected the increasing emphasis on strategic planning at regional and national levels, re-emphasised after 1964 under the incoming Labour government. The Town Development Act, central to the initial postwar phase of expansion, remained an important device for development purposes, giving certain financial advantages. The policy impetus for this second phase of development derived much more, however, from strategic planning concerns and regional policy than the narrower concerns of slum clearance and overspill which underlay the 1952 Act. It seems to have been in this context, as well, that the explicit idea of expanding Swindon not only to city scale but also city status was conceived, in contrast to the earlier phase of 'town development'.

M4 Corridor magnet

Important as well in contextual terms, the government had initiated a second major wave of New Town development in the 1960s. Policy aims included both regional redevelopment, as with Washington New Town in the North East, and New Towns linked to overspill and renewal policies in the West Midlands, Merseyside and Glasgow conurbations, such as Redditch, Skelmersdale and Cumbernauld. Overspill policy with relation to London shifted towards larger counter-magnets at a greater distance from the capital than the first generation of New Towns. Milton Keynes, 45 miles from London and designated in 1967, was the first 'new city' to be created in the UK, expected to grow from around 40,000 in 1967 to 250,000. Two others, Peterborough designated in 1967 and Northampton in 1968, were more similar in some ways to Swindon. Although designated as official New Towns under the 1946 Act, both, like Swindon, had a substantial existing population and both, like Swindon, were further from London than the norm for earlier New Towns. Peterborough, an old Cathedral City 72 miles from London, had a population of 84,000 in 1968 which, it was planned, would expand to 185,000 predominantly through in-migration from London (Schaffer, 1972). Northampton, a County Borough at the time and 66 miles from London, already had a population of 130,000 in 1968, and planned to expand to around 230,000.

As already noted, based on the *Silver Book* proposals, the Ministry of Housing and Local Government recommended that Swindon be expanded from 121,000 in 1966 to around 200,000 by 1981 and about 250,000 by the end of the century (see Chapter Six, Table 6.1). Swindon's planned growth trajectory was therefore equivalent to that of the three major official counter-magnets. Although not designated under the 1946 Act, it was essentially the fourth counter-magnet. Unlike the officially designated New Towns, however, it operated with the more restricted powers of the Town Development Act, with normal planning powers and under the control of a democratically elected local council – Milton Keynes had an autonomous development corporation; in Northampton and Peterborough, a development corporation, responsible for expansion, was established to work in partnership with the local authorities. It is also interesting to note that the consultants Llewelyn-Davies, Weeks and Partners, who produced the follow-up to *The South-East study* and later contributed to plans for the implementation of the *Silver Book* proposals in the form of Swindon's western expansion, were also key contributors to the Milton Keynes Master Plan and, prior to that, had produced the Washington New Town Master Plan. The *Silver Book* itself, in many ways the key document, had, however, been produced by a joint team of officers from Swindon Borough Council, Wiltshire County Council and the GLC. In April 1970 the government suggested that further expansion of Swindon should be on a somewhat reduced scale compared with the *Silver Book* proposals, indicating a target population of around 200,000 by 1986 (compared with 240,000). This still represented major expansion, from around 139,000 at that time. The sequence of major studies, moreover, rooted in the strategic planning of the mid-1960s, provided, in effect, the outline plan for Swindon's development over the next two decades and more. Similar debates as to how forecast population growth was to be accommodated would, moreover, be a recurrent theme in the era of structure plans and structure plan review in the 1980s and 1990s and beyond.

Nationally, the policy context which had driven town expansion early on had shifted through the 1960s. Housing conditions remained an issue in London but the GLC had become increasingly concerned at the scale of manufacturing job loss. The 1969 Development Plan for London actually proposed an increase in manufacturing floorspace. Economic growth was slowing down nationally and the impacts of growth pressures on the South East were easing. Policy at the national level to encourage decentralisation from London and other major conurbations to New and Expanded Towns had largely been abandoned by the late 1960s in the face of increasing concern over inner-city decline. The overall policy context for the western expansion was essentially therefore driven by the strategic planning framework of the mid-to-late 1960s. The Town Development Act was of some minor relevance in implementing the western expansion early on. Official overspill policy as an explicit driver of expansion and a key mechanism linking employment growth and population growth was, however, of decreasing relevance. The GLC was unwilling to commit itself to a new scheme in West Swindon under the Town Development Act, signing up instead to a series of interim agreements (Harloe, 1975, p 281). By the early 1970s, however, it was the increasing attractiveness of the M4 Corridor and Swindon in particular, and its capacity to generate self-sustaining growth, which was the critical factor driving continued expansion.

The major strategic planning studies in the 1960s had already anticipated the impact of the M4, routed past the southern fringe of the town. Opened in 1971, this confirmed the town's nodal position within a high-speed road and rail corridor running west from London, past the expanding Heathrow international airport to Bristol, South Wales and the South West. The routing of the M4 emerged from protracted negotiations over options, in which Swindon's status as an expanded town was a relevant factor (Hall et al, 1987, p 165). Both the overall routing of the M4 adjacent to the town and the detailed links between town and motorway were crucial. Provision of two separate motorway junctions with feeder routes into the town created development potential over massive areas of land both to the east and to the west of the existing developed area. The development of the western expansion in particular was closely tied to the location of Junction 16, some 3 miles west of the town centre. The M4 became increasingly important over time, both in terms of the massively increased role of road-based freight transport and also the ability of employers locally to draw on the extended M4 Corridor labour market. The early upgrading of the rail line and introduction of the high-speed rail service in the early 1970s was again a critical factor both in terms of business travel to London and in terms of labour catchment area. Decisions made at national level with regard to infrastructure development were therefore crucial in terms of Swindon's future development and that of the M4 Corridor in general.

The Llewelyn-Davies, Weeks and Partners report, as quoted earlier, had recognised the critical importance of location in relation to Swindon. The *Silver Book* report similarly noted the potential for self-sustaining growth over and above official town development scheme and overspill arrangements:

> ... it is not difficult to understand why the town's efforts at attracting industry have been so successful. In the future, its strategic position, a young and fertile population and several growth industries are likely to be sufficient to stimulate a continued and substantial growth of the town, quite independently of planned migration. (Swindon Borough Council et al, 1968, p 24)

Reviewing the activities likely to be attracted, it noted the likelihood that "the town will become a major distribution centre and centre for office organisations" (Swindon Borough Council et al, 1968, p 29). Harloe later observed that:

> Since 1965, housing, industry and commerce have continued to expand ... the obvious locational advantages of the town, and its accumulated expertise in attracting new jobs, results in a pressure for growth which is no longer dependent on the existence of a town development agreement. (Harloe, 1975, p 281)

Detailed plans for the first stage of the western expansion were drawn up in 1971 by a joint team from the Borough Council, the County and Llewelyn-Davies, Weeks and Partners consultants. This formed the basis, initially, for the development of Toothill, the first planned urban village with a projected population of around 7,000 by 1975. The subsequent development of the western expansion is discussed in more detail in Chapters Five and Six.

Politically, Labour had controlled the Borough Council from 1951 onwards, with 'Independents' the main opposition. The latter, however, tended to be very much locally oriented and contributed to strong non-partisan support on the Council for town expansion. Policy tended to be developed and implemented by key officers, in particular, the town clerk, David Murray John and a relatively small group of Labour members. This grouping was able to sustain wide support both within the Council and from a broader range of interests locally, including the unions and rail works management. From the late 1960s, elections were increasingly fought on national party lines. The 'Independents' were displaced by Conservatives. Many Conservatives were at this time younger and represented the newer industries moving into the town. They actually took control of the Council in 1968 at a potentially crucial stage in relation to the western expansion. The Conservative Group remained, however, politically committed to continued growth and supported the planned development.

Financially, town expansion had been funded by significant levels of borrowing, together with capital receipts from the sale of assets (primarily land). Interest would typically be deferred and paid out of the revenue generated once development was complete. The Brunel Centre, for example, a major component of comprehensive town centre redevelopment in the mid-1970s and costing £19.9m, was funded entirely out of borrowing. Capital receipts were also ploughed back into continued expansion and development projects. In the 1970s, the South Dorcan development in east Swindon, for example, cost £5.1m to develop but generated capital receipts of £2.2m (Thamesdown Borough Council, 1976). In the western expansion, development costs of £34.6m were partially offset by capital receipts of £25m (Thamesdown Borough Council, 1986).

Revenue expenditure, funding local authority services, was financed, as elsewhere, by domestic and business rates and by central government grant. In Swindon's case this was augmented a considerable degree by a range of other sources, including income from property rent and charges from car parking, for example. This supported levels of revenue and capital expenditure on services such as leisure and community development well above the average. In 1985/86, for example, spending per head on recreation services was £26.05 per head compared with the average for non-metropolitan authorities of only £9.88. Spending on housing was £8.43 per head compared with only £3.51 nationally, partly reflecting the subsidy rent levels out of general Council resources. With considerable experience of large-scale development and project funding associated with town expansion, the local authority developed significant expertise in finance and debt management and in rescheduling its commitments in order to maximise the benefits extracted from its resources.

With falling birth rates and slower economic growth nationally, development of the western expansion was slower than anticipated. Collapse in manufacturing employment and sharply rising unemployment in the 1970s led to high profile marketing and promotion by the Borough in an attempt to boost inwards investment (see Chapter Four). It also used its land ownership and planning powers to boost the provision within the western expansion of sites which would be attractive to inward investors, including campus-style business parks. Growth in the 1970s and early 1980s fell significantly short of the rates required to realise the more grandiose 'new city' plans of the 1960s, which had seen the town's population reaching the 200,000 mark by 1986 (Figure 2.3).

Figure 2.3: Population growth, Swindon (1981-95)[1]

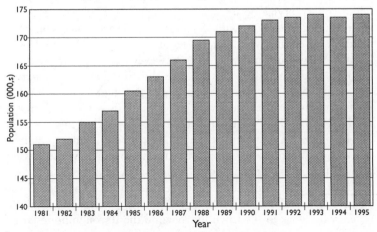

Year

[1] Mid-year estimates for area of modern Swindon Borough

By the late 1970s, moreover, strategic planning at regional level, which had essentially provided the context for town expansion in the first place, had, in effect, been abandoned at national level. The pace of growth was now largely dependent on the strength of the national and international economy and the extent to which this generated growth pressures along the M4 Corridor. With rates of growth slower than anticipated, plans laid for the western expansion were, in practice, to provide the basic policy framework for town expansion over a much extended time-frame – later stages of development continuing well into the 1990s. Even as the western expansion proceeded, however, the 1980s saw the start of a major rethink of policy direction at the local level and the opening up of debate as to future directions for the overall development of the town. The vision which had guided and sustained town expansion throughout the postwar years started to be questioned.

New vision

Having regained control of the Council in 1971, Labour have retained control ever since, except for a brief period of Conservative resurgence when they lost overall control. This in itself is significant. The 1970s saw the collapse of blue-collar, unionised, manufacturing employment and a rapid expansion of white-collar, service occupations. In-migration of new households with little connection with Swindon's industrial, working-class history and culture was a major feature of the 1970s and 1980s. Labour party support was not, however, as might have been thought, undermined by this massive shift in terms of population and social mix. Support for Labour, at Borough Council level at least, actually strengthened from the late 1970s with a majority of 22 in 1986. This partly reflected the particular mix of new employment. Expansion of public sector employment, manual labour in warehousing and distribution, together with massive growth in routine clerical work, represented, in a sense, a 'white-collar proletariat' generating continued support for Labour. Given patterns of residential location as well, many potential non-Labour voters who work in the town live beyond the Borough boundaries. Successive Labour councils had also been identified with promoting the town, successfully managing expansion, job creation and the provision of physical and social amenities (Bassett et al, 1989), which is likely to have increased their support. The Conservatives did win the Swindon parliamentary seat in 1983. This was a surprise result at the time in what had been a long-held Labour constituency, but was repeated in subsequent elections.

There was growing concern locally over the scale of the western expansion and the extent to which it pre-empted resources which could have been directed to other parts of the town. Questions were also raised over continued high profile marketing of the town, the emphasis on attracting new private sector employers and providing for their needs. A stronger left-wing presence within the ruling Labour Group on the Council provided a focus for some of these concerns. Initially, the consensus behind expansion held together, but by the mid-1980s more serious doubts started to be expressed, marking a significant turning point in the town's postwar history (Bassett and Harloe, 1990). The very future of Swindon as an expanding town and potential new city, which had underlain its development in the whole of the postwar period, came under scrutiny.

These new uncertainties were initially articulated in the Council's 1984 consultative document, *A new vision for Thamesdown* (Thamesdown Borough Council, 1984). Although it was a relatively brief document, it nevertheless represented the first major reappraisal of overall strategy for the town since the *Silver Book* in 1968, which had laid the framework for the western expansion and, indeed the northern sector. It appears to have originated largely from a group of officers of the Borough Council who saw it as a means of encouraging politicians to face up to the changing context for growth and town expansion for the future (Bassett and Harloe, 1990, p 50). It was argued that up to the end of the 1970s there had been a clear vision of what the town was trying to achieve, together with the means to achieve it. There was strong local support from virtually every quarter for expansion. The Borough Council as a major landowner had been able to exert considerable control over the overall development process, ensuring a balance between population growth and employment. It could ensure high standards of development and high quality provision of publicly funded community facilities. It could also plough back financial returns from development to finance the ongoing programme of expansion and to provide community facilities, while keeping levels of local taxation down. Continued expansion, building on town expansion in the early postwar years and articulated again in the *Silver Book*, with new housing, new jobs and new community facilities, had clearly benefited the town and its residents. It also made sense financially. This vision of continued expansion, the attainment of city scale and city status had held good over many years.

By the early 1980s, however, this far-sighted vision which had sustained expansion and growth throughout the postwar years had, it was argued, become increasingly blurred, and no longer provided a clear view of the way ahead. The financial context as far as the Borough Council was concerned had become increasingly hostile. Central government cuts and controls over local government spending became, under the Thatcher government (elected in 1979), increasingly tight, progressively constraining over a number of years the Borough's room for manoeuvre. The County Council was also finding it increasingly difficult to see how it could fund its share of the infrastructure costs of new development. Critically, as well, the Borough's existing stocks of land had largely been used up or were already committed for development. Previously, the Borough had been able to buy up agricultural land in advance of development. Land values, however, had increased significantly, driven up ironically to a considerable extent by the Borough's past success in terms of town expansion and economic growth. Now the private sector was increasingly cashing in on the success, buying up land or taking out options to control future development. With limited financial resources to draw on, the Council was being priced out of the market. It had been unable, therefore, to restock its landbank as development proceeded.

Public opinion was also, in some quarters, becoming increasingly hostile to further expansion. This included those who saw expansion draining away resources that could have been used to renew and upgrade facilities in the older parts of the town. It also included residents' groups in the newer parts of the western expansion itself, relatively new arrivals with 'nouveau-NIMBYist' tendencies, who formed the 'Northern Action Group', opposed to further development and encroachment into adjoining areas of land including the planned northern expansion. As this suggests, the social and economic structure of the town had become more complex with new neighbourhoods and successive waves of in-migrants as well as more established neighbourhoods and communities reflecting earlier phases of town development. This increasingly posed the question of 'growth for whom', with the apparent benefits of growth, new employment possibilities and prosperity seemingly passing certain groups by. The benefits of attracting yet more new employers and further waves of in-migration to the town were no longer universally self-evident.

Under pressure financially, and with limited land stocks, the Borough's ability to control and to shape the overall process of expansion and to ensure provision of community facilities was significantly reduced. Future provision of jobs, housing and community facilities would increasingly depend on the private sector with the Borough Council increasingly on the sidelines. *A new vision* identified various mechanisms and resources which the Council *could* mobilise in order to intervene in and influence the development process. These included the use of statutory planning powers, and partnership arrangements with the private sector. It could also seek to strengthen its role in terms of lobbying and seeking to influence central government. It saw the Council's role increasingly as one of advocacy rather than direct intervention, dependent on "outside agencies for the powers, resources, employment, investment and much of the infrastructure needed to achieve its vision." (Thamesdown Borough Council, 1984, p 61). *A new vision* also set out a range of high and low growth scenarios. It recommended continued growth in employment and housing up to the 1990s – a time-frame expected to include the northern expansion, long anticipated by developers and representing in a sense the final stage of planned expansion as envisaged in the *Silver Book*. This, it was argued, should be followed by a period of consolidation or carefully controlled physical growth.

Financially, the situation deteriorated. Initially Thamesdown was able to exercise considerable ingenuity in order to maintain town expansion and levels of service provision. The Borough's aim in the mid-1980s remained that of maintaining and, where possible, enhancing local services while at the same time avoiding job cuts, forced sale of assets or any increase in the rates in real terms. This required some juggling with its spending plans but was largely achieved. Spending per head of population had generally been rising since the mid-1970s at a time when the town's population had itself grown to a significant degree. This was despite ongoing reduction in government grant – cut by £2.5m between 1980/81 and 1985/86.

From 1984/85 central government also, however, limited the extent to which local authorities could spend the receipts from selling land and other assets to 50% of the amount received (40% in the case of housing) – a significant threat to Thamesdown which had relied on this as a mechanism to fund continued development and town expansion. In 1985/86, moreover, the Council became one of the first 12 local authorities to have their discretion over the level at which they set the rates removed by central government 'rate-capping'. This was essentially designed to curb what were seen as high-spending Labour controlled authorities and was widely seen as an overtly political measure by the then Thatcher government. The fact that Swindon was caught in the rate-capping net was largely attributable to the high cost of interest charges on the capital debt associated with town expansion. Initially, along with other Labour councils, Thamesdown refused to set a rate as part of the political battle with central government. As elsewhere this was not found to be a sustainable course of action and at the last minute a legal rate was set.

The Council's experience of 'creative accounting' had already been quite highly developed through its experience in funding town expansion and it was at this time fairly confident that it could still meet its spending objectives. In 1985/86 it adopted a series of other 'financial adjustments' and drew on its accumulated reserves to the sum of £1.9m in order to maintain spending levels. It continued to protect expenditure levels and even fund new initiatives through the rest of the 1980s. In successive years it established its likely income based on the level of grant income and rates allowed by central government and, at the start of each year, set spending levels in excess of income. It then aimed to close the resulting gap over the course of the year by a range of savings, financial adjustments and meeting any shortfall from reserves. Despite continued rate-capping the Council was able to maintain levels of spending significantly above a level which could be supported by local taxation together with central government grant – and well above the level at which central government calculated it should be spending. Throughout the late 1980s, however, while major crisis was averted, the finance director was increasingly sounding warning bells to the effect that the Council was running out of room for manoeuvre.

The situation deteriorated further in the early 1990s, with the Thatcher government determined to tighten the screw on local government. There were further cuts in government grant and additional controls on capital spending. Compounding the problems, recession increased the amount the Borough needed in order to meet the costs of housing benefit and homelessness. The downturn in the property market, coupled with low interest rates, also reduced the flow of capital receipts and investment income. Reserves, moreover, were depleted. The crunch came in 1993/94, forcing the Council to seek spending cuts of just over £4m. Its aim was "... to produce a balanced budget which minimises redundancies and protect front line services as far as possible" (Thamesdown Borough Council, 1993c). Committees were required to prepare budgets incorporating cuts adding up to the required total. This seems, however, to have represented in effect a one-off adjustment and significant cuts were avoided in subsequent years. Limited new initiatives were restored and, with some ingenuity, capital spending, including refurbishment of the Brunel Centre, was maintained.

Expenditure commitments for infrastructure in the new northern sector expansion, however, totalled some £5m. Spending levels (both revenue and capital) remained tightly controlled by central government, as did the level of local taxation which the Council could levy via the Council Tax. Swindon illustrates very dramatically, the extent to which local government's discretion over the use of resources has been progressively and increasingly severely restricted since the mid-1970s. It also demonstrates the extent to which the discretion and capacity of local government to take an active role in economic and social development has been curtailed by the impact of financial cuts and controls imposed on local government. That Thamesdown was able to maintain and to some extent develop services and to support continued development in the northern sector largely reflected the assets and capacity for income generation created and accumulated by its earlier involvement in town expansion.

The Council went through a process of public consultation following *A new vision* and the various scenarios, opting in the end for a strategy described as 'selective intervention', based on a combination of the mechanisms identified in the report. The mid-1980s was in many respects, therefore, a turning point in terms of policy at the local level. 'Consolidation' as a strategy was revisited and reworked in a number of different contexts. The Borough Council itself sponsored a conference on 'The Limits to Growth' in 1990, with invited representatives of a range of private sector bodies, the voluntary and community sectors, to debate the issues. Consultation exercises were again carried out with local residents and with businesses in 1991, the results of which were seen by the Council as providing support for consolidation rather than further expansion. In 1991, a policy of 'consolidation and improvement' was formally adopted as the Council's planning strategy for the period after 2001. There were major shifts in terms of economic development policy, including the winding up of the high profile marketing in pursuit of inwards investment (see Chapter Four). Official Council policy and Labour members stressed that 'consolidation' did not mean no growth or a freeze on new development. There was, however, heightened political conflict between the parties and tension to some extent within the ruling Labour Group over the issues raised. There was also concern from private sector interests, including the Chamber of Commerce representing local businesses, expressing concern that the Council's stance threatened the continued prosperity and the future of the town.

In practice, recession and a major reduction in development pressures in terms of inwards investment and the housing market meant that there was little to challenge the de facto policy framework on the ground. Population growth had, in fact, levelled off in the early 1990s (see Figure 2.3). There had been very significant growth, particularly in the early part of the 1980s and the peak years of the western expansion. Thamesdown was the sixth fastest growing district in England in the decade to 1991 measured in terms of absolute population growth (Table 2.1). In terms of growth *rates* it was only nineteenth fastest expanding by 14% compared with Milton Keynes which expanded by 42% for example and Wokingham, up by 21% over the same period. Policy remained to support development to the extent that this was consistent with the existing planning framework and land already allocated for development purposes. This in itself, the Borough argued, provided for a significant level of continuing growth up to 2001 at least and could accommodate projected growth. Sites remained in West Swindon and the northern expansion was coming on stream in the 1990s. The critical battles around consolidation were, in fact, being played out in relation to the new Swindon Local Plan and the Structure Plan, with the Borough Council fighting to hold the line against commitment to further expansion on any significant scale (see Chapters Five and Six). Historically, the Borough had tended to find itself battling to secure growth and development in the face of opposition from the County Council and other interests. Now, in what was in some respects a remarkable about face, it found itself fighting to resist the levels of development which the County Council wanted to impose on Swindon and battling against private sector development interests seeking to prise out additional development opportunities well in excess of existing commitments.

Table 2.1: Fastest growing districts in England (1981-91)

Local authority[1]	Population (1991)	Population change (1981-91)	Population change (1981-91) (%)
Milton Keynes	179,232	53,276	42.3
Northampton	184,610	25,751	16.2
Wokingham	142,032	25,071	21.4
Tower Hamlets[2]	168,097	22,894	15.8
Huntingdonshire	146,538	21,604	17.3
Thamesdown	172,948	21,345	14.1
Peterborough	155,029	20,919	15.6
Suffolk Coastal	114,585	17,963	18.3
Woodspring	179,830	16,966	10.4
Newbury	139,328	16,682	13.6

[1] Area defined by 1991 boundary; [2] includes Docklands.
Source: NOMIS, Population Estimates, OPCS

In terms of overall policy, while continuing to emphasise that consolidation did not equate with opposition to development as such, the Council did not envisage further planned expansion on the scale of earlier years. To this extent the mid-1980s clearly represented a turning point, with a definite shift in policy at the local level. The extent to which the Council is able, in practice, to hold the line against renewed pressures for development and further expansion and the extent to which it can itself intervene in and shape the process remains to be seen. The Council's stance in relation to the planning framework, described in Chapters Five and Six, may prove, pragmatically, to be the most effective means of maximising its leverage and influence for the future in a situation where it is acknowledged that outright opposition is unlikely to succeed in the longer run.

City for the 21st century?

At the same time, there was increasing collaboration and partnership between the Borough Council and other bodies. A joint initiative was established with the Chamber of Commerce in 1993 under the title, 'Swindon: City for the 21st Century'. Initially this reflected the sort of concerns noted earlier in the wake of *A new vision*, particularly on the part of the private sector, with the profile of Swindon and a desire to emphasise that Swindon was still 'open for business'. The Chamber of Commerce supported a joint exhibition in London to this end. However, the partnership also provided the basis for continuing dialogue. This partly reflected the status and standing of the Chamber which had been enhanced by the involvement of major local employers as 'corporate members'. A workshop and conference was held in 1995 and 1996 with the objective of developing long-term strategic thinking on the future of Swindon, to promote the town and to develop a shared vision for the future across all sectors. This initiative also provided a boost to the campaign to achieve formal city status for Swindon in the next millennium, discussed in more detail below.

Other specific initiatives provided a focus for joint working in the 1990s. The 'Higher Education Initiative' involved the Borough Council in partnership with other local bodies. As well as enhancing the skills and opportunities available to employers and individuals locally, this was seen as offering economic and employment benefits and enhancing the cultural infrastructure and status of the town. Initial plans for a 'University of Swindon' along more traditional lines made only limited progress and specific plans for a campus of Cranfield Institute of Technology fell through, but the overall objective of enhancing higher education locally remained alive.

The Swindon Transport Plan (Wiltshire County Council and Thamesdown Borough Council, 1992) set out policy in what had become an increasing area for concern for business and the local population, particularly in terms of commuting flows, congestion and parking issues. Town centre refurbishment went ahead as a major project funded on a partnership basis with the private sector, in parallel with the development of the northern sector, as did redevelopment of part of the Council's Greenbridge industrial estate as a retail park. Symbolically, John Lewis opened their first new store for five years in the refurbished Brunel Centre. Redevelopment of the massive former GWR rail works in the heart of the town, now owned by Tarmac properties, was slowed up by the recession but perhaps fittingly attracted the headquarters of the Royal Commission for Historic Monuments occupying part of Brunel's former administrative buildings. Even more symbolic, perhaps, of the massive shifts both economic and social which had impacted locally, the designer shopping mall, 'Great Western Designer Outlet Village', with a hundred stores and decorated with railway memorabilia, colonised a major part of the former locomotive and wagon works – truly, as the sign board outside proclaimed, 'From the Golden Age of Steam to a Golden Age of Shopping'. The Council subsequently secured £7.9m from the National Lottery Heritage Fund for a railway heritage centre on an adjoining site.

Through the 1990s, however, the Council was increasingly preoccupied with local government reorganisation, initiated by central government under the 1992 Local Government Act, and with its local implications. The process in relation to Thamesdown itself was essentially uncontroversial with proposals for a unitary, single-tier authority on Thamesdown's initial boundaries, supported by Thamesdown itself, receiving general support locally and indeed at County level. This reflected Swindon's distinctive nature both in terms of economic structure and in terms of its size and physical structure, but also in political terms as a Labour stronghold. A local opinion poll conducted for the review by MORI also indicated the general support of the local population for this option. The Local Government Commission recommendation of single-tier government for Thamesdown with two-tier structures retained elsewhere was accepted by Parliament. The process of reorganisation was itself, however, time-consuming, diverting significant resources within the Council. As elsewhere, the Council has, to an extent, therefore inevitably tended to be somewhat inwards looking over this period. It also

involved redesign and restructuring of committee and depart-
mental structures together with major personnel changes at senior
management level and recruitment of new senior officers from
outside of the Borough, including a new chief executive. The
Borough Council also took the opportunity to consider the name
appropriate to the new authority. Thamesdown itself had only
been created 25 years previously in 1974, with the merger of the
former Swindon Borough Council and Highworth Rural District
Council. Consultation locally confirmed Swindon as the leading
contender for the new authority by a massive majority, favoured
by 84% of respondents. Only 6% wanted to retain the name of
Thamesdown, while alternatives, such as North East Wiltshire,
received minimal support. The decision was therefore taken to
rename the authority Swindon as from April 1997.

April 1 1997, therefore, saw the inaugural meeting of the new
Swindon Borough Council, complete with new corporate coat of
arms, new logo and bright orange paintwork. Labour had swept
the board in the May 1996 elections for the new unitary authority,
with a majority of 32 over the Liberal Democrats, the next largest
party with 8 seats, while the Conservatives retained only 3. As a
new unitary authority, Swindon now had responsibility for the full
range of local services within its boundaries. Its total budget
increased by a factor of five to £117m with total staff of around
5,000 compared with around 2,000 previously. The major new
service areas acquired by Swindon include the high spending and
politically high profile areas of education and social services. This,
in itself, will tend to shift the overall policy focus and the balance
of power and influence within the Council and the officer
structure away from the more centralised planning and
development functions which had characterised the former
Thamesdown Borough. In particular, it represents a major
contrast with the heyday of town expansion and the development
of the western expansion when the authority was very much
focused around town development and expansion. Financially, it
was initially anticipated that the new unitary authority would, if
anything, be slightly better off. Indicative spending levels, as set
by central government, suggested that the new authority would be
allowed to spend slightly more than the County and District had
previously spent jointly within the Thamesdown boundary. This
supported the Borough's contention that the County had
underspent on services locally, favouring instead the more rural

areas. In practice, the government set the spending level for the new Council below what was thought to be the current cost of services, leaving it to cut its initial budget by around £11m.

Unitary status is seen as having significant benefits in terms of strategic planning. Responsibility for these former County services and the cost of providing them will, in the future, however, fall squarely on the Borough itself. The implications for future levels of service provision of demographic change and the implications, for example, of any further expansion and development locally, will also impact directly on the Borough Council. A degree of joint working with the County is required in principle, particularly in relation to planning, and this is very likely to be a source of conflict in terms of planned levels of development into the next millennium. Generally, however, the future development of services locally and of the urban area of Swindon overall, is now more clearly down to the Borough Council – it can no longer point the finger at the County in terms of any shortcomings in the major service areas and policies for which it now has responsibility. On the other hand, the new Swindon Council inherited several hundred acres of land from the County Council which lay within the Borough boundary. With part of this being potentially prime development land – but ruled out by the Council's current planning policies – this may pose an interesting and controversial challenge to the Council's strategy in relation to 'consolidation'.

Local government reorganisation also gave added impetus to the idea of securing formal city status for Swindon for the next millennium. The Council itself had expressed a desire to achieve city status in 1993. Public consultation on the issue at the time of the consultation on local government reorganisation, revealed strong support for city status with just over two thirds in favour and just under a quarter against. Those expressing doubts were particularly concerned as to the possible cost involved and questioned whether Swindon had the amenities, infrastructure or retailing to justify city status. Local businesses surveyed by the Chamber of Commerce were generally in favour. The Council saw city status in part as a means of enhancing the status of Swindon. The initiative itself was also seen as a vehicle through which to debate and address issues around the institutions, amenities and facilities offered – or lacked – by Swindon, including, for example, a university or a cathedral as typical symbols of city status. In formal terms, grant of city status rests with the monarch, as advised by the Home Office, and is normally linked with significant occasions – the last being the 40th anniversary of the Queen's accession to the throne. For the moment, the outcome of this particular initiative remains unresolved. The idea of Swindon as a 'City for the 21st Century' – and quite what that might mean – is, however, central to the ongoing debate as to Swindon's future, into the next millennium.

three

Economy and employment

The last 25 years has seen a massive transformation in the overall structure of industry, economy and jobs in the country as a whole. Major decline in older manufacturing industry has been juxtaposed against the enormous expansion of jobs across a wide range of service-based activities. New high-growth manufacturing sectors have emerged, based on new technologies, new processes and materials, and with an increasing emphasis on electronics, information and a convergence around digital technologies. In an increasingly competitive global economy, there has also been major growth in import penetration and competition from overseas manufacturers in countries such as Japan and Germany. There has been strong growth in direct investment by overseas companies into the UK, in part, as a stepping stone into European markets. More recently, competition from the newer economic 'tiger economies' of South East Asia has accelerated, as has foreign direct investment into the UK and mainland Europe. Domestically, the drive to cut public sector expenditure and to privatise an ever-widening set of public utilities and services since 1979 has itself had major implications for jobs, industry and employment.

The transformation in terms of jobs and in employment structure has been equally far reaching, with job losses concentrated in more traditional male manual employment sectors. Much of job growth has represented female employment, much of this part-time. Impacts on different parts of the country have also differed very greatly over this period, dependent among other things on the existing employment structure of different localities, their vulnerability to change, but also their capacity to take advantage of successive waves of change and investment over what has been a very critical period for the economy of the country as a whole. The overall trajectory of change over this period has been marked by pronounced periods of boom and slump at the level of the international and national economy. Domestically, this pushed unemployment through successive thresholds historically unprecedented in the postwar period passing the 3 million mark by the mid-1980s. Unemployment rose sharply again with renewed recession in the early 1990s. Economic transformation at national and international levels clearly impacted on Swindon as elsewhere in a very major way. These impacts were, if anything, more intense and far reaching locally than elsewhere in terms of the transformation in the local economy over this period. This chapter provides an analysis of economic and employment change in Swindon in the context of change at the level of the national and international economy.

Like many other localities, Swindon was, in the late 1960s, still heavily dependent on the older manufacturing industry. It was therefore hit to an exaggerated degree by the collapse in manufacturing in the 1970s in particular (Table 3.1).

Table 3.1: Manufacturing and service employment as a proportion of total employment, Swindon and Great Britain (1965-93) (%)

Year	Manufacturing		Services	
	Swindon	Great Britain	Swindon	Great Britain
1965	47	37	40	48
1971	45	38	46	53
1981	27	28	64	62
1991	21	21	71	71
1993	19	18	75	75

Source: NOMIS, Employment Department

Also exceptional, however, was the rate of growth in service sector employment and in some areas of new manufacturing. It is this combination of well above average loss of manufacturing jobs with exceptional growth in service sector employment which marked out Swindon and was critical to its continuing success in subsequent years. As a case study, therefore, of the processes of economic restructuring which impacted nationally over this period, it is particularly pertinent. The extent of change at the local level has been remarkable, particularly when measured against the persistent dominance of engineering employment right up to the late 1960s, despite at least three decades of concern at overdependence on a narrow economic base – circumstances which had major adverse impacts in many other localities built around and economically dependent on, for example, coal, steel or shipbuilding. The impacts of inwards investment on job growth have been particularly significant. The impacts of globalisation on the local economy, which has become increasingly tied in to national and international economic forces, are also very evident. The first part of this chapter provides an analysis of economic and employment change and examines some of the implications of this change. Drawing on research conducted specifically for this study, the latter part of the chapter then focuses on the views of employers and the factors which have shaped corporate decision making in relation to the local economy.

Precursors to change

Britain's high point as a manufacturing economy was the mid-1960s. Thereafter, manufacturing was to account for a declining share of total employment nationally. Emphasising Swindon's continuing historic dependence on the manufacturing sector, manufacturing jobs did not peak locally until 1970, some four years after decline set in nationally. In the 1960s there were already, however, changes indicative of the massive restructuring to follow. The mid-1960s saw the town still heavily dependent on manufacturing and on the three main engineering employers, British Rail Engineering, the Pressed Steel car body plant and Plessey's electrical engineering works. British Rail's short-lived modernisation plans had temporarily staved off major decline in rail engineering, leaving employment still at around 10,000 in the early 1960s, compared with around 12,000 in 1950. Engineering and vehicles accounted for over 26,000 jobs locally in 1965, 83% of all manufacturing jobs, 39% of all jobs in the town. Nationally these sectors accounted for less than 14% of all jobs, emphasising Swindon's dependence on this narrow group of employers. Other manufacturing concerns, smaller scale in employment terms, included wartime employers Marine Mountings, Vickers, together with Wills Cigarettes, Garrard Engineering and a number of clothing and uniform manufacturers. There was also, already, a significant flow of new firms relocating to Swindon, many of these on the Borough's Cheney Manor and Greenbridge Estates. Up to the early 1970s these represented mainly manufacturing activities, reinforcing the town's existing dependence on this sector. Service sector employment, including retailing and financial services, were under-represented locally, accounting for only 40% of all jobs in 1965 as against 48% nationally. Manufacturing as a whole accounted for 47% of all jobs locally compared with only 37% nationally.

The picture was to change significantly, however, over the coming years (see Table 3.1). Initially, employment in the rail works fell by around 4,000 between 1965 and 1967, to just over 5,000. This reflected 'rationalisation' of the national rail network under Beeching. With modern locomotives and rolling stock there was also less demand for maintenance and replacement. Railway carriage production ended and the works was reorganised as a result. Beeching's plans represented the end of the railway era and the accelerating shift from rail to road transport both for people and goods. Pressed Steel and Plessey continued to grow in the 1960s – Pressed Steel employed around 6,500 by 1965 and was soon to be more important in employment terms than the rail works. Aircraft production, however, was phased out at Vickers in the mid-1960s, and with recession in the mid-1960s there was short-time working at Pressed Steel and some redundancies in local firms. Clearly the latter part of the 1960s was a critical period for the town, with older manufacturing looking increasingly vulnerable.

Economic transformation in the 1970s

With the onset of recession, growth nationally was considerably slower in the 1970s than in the previous decade. The context, internationally as much as nationally, was one of economic turbulence and volatility, which was to extend through the 1970s into the early 1980s. Key factors impacting at the international level were the collapse of the Bretton Woods system of monetary regulation, abandonment of exchange rate controls and the liberalisation of international financial markets; the OPEC oil price hikes in 1973 and again in 1979; and the impacts, internationally of US involvement in the Vietnam war. Added to this were the effects of policy failure in the advanced economies which added to rapidly rising inflation, further undermining economic stability (Hirst and Thompson, 1996). The impacts of these processes reverberated throughout international economic and financial systems. It was also a period of growing 'de-industrialisation', the rapid shrinkage of manufacturing industry in the US, Britain and mainland Europe, rising unemployment, and increasing concern over foreign competition both from Japan and from newly industrialising countries,

Locally as well, the 1970s were very much a decade of turbulence and transformation. There had been precursors to the massive changes to come in the 1970s, and there had already been a significant flow of inward investment to the town. While much of this was in engineering and traditional areas of manufacturing, newer manufacturing sectors, such as pharmaceuticals and electronics, were represented, for example, by Roussel, Emerson Electrical and Spectrol-Reliance, which survive as employers locally. The growth potential of warehousing and distribution functions was also anticipated early on, with facilities established locally by WHSmith and the Post Office Supplies Division. The major shift took place, however, in the decade or so from the early 1970s in what was, in many ways, the most critical period of the town's postwar transformation. It was in this period, against the background of major recession and rising unemployment nationally and internationally, that Swindon successfully accomplished the key shift from manufacturing dependence to broadly based, self-sustaining growth based on service sector employment and modern manufacturing. Unemployment climbed locally in the 1970s as elsewhere (Figure 3.1).

Heavy manufacturing job losses were sustained, pushing unemployment rates temporarily above national levels from 1974 to 1979. This coincided, however, with increased inwards investment by new companies and by marked growth in service sector employment. It was during this critical period in the 1970s that the town, in effect, finally broke free of its long-term historical dependency on rail engineering and more traditional engineering activities.

Despite rising unemployment, the local economy, in fact, performed particularly well, at least in overall terms, compared with the national picture, and was in much better shape at the end of the decade than at the start. Total employment expanded by 10% in the decade to 1981 compared with a drop of 3% nationally. Underlying this, however, was a truly massive shift in the very economic basis of the town. A third of the town's manufacturing employment was lost in the space of a decade – the long feared 'melt-down' of manufacturing (Table 3.2).

Figure 3.1: Unemployment, Swindon and Great Britain (1974-97)

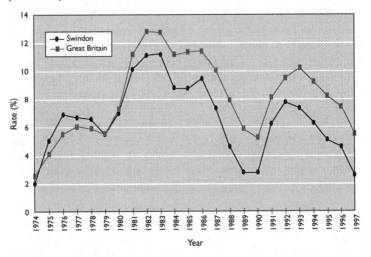

In point of fact, *more* than a third of manufacturing jobs disappeared, given that new manufacturing employment partially offset some of the losses. On the other hand, and even more remarkably, service sector jobs more than doubled in the decade to 1981. Change on this sort of scale, moreover, had massive consequences in social as much as economic terms for the town. Job losses impacted in particular on older, male manual workers. Much of the increase in jobs, as nationally, was in part-time female employment in the service sector. Women were also hit hard by job losses in manufacturing – in percentage terms more so than men. And the rate of increase in male employment in services often seen as dominated by female employment was, moreover, little short of that for women.

Table 3.2: Employment change, Swindon[1] and Great Britain
(1971-91)

Category	Employment change (1971-81)		Employment change (1981-91)	
	Swindon	Great Britain	Swindon	Great Britain
All	+10	-3	+28	+1
Manufacturing[2]	-34	-24	+2	-25
Services[3]	+52	+14	+42	+17
Male	-1	-10	+18	-9
Female	+28	+9	+43	+15
Male manufacturing	-31	-23	-3	-26
Female manufacturing	-44	-27	+22	-22
Male services	+43	+5	+40	+8
Female services	+60	+24	+43	+24
Female part-time	+51	+35	+35	+24

Notes: [1] Swindon defined as the travel to work area; [2] manufacturing defined
as SIC 1968 Orders 3-19; SIC 190 Divisions 2-4; [3] services defined as SIC 1968
Orders 22-27; SIC 1980 Divisions 6-9.
Source: Census of Employment, NOMIS

The major job losses were in electrical engineering, vehicles and
other engineering (Table 3.3(a)). Employment in the rail works
was, in fact, relatively stable after major losses in the mid-1960s.
Plessey, on the other hand, still one of the town's major employers, disposed of all but one of its Swindon companies. These
included Garrard which was hard hit by Japanese competition in
the expanding electrical hi-fi market. Employing 4,000 in 1973,
Garrard finally closed down in 1979. Plessey, having divested
itself of largely old technology electrical product lines, was to
move heavily into the emerging semiconductor sector with some
considerable success, and was eventually transformed into GEC
Plessey Semiconductors. There were also major losses in Pressed
Steel, subsequently part of Rover Group, as the domestic car
industry ran into increasing problems of competition in both home
and export markets. Employment in the Swindon plant fell from

Table 3.3(a): Industrial structure, Thamesdown and Great Britain (1971-81) (%)

Industry	Swindon (1971)	Great Britain (1971)	Swindon (1981)	Great Britain (1981)	Swindon, change (1971-81)	Great Britain, change (1971-81)
Agriculture and fishing	2.3	1.9	1.8	1.6	-15.8	-18.4
Energy and water	1.3	1.7	1.3	1.6	12.2	-8.3
Manufacturing	45.4	38.3	27.3	29.9	-34.1	-23.9
Construction	5.0	5.6	5.8	5.3	26.1	-8.1
Distributive trades	13.2	11.8	18.3	12.7	52.4	5.0
Transport, communications, banking, finance	18.9	25.1	30.7	30.3	78.1	17.7
Public administration and defence	5.6	6.8	3.7	6.6	-28.0	-5.0
Miscellaneous services	8.3	8.8	11.2	11.9	48	31.0
All manufacturing	45.4	38.8	27.3	29.9	-34.1	-23.9
All services	46.0	52.5	63.9	61.5	52.4	14.2
All industries	100.0	100.0	100.0	100.0	9.8	-2.7

Table 3.3(b): Industrial structure, Thamesdown and Great Britain (1981-91) (%)

Industry	Swindon (1981)	Great Britain (1981)	Swindon (1991)	Great Britain (1991)	Swindon, change (1981-91)	Great Britain, change (1981-91)
Agriculture and fishing	2.3	1.7	1.2	1.3	-32.2	-21.8
Energy and water	1.4	3.3	2.8	2.0	161.9	-38.8
Manufacturing	26.7	28.4	21.4	21.2	2.3	-24.5
Construction	5.8	5.1	3.6	4.5	-19.9	-10.9
Distribution, hotels and catering, repairs	24.3	19.2	24.0	21.5	25.8	13.0
Transport, communications, banking, finance	15.2	14.7	21.9	18.3	83.5	25.8
Public administration and defence	4.0	7.3	4.6	6.3	44.5	-12.8
Other services	20.2	20.2	20.4	24.9	28.6	24.9
All manufacturing	26.7	28.4	21.4	21.2	2.3	-24.5
All services	63.9	61.5	70.9	71.0	41.6	16.9
All industries	100.0	100.0	100.0	100.0	27.5	1.2

Table 3.3(c): Industrial structure, Thamesdown and Great Britain (1991-93) (%)

Industry	Thamesdown (1991)	Great Britain (1991)	Thamesdown (1993)	Great Britain (1993)	Thamesdown, change (1991-93)	Great Britain, change (1991-93)
Agriculture and fishing	0.2	1.4	0.1	1.6	-62.2	7.3
Energy and water	2.5	1.7	2.7	1.3	1.3	-21.9
Manufacturing	19.4	19.3	18.8	18.1	-10.3	-8.3
Construction	3.5	4.7	3.3	4.0	-12.7	-16.1
Distribution, hotels and restaurants	24.0	21.9	25.6	22.3	-1.1	-0.6
Transport and communications	8.3	6.3	8.6	6.2	-4.3	-3.8
Banking, finance and insurance, etc	20.6	15.6	19.2	16.3	-13.8	1.8
Public administration, education and health	18.3	25.1	17.9	25.8	-9.6	0.9
Other services	3.2	4.1	3.9	4.5	13.2	7.2
All manufacturing	19.4	19.3	18.8	18.1	-10.3	-8.3
All services	74.4	73.0	75.1	75.0	-6.4	0.6
All industries	100.0	100.0	100.0	100.0	-7.4	-2.2

around 5,000 in 1979 to 3,400 by 1981. This partly reflected investment in new technology and major productivity gains introduced in the face of fierce global competition for market share.

The major job gains in the 1970s were in financial services, distribution and professional and scientific services, including education and medicine (Table 3.3(a)). There were also gains in some areas of manufacturing, although this was more than offset over the period as a whole by the major job losses detailed earlier. In-migration accelerated through the 1970s, with an increasing emphasis on office-based employment and on warehousing and distribution. It was also in the 1970s that several of the key headquarters functions now established in the town were initially set up. Many of what are now the town's major employers were established locally in the 1970s (see Table 3.4) and several of these grew strongly over this period. WHSmith had set up its national retail distribution centre on the Council's Greenbridge Estate in 1966 and started expanding office-based employment locally in the mid-1970s. Book Club Associates, now the largest UK operator of book clubs and related activities, similarly established national distribution facilities in the town in the 1960s. It then grew strongly throughout the 1970s, adding a succession of office-based functions. Specialist plastics manufacturer Raychem, initially established on a small scale in the 1960s, expanded from 200 employees in the early 1970s to around 1,200 by the early 1980s.

Financial services specialists, Allied Dunbar, established what was to grow into their national headquarters and main employment centre locally in 1971, while Burmah Castrol set up divisional and UK headquarters functions in its major office development in 1973. Nationwide Building Society initially set up computing and technology functions in the town in 1974, followed by major employment expansion in a series of town centre offices; subsequently it established new purpose-built premises and employs around 2,200 locally. The government-funded research councils, the Science and Engineering Research Council and the Natural and Environmental Research Councils, relocated their administrative functions to Swindon in 1978 in what was, in effect, a public sector office relocation – one of the few in the town's history of expansion. US-owned semiconductor company, Intel Corporation, established a temporary base in the town in 1979, subsequently expanding in purpose-built premises

Table 3.4: Incoming companies and employment generation

Company	Established in Swindon	Activity	Employment (1996)
Allied Dunbar	1971	Financial services, head office	2,730
Anchor Foods	1979	National warehouse, packaging and distribution centre for butter and other food products	450
Book Club Associates	1968	National administrative centre, warehousing and distribution centre	600
Burmah Castrol	1973	Head office	750
EMI Compact Disc	1987	CD manufacture	240
Galileo	1987	Computerised airline reservation systems operator	640
Hoechst Roussel	1970	Pharmaceutical products manufacture	480
Honda of the UK Manufacturing	1986	Engine and car manufacture	2,040
Intel UK	1979	Microprocessor sales, marketing, warehousing and distribution, UK and Europe	650
Motorola	1989	European headquarters and manufacturing facility, cellular communications infrastructure	1,400
National Power	1989	Administrative centre	1,000
Nationwide Anglia Building Society	1975	Head office	1,800
PHH Europe	1980	Vehicle fleet management and property services	820
Raychem	1966	Specialist plastics manufacture, and European technology centre	1,050
Renault UK	1983	National parts distribution centre	230
Research Councils	1978	Offices if five government-funded national research councils	1,000
Royal Commission on Historical Monuments	1994	Headquarters and archive	260
RP Scherer	1982	Pharmaceutical products manufacture	600
WHSmith	1966	Retail group headquarters and distribution centre	1,450

Source: Thamesdown Borough Council and individual companies. Employment totals are as at the time this study was undertaken. Totals have been rounded to the nearest 10.

completed in 1983. Finally, New Zealand-owned Anchor Butter set up their national warehouse, packaging and distribution centre in 1979, taking advantage of Swindon's key location on the motorway network.

The 1980s expansion fast track

The trajectory of the national economy since the early 1980s has been something of a roller-coaster ride. Recession in the first half of the 1980s saw unemployment (measured in terms of unemployed claimants) rising to historically unprecedented levels to a peak of well over three million by 1986 – a rate of 12% (see Figure 3.1). Recovery in the latter part of the 1980s saw unemployment almost halved to just over one and a half million (5.4%). Sharp recession in the early 1990s, however, drove up unemployment again to barely short of three million by 1993. Slow recovery followed from 1994, with unemployment down to just under 7% by early 1997. Actual employment growth nationally over the decade as a whole to 1991 was minimal.

Swindon's economy followed a similar trajectory – deepening recession and rising unemployment in the first half of the decade, recovery in the late 1980s, a sharp rise in unemployment in the early 1990s followed by recovery. However, there were key differences between Swindon's trajectory and that of the economy as a whole, which suggest a significant shift in the structure of the local economy between the 1970s and the 1980s. In the recession of the 1970s, accelerating unemployment, driven upwards by heavy manufacturing job loss, overshot national levels (see Figure 3.1). There was little similarity over this period between the trajectory of unemployment locally and nationally. Unemployment rose sharply again in the 1980s and in the early 1990s. In marked contrast with the 1970s, however, unemployment locally peaked well short of national levels. In this later period the trajectories of unemployment at local and national levels were much more similar than in the 1970s. Unemployment locally has tended to track changes at the national level quite closely. This suggests that, having gone through the major period of restructuring in the 1970s described earlier, the Swindon economy is now much more closely tied in with, and more or less mirrors, national economic trends. Measured, somewhat simplistically, in terms of unemployment at least, it seems now to respond much more closely to the national and international forces driving the national economy and determining economic competitiveness at national level. It would seem, however, that the economic structure which emerged by the early 1980s was significantly stronger than it had been in the 1970s and able to perform significantly better than the national average.

This is evident from unemployment levels locally, which have remained consistently below national levels since 1979 (Figure 3.1). The local economy also performed particularly well in terms of overall employment growth. Employment as a whole grew by nearly 30% in the decade to 1991, compared with only 1% nationally (Table 3.2). Female employment grew by 43% – well above the national rate. Male employment, however, also grew significantly, up by 18% in marked contrast with male job *loss* of 9% nationally. And while there was significant growth in female part-time employment locally, two thirds of the increase in female employment in Swindon represented *full-time* jobs – compared with little more than a third nationally. The economy locally was therefore generating male employment as well as female, and full-time female employment more than part-time.

As in the previous decade there were also major shifts in underlying structure of the local economy. Service employment, which had more than doubled in the 1970s, expanded by a further 42%, well ahead of the national growth rate (Table 3.2). More remarkable in a way, however, was the turnaround in manu-facturing employment. Over a third of the town's manufacturing jobs had disappeared in the 1970s, well ahead of national rates of decline. At the national level, moreover, manufacturing decline continued unabated in the 1980s with the loss of nearly a quarter of the country's manufacturing jobs. Swindon, on the other hand, actually achieved a modest increase in manufacturing jobs against the background of the continuing collapse of manufacturing employment at the national level. This was all the more remarkable given the pace of manufacturing job loss locally in the previous decade. So, alongside continued growth in a wide range of service industries, the town had also, therefore, turned back the tide of manufacturing job loss.

Job loss in older manufacturing sectors continued during the 1980s (Table 3.3(b)). The rail works, central to the town, its economy and culture for so long, finally closed in 1986 with the loss of the remaining 2,400 jobs. Closure reflected a change in British Rail's purchasing policy, moving to competitive tendering from a range of manufacturers. British Rail also decided to concentrate the shrinking volume of maintenance work at Derby and York. There were views, locally, that a slimmed down British Rail Engineering Limited represented a better candidate for privatisation and it would seem likely that British Rail saw more possibility of returns from land disposal in Swindon than its other sites and possibly thought that closure would be politically less difficult to manage in an economically more buoyant area such as Swindon (Bassett, 1987).

In overall terms, however, much of the remaining employment locally in older, more vulnerable manufacturing sectors had already been shaken out in the 1970s. Job loss in these older manufacturing sectors was more than offset over the decade as a whole by employment growth in newer, expanding sectors of manufacturing, including electronics, chemical and plastic products. New inwards investment was a significant source of manufacturing growth, including pharmaceuticals manufacturers Scherer, EMI Compact Disc, together with a wide range of smaller companies. Honda was an increasingly significant employer in the latter part of the decade with its pre-delivery inspection facility operational by 1986 and its engine plant up and running in 1989. Cellular phone company, Motorola, had set up an initial operation locally in 1989 with 45 people, although major job growth linked to the expansion of digital phone technology came later on. Increasingly significant as well over this period was continuing employment growth in manufacturing companies which had already established an initial presence in the town, such as advanced plastics manufacturer, Raychem and pharmaceuticals company Roussel. Plessey, moreover, after heavy job losses in the group as a whole, had now pulled out of older technology sectors and refocused its activities in high growth, advanced micro-processors, becoming part of the GEC group in 1990.

The major job gains, however, were concentrated in a range of service industries (Table 3.3(b)). Growth in service employment overall included the expansion of jobs and activities needed simply to support a fast growing population. But it also included major growth in service sector employers serving regional, national and international markets, companies and therefore 'exporting' services from the local economy, and generating growth locally. It included, as well, significant growth in a wide range of local 'business' services supporting the needs of businesses locally.

The early 1980s saw a major influx of inwards investors across a range of service sector activities, including warehousing and distribution, finance and other office-based activities. 1980 alone saw the arrival of Man VW's national distribution centre, Readers Digest book club's national warehouse and distribution centre, PHH vehicle leasing company, the national Water Research Council and insurance company NEM. Renault established their UK parts warehouse and distribution centre in the striking Norman Foster designed building on the Rivermead Estate in 1983 (see Figure 5.1). WHSmith set up their retail office headquarters on the Council's Greenbridge Estate alongside their distribution centre. National Power centralised much of its UK employment on the Windmill Hill Business Park in 1988, with around 800 staff initially. British Telecom established a major office complex locally. Galileo, operators of an international air-line reservation system on behalf of a range of airline companies, set up purpose-built premises including major computing facilities on Windmill Hill Estate in 1988, employing around 250 people by 1989 and up to 950 at their peak in 1993. As with manufacturing there was also major growth in the 1980s in companies which had established a base in the town in earlier years, including financial services specialists Allied Dunbar, Book Club Associates and Readers Digest. Nationwide Building Society grew strongly throughout the 1980s. American-owned semiconductor company Intel Corporation, set up locally in 1979 and moving into purpose-built premises in 1981, expanded throughout the decade.

Much of this job growth, particularly in relation to new inwards investment, occurred locally in the first half of the 1980s against a background of national economic recession and rising unemployment. Unemployment did rise locally, despite the scale of employment growth locally. Job growth locally was unable to keep pace with the rapid expansion of the potential labour force, which was growing rapidly through a combination of in-migration and indigenous growth in the town's relatively young population. Nevertheless, economic expansion was achieved locally against the background, in the first half of the decade at least, of national recession.

Table 3.5: Employment structure, Swindon[1] and Great Britain (1971-93) (%)

Category	1971		1981		1991		1993	
	Swindon	Great Britain	Swindon	Great Britain	Swindon	Great Britain	Swindon	Great Britain
Manufacturing[2]	45	38	27	28	21	21	19	18
Services[3]	46	53	64	62	71	71	75	75
Male	63	62	56	57	52	52	52	51
Female	37	38	44	43	48	48	48	49
Male manufacturing	54	44	38	39	30	29	26	25
Female manufacturing	32	29	14	19	12	13	11	11
Male services	34	43	49	50	59	59	66	64
Female services	66	68	83	78	84	84	85	86
Female part-time	15	13	20	18	21	22	19	22

Notes: [1] Swindon defined as the travel to work area (1971-91). Thamesdown Borough Council, 1993; [2] manufacturing defined as SIC 1968 Orders 3-19; SIC 190 Divisions 2-4; [3] services defined as SIC 1968 Orders 22-27; SIC 1980 Divisions 6-9. Manufacturing and services represent less than 100% of all employment, which includes agriculture and fishing, energy and water supply and construction. All figures show percentage of total employment.
Source: Census of employment, NOMIS

Table 3.6: Leading employment sectors, Swindon[1] (1991)

Employment sector	Employment	% of total employment	Multiple of national average[2]	Change 1981–91 (%)
Retail distribution	12,980	12.5	1.16	+50
Business services[3]	8,710	8.4	1.15	+154
Education	6,960	6.7	0.83	+7
Banking, finance, insurance[3]	6,570	6.3	1.55	+93
Motor vehicles and other mechanical engineering[3]	6,540	6.3	1.51	+4
Medical and other health services	5,850	5.6	0.80	+19
Wholesale distribution	6,200	5.9	1.46	-9
Electrical and electronic engineering	5,470	5.2	2.28	+45
Services to the general public and recreation[3]	5,370	5.2	0.79	+127
Hotels and catering	4,940	4.7	0.85	+47
Public administration	4,740	4.6	0.73	+82
Construction	3,790	3.6	0.81	-16
Postal services and telecommunications	3,310	3.2	1.60	+9
Chemicals, rubber and plastics processing[3]	2,940	2.8	1.19	+48
Production and distribution of energy and water[3]	2,640	2.5	2.31	+161

Notes: [1] Swindon defined as the travel to work area. [2] Shows the extent to which Swindon specialises in a particular employment sector compared with the national average; a figure above 1.00 indicates an above average share of employment in a particular sector, and less than 1.00 below average: thus, for example, a figure of 1.5 would indicate that Swindon has 1.5 times the percentage of employment accounted nationally for by this particular sector. [3] Classes merged in order to ensure confidentially

Source: NOMIS, DfEE, SIC 1980 Industrial Classes

In the space of two decades, the town's over-reliance on manufacturing employment and male manufacturing employment in particular, had been thoroughly transformed. By the early 1990s, its employment structure was very close to the national picture – slightly less part-time female employment, slightly more male service sector employment, but very little difference overall (Table 3.5).

Dominant employment sectors include activities essentially serving the needs of the local population, for example, education, public administration and much of retailing. Other major service-based industries, including, for example, banking and finance, business services and wholesale distribution are very much drivers of the local economy (see Table 3.6). The importance of motor vehicle manufacturing, electrical and electronic engineering and processing of chemicals and plastics is also very evident from Table 3.6.

Equally apparent is the major shift in terms of occupations generated largely by the transformation in the town's economic base (Table 3.7). Again, comparison with national trends is instructive, showing the particularly rapid growth locally, of managerial, professional and related activities, and of clerical and sales. Reflecting this, by 1991, the proportion of local residents working in clerical and sales activities and also in the various process industries was higher than average. The proportion in managerial and professional activities was still, however, despite growth in the 1980s, below average. This partly reflected the fact that those in managerial and professional occupations working in the town were more likely to live beyond the Borough boundary.

Table 3.7: Occupational structure, Thamesdown, England and Wales (1981-91)

Occupational order	Order no	England and Wales (1991) % of total	Thamesdown (1991) % of total	England and Wales, change (1981-91) %	Thamesdown, change (1981-91) %
Professional and related supporting management	1	6.8	6.6	62.7	157.6
Professional and related, education, welfare, health	2	9.2	6.8	16.7	33.6
Literary, artistic and sports	3	1.4	0.9	38.0	48.1
Professional and related, science and engineering	4	4.8	6.2	13.1	75.1
Managerial	5	12.2	11.5	25.5	76.2
Clerical and related	6	16.7	19.8	0.6	32.4
Selling	7	6.2	6.8	7.4	52.0
Security and protective services	8	2.1	2.2	-4.7	-9.7
Catering, cleaning, hairdressing, etc	9	10.9	9.3	5.7	19.6
Farming, fishing and related	10	1.2	0.6	-11.6	-6.9
Materials processing, making and repairing	11	5.9	4.8	-14.0	9.0
Processing, making, repairing and related	12	8.8	10.1	-22.9	-14.9
Painting, repetitive assembling, product inspecting	13	3.2	4.2	-14.0	6.8
Construction, mining and related	14	3.2	2.9	-1.1	19.9
Transport operating, materials moving	15	5.5	6.3	-11.5	7.8
Miscellaneous	16	0.9	0.4	-47.9	-74.8
Inadequately described	17	1.1	0.6	23.9	48.6
All industries		100.0	100.0	2.8	26.5

Source: NOMIS, DfEE

The 1990s: recession and recovery

Inwards investment and local job growth drove unemployment down to only 2.5% in Swindon in the late 1980s – less than half the national rate and close to what might be considered on some definitions 'full employment'. There were complaints, then, of labour and skills shortage and a handful of manufacturing companies reliant on low-cost, unskilled labour relocated elsewhere, citing rising costs and recruitment problems. It was against this background that the emphasis of the Borough Council's economic development strategy shifted away from promotion and marketing and more towards consolidation and support for existing employers (see Chapter Four). This also formed the background for initial debate around consolidation mentioned in Chapter Two, initiated in *A new vision for Thamesdown*. At the time, circumstances seemed to justify the switch in policy. In fact, however, the context was to change rapidly.

While job growth continued in established companies, the major pressure from inwards investment and relocation fell away rapidly in the early 1990s, with the rapid onset once more of recession and rising unemployment nationally. There was a significant wave of closures and job cuts locally. Unemployment rose very rapidly, from under 3,000 locally at the end of 1989 to nearly 11,000 by 1993. Figures also suggest that there was actually a net loss of employment in the town of nearly 4,000 in the two years, 1991 and 1992, unprecedented in the town's postwar history (Thamesdown Borough Council, 1993a). This included a net loss of service sector employment. The Borough Council spoke of 1992 as the worst year on record, with the net loss of 460 (mostly small) businesses and employment down by around 1,900 (see Table 3.3(c)). In this context, the wisdom of consolidation and putting the brakes on growth and inwards investment came into question locally.

In the early 1990s a particular feature of recession, nationally, was its impact across a wide range of activities, including services as well as manufacturing (Table 3.3(c)). Its impacts were also more generalised across the country as a whole, affecting the traditionally more prosperous parts of the country. This was particularly the case in Swindon, where cuts and closures extended to financial services, sales and marketing, warehousing and distribution, as well as engineering and other manufacturing sectors. Insurance company NEM ran down its workforce and subsequently closed. Leasing company PHH and the Royal Mail both shed jobs. Marconi and National Semiconductors closed their facilities in the town. There were job losses in the town's blue chip growth companies, including Raychem, Galileo and GEC Plessey. In the more traditional engineering sectors, engine and generator manufacturers Lister Petter, set up originally for wartime production, but now under strong competition from overseas manufacturers, shut down their Swindon factory, with the loss of 250 engineering jobs. Rover Group was investing heavily in new press equipment, but also shed around 500 jobs as part of its strategy to increase productivity and competitiveness.

While the net effect of the recession locally was reflected in the stalling of employment growth, the flow of inwards investment did not dry up completely. It included overseas firms such as Pentel and Dolby. Much of what there was, however, represented smaller firms, branch offices or support services of companies based elsewhere, and total employment generation was small compared with the peak years of the 1980s. Among the more significant, the Royal Commission for Historic Monuments relocated its headquarters and archive appropriately to a refurbished building in the conservation area of the rail engineering works. Iceland also set up a frozen food warehouse and distribution centre on former railway land, expected to employ up to 500 people. Both were seen as a welcome boost to the Churchward development, which had been very slow to get off the ground (even if Iceland, providing relatively low-skilled service sector jobs, was not seen as ideal in terms of the type of employment the Council would have wanted to see on the site). Private ownership of the Churchward development meant, however, that the Council's influence was in any case limited. There was also significant growth in retailing, hotels and catering. Again on the Churchward development the Great Western Designer Outlet Village created an estimated 700 jobs. Overall, however, there was no return to the spectacular growth levels of the past, driven by inwards investment and relocation.

More important was continuing job growth in a number of major established employers. Honda, having set up an engine plant in 1989, went into full car production in 1993. Output and employment continued to expand with employment rising from

650 in 1990 to nearly 1,800 by the end of 1994 and 2,040 by 1996 with Honda intending to add press capacity to its range of activities locally. Employment growth in Motorola took off in the 1990s, with its success in the mushrooming global market for digital cellular phone equipment, from its initial employment base of 45 in 1989 to around 1,400 by 1996. Further growth was anticipated following its move to new purpose-built premises in late 1997 or early 1998. By the mid-1990s there was also growth in firms such as Intel, EMI Compact Discs, Intergraph and Scherer.

The recession of the 1990s showed the town to be increasingly vulnerable to wider economic forces. The Borough Council's policy of 'consolidation' was, in effect, achieved with little effort on its part, as major growth pressures abated. Overall, however, the town did not suffer as badly as many parts of the country. Unemployment peaked at less than 9%, 2% below the national figure. There was some continued inwards investment alongside job growth in already established employers. Recovery in the mid-1990s was faster and more successful locally than nationally – by 1996 unemployment was back down below 4% compared with over 6.7% nationally. Whatever the Borough Council's strategy, however, actual employment growth was effectively stalled by national recession in the 1990s. This demonstrated that continued employment growth could no longer be relied on locally as it had been in the past, almost as a fact of life and, at times, in the face of national recession. On the other hand, the town's economic structure and its attractiveness to inwards investment are such that pressures for growth and inwards investment are likely to be strong when economic growth is again buoyant nationally and internationally.

Inwards investment and job growth

It is, above all, the scale of inwards investment and its subsequent contribution to job growth which has fuelled Swindon's spectacular expansion in recent decades. Exact numbers are difficult to determine, but several hundred new employers, large and small, set up since the 1950s, still operated locally in the latter part of the 1990s. A survey in 1986 found that almost half of all local employers reported an increase in employment over the previous five years. This compared with only 17% who reported that employment had fallen over the same period, demonstrating the key contribution of job growth among incoming companies (Bassett et al, 1989, p 52). Larger incoming employers are listed in Table 3.4. In a number of cases, inwards investment involved the relocation of significant numbers of jobs and employees from elsewhere, typically London and the South East. This was the case, for example, with Burmah Oil and WHSmith. In Burmah's case, the move involved the major relocation of many of their London-based staff with the aim of achieving substantial cost savings. WHSmith's retail distribution centre similarly replaced its existing facilities in London and subsequent expansion in Swindon saw much of the Group's London-based office staff relocated in stages to Swindon. Relocation, as was the case with WHSmith for example, typically involved local recruitment of additional employees, either to replace staff who chose not to move or to meet immediate expansion needs, rather than simply moving staff in from elsewhere.

Many of what are now the leading employers in the town, however, were set up initially with few employees. Several of these were to capitalise on rapidly expanding markets, nationally and internationally, in key growth sectors, and it is the scale of this subsequent growth and expansion, in some cases quite spectacular, that has contributed to overall employment growth in the local economy. The 1986 study (Bassett et al, 1989) referred to above, found that 70% of larger private sector employers reported increased demand for their products or services over the previous five years. This itself was seen as the overwhelming factor likely to lead to future job growth. Swindon was selected as a location by many of these employers specifically because it seemed to offer the potential to support rapid expansion. Advanced plastics manufacturer Raychem, set up in 1966 with only 17 employees, had expanded its workforce to around 1,300 by 1986. Financial services company Allied Dunbar, with around 100 employees when set up in its initial town centre offices, employed around 2,500 locally by 1996. Book Club Associates, set up with a handful of employees in 1966, initially under the wing of its then part-owners, WHSmith, expanded rapidly in the 1970s in particular, to a peak of around 900 by the early 1980s, and still accounted for around 750 in 1996. Nationwide Building Society grew in stages following the initial transfer of around 200 staff from London to its newly established computing and data centre in 1974. There was additional recruitment locally at the time, but the major expansion came in the 1980s, with the expansion in the Society's savings and investment business in particular and major recruitment of staff locally. With continued expansion and the move into new purpose-built premises in 1993, total employment had reached nearly 1,800 by late 1996. Intel, with around 200 staff when they moved into the initial building on their current site in 1983, employed around 360 in 1986, rising to some 700 by 1996, having added a further two buildings. Among the most spectacular growth stories was Motorola who came to Swindon in 1989 with only 45 employees. Seven years later, in 1996, following the takeoff in the market for digital cellular phone equipment, it employed 1,400 and was investing in its new £116m European headquarters building in the town.

Initial investment decisions and choice of location have clearly been critical to Swindon's success. Its ability initially to attract employers and in particular those which were moving in order to expand or which were linked to key growth sectors and about, therefore, to be launched on a trajectory of investment and rising employment was of key importance. It has, however, been the ability of the town to cater for and to continue to attract subsequent waves of investment, expansion and employment growth following the initial establishment of companies locally, that has accounted for a major part of economic and employment growth. This has been particularly evident in the case of those employers, some of which are identified above, which achieved spectacular growth from modest investment and employment initially. Even when relocation of existing employment has represented a significant part of an employer's initial workforce, subsequent stages of relocation and significant additional job growth locally have been of major importance – the staged relocation of WHSmith is a key example. This overall process of 'second-wave' expansion and employment growth, identified elsewhere as an important aspect of industrial relocation, appears to have been particularly significant in the case of Swindon.

Globalisation

The late 1990s saw the Swindon economy much more closely tied in to national and, increasingly, international level economic structures and processes of change. The Borough Council itself recognised the implications of this, observing in 1995 that:

> International and global factors, now exert over-
> whelming influences on national and regional
> policies and performance. Individual govern-
> ments and agencies have diminishing capacity to
> respond.   (Thamesdown Borough Council,
> 1995a)

There is increasing competition between and within the major trading blocs and significant shifts in the pattern of growth at the international level. Processes of globalisation have also generated greater turbulence in terms of economic structures. Again, quoting the Organisation for Economic Cooperation and Development, the Borough Council noted that:

> ... globalisation has entailed a turbulent process
> of birth and death of firms, the rise and fall of
> whole sectors of activity, and the re-allocation of
> production within, as well as between, regions
> and countries. (Thamesdown Borough Council,
> 1995a)

The impact of increasing turbulence was particularly evident in Swindon in the 1990s, with considerable flux underlying the broader shifts in economic and employment structure.

As the previous section illustrates, much of inwards investment and job growth locally has been generated by overseas companies, including multinational corporations (MNCs) such as Intel, Honda and Raychem. This in itself is indicative of what has been seen as the growing trend over recent decades towards the increased internationalisation or globalisation of economic activity. While commentators have warned against the over-enthusiastic assumptions as to the extent of true globalisation at the economic level, it is clear that much has changed in the postwar period at the international scale. International trade and competition in domestic and export markets has increased markedly, with increasing import penetration in UK markets and increased competition for overseas sales. Multinational companies have become increasingly dominant components of national economies. Overseas direct investment by companies extending production, marketing, sales and support and other functions beyond their host-nation has increased, particularly between the dominant economic blocs of Europe, Japan and North America, but with increasing diversity more recently. Foreign direct investment has also taken the form of takeover of domestic companies by overseas MNCs. Liberalisation and internationalisation of financial markets and markets for financial products has also created both new challenges and new opportunities.

Listings of major employers in the 1960s show the Swindon economy to have been almost entirely UK-owned. An early exception, identified in the Silver Book (Swindon Borough Council et al, 1968) was US-owned Union Carbide still operating locally in the 1990s. US-owned plastics company Raychem set up a small plant locally in 1966, although its major expansion came later. Subsequent decades saw the increasing growth of foreign direct investment into Swindon by overseas MNCs, and an increasing scale of employment in foreign-owned enterprises (see Table 3.8). Much of this investment has been concentrated in electronics, plastics, pharmaceuticals and, with BMW's takeover of Rover and Honda's growing investment, the car industry. It extends, however, to a range of other industrial sectors, including service industries. US-owned MNCs accounted for around 6,500 jobs locally by 1985, an estimated 27% of all manufacturing employment, compared with around 15% in 1979 (Bassett et al, 1989). In 1995, the Borough Council identified 23 foreign-owned companies employing over 100 employees, including 14 US-owned enterprises. There were a further 21 smaller US-owned companies locally, employing less than 100 employees.

A number of these represented continued investment and expansion, following the initial establishment of facilities locally. This has been the case, for example, with what are now major local employers such as Raychem, Intel and, more recently, Motorola, all US-owned. The same is true of Japanese car manufacturer Honda, which has undertaken a staged build up in its investment, employment and range of activities at the old Vickers airfield site. US-owned vehicle leasing and business

Table 3.8: Foreign-owned enterprises in Swindon

Company	Owner	Country	Employment (1996)
Anchor Foods	New Zealand Dairy Board	New Zealand	450
Book Club Associates	Bertelsmann AG	Germany	600
Clarion Shoji	Clarion Co Ltd	Japan	100
Dana Holdings	Dana Corporation	USA	200
Emerson Electrical Industrial Controls	Emerson Electric	USA	200
Galileo International	The Galileo Co	USA/ European	640
Honda of the UK Manufacturing	Honda Motor Company	Japan	2,040
Intel Corporation UK	Intel Corporation	USA	650
Intergraph (GB)	Intergraph Corporation	USA	290
Motorola	Motorola Inc	USA	1,400
PHH Europe	PHH Corporation	USA	820
Praxair Surface Technologies	Union Carbide Corporation	USA	250
Raychem	Raychem Corporation	USA	1,050
Readers Digest Association	Readers Digest	USA	670
Renault UK	Renault SA	France	180
Rover Group	BMW	Germany	4,500
Sauer Sundstrand	Sauer Inc	USA	440
RP Scherer	RP Scherer Corporation	USA	670
Spectrol Reliance	Dyson, Kissner, Moran	USA	240
Triumph International	Triumph International Spiesshofer & Braun	Switzerland	270
Zimmer	Bristol, Myers, Squibb	USA	160

Source: Thamesdown Borough Council and individual companies.
Employment totals are as at the time this study was undertaken, and have been rounded to the nearest 10.

services group PHH Europe, set up in 1980, represents significant inwards investment in the service sector, with over 800 employees in 1996.

In other cases, inwards investment took the form of overseas companies taking over or buying into existing concerns, with Rover Group, acquired by BMW from British Aerospace in 1994, the prime example. At one level, this represented a transfer of resources from BMW to British Aerospace, rather than wholly new investment as such. The takeover and new ownership structure clearly, however, has potentially major implications for the former Rover press works. An immediate consequence was, in fact, continued investment in new plant and it may well be that the Swindon works, now employing around 4,000, will benefit from BMW's longer term investment strategy and commitment to car manufacture – the latter having been a weakness under British Aerospace ownership. On the other hand, BMW's purchase has also had implications for Rover's relationship with Honda. Honda remained in the mid-1990s a significant customer, but the longer term strategic partnership between Honda and Rover Group as a whole, envisaged in the early 1990s, is unlikely to be realised. In the service sector, Book Club Associates was originally set up by WHSmith and the US Doubleday Corporation. Doubleday were subsequently acquired by the German media group Bertelsman, who now run the book club business from Germany. WHSmith subsequently sold their interest to UK publishing and media group Reid Elsevier.

Computerised airline reservation system operator Galileo, set up locally in 1988, was itself a product of intense competition between international airline companies on a global scale. Reservation systems, highly dependent on advanced computing and electronic communications capacity, became in the 1980s, a key (some would say *the* key) to airline profitability. Groups of airlines set up highly competitive reservations systems, attempting to secure competitive advantage in marketing terms and to tie in customers to products sold through their own systems. The Galileo system was itself set up a grouping of eight European airlines, including British Airways, KLM and Alitalia, in order to counter the threat of American dominance of reservation systems. After initial development work, collaboration with the US-owned Covia system, operated by United Airlines and US Air, led in 1993 to the merger of Galileo and Covia. Some parts of the operation were relocated to the US, and employment fell from its peak of around 950 to around 640 in 1986. Galileo remains, however, a significant employer locally with an international US–European ownership structure.

In terms of trade and international market competition, Swindon firms such as Plessey, Garrard and Rover itself, had, in fact, suffered severely in the 1970s from trade liberalisation and increased competition in overseas and domestic markets, resulting in the major rationalisation and manufacturing job loss referred to earlier. This included strong competition from Japanese manufacturers in electrical goods, electronics and cars. Plessey, taken over initially by Ferranti and subsequently in 1990 by GEC, underwent major restructuring and, as noted earlier, successfully refocused its activities in high growth, high profit, custom chip design and manufacture. Rover survives as a component now of BMW with a potentially secure future. Employment in both, is, however, well down on peak figures attained in the 1950s and 1960s. Plessey, for example, now employs around 1,200 compared with around 9,500 across all Plessey-owned companies (including Garrard) locally at the peak. Both, however, have seen some growth in employment most recently and employment, though smaller, is now more secure than in the past.

In terms of markets, a number of major companies are tied primarily to the domestic UK market. This is the case, for example, with domestic companies such as Allied Dunbar and WHSmith, as well as foreign-owned companies with facilities located in Swindon primarily to access and service the UK domestic market. The latter would include Renault's national part distribution centre, for example, and New Zealand-owned Anchor Foods. Others companies including Intel, Raychem, Honda, Burmah and Motorola partly relate to the domestic UK market. Their operations are also geared to a considerable extent to mainland Europe and wider international markets. Regional (in the sense of Europe-wide), and in some cases global corporate functions, are also in some cases located in Swindon. Some have seen the UK specifically as a stepping stone to mainland Europe. Honda, as with other Japanese-owned car manufacturers, has seen the UK as a platform for accessing and serving the European market as a whole, and accommodating European Union pressures for European-based production rather than market penetration by imported products. Global processes have thus resulted in an increasingly complex set of linkages between the economy and employment at local, national and international scales with far reaching implications.

Swindon as a location: the corporate view

The second part of this chapter examines some of the factors in terms of corporate decision making which have driven expansion and have transformed the economic and labour market structures as described above. It looks in particular at the factors which have impacted on the investment decisions of major employers which have established themselves locally. It draws on a programme of interviews conducted with senior managers in twelve leading companies conducted by the authors in 1996 for this study. The scale of Swindon's growth and its continuing success reflects the positive attractions of the local area to a range of different industries and employers over an extended time period. Common factors stand out. These include access and communications, the availability of sites and premises together with the Borough Council's active commitment to and involvement in expansion and development and, finally, the ability to draw on and to combine particular types of labour and skills. While it is possible to separate out these individual factors, to some extent, it has been very much the combination of these factors in a particular location which accounts for Swindon's capacity to capture and to hold down economic investment and employment over an extended period of time. It is also evident that many employers, having initially located in Swindon, have continued to invest and to increase the scale and their operations and employment locally.

Access and communications

Access and communications, particularly in terms of the motorway network, but also the London to Bristol high speed rail link, have been a critical component of Swindon's magnetic attraction for industry and employment particularly since the early 1970s. The immediate proximity of the M4 and ease of access from most of the town's main employment areas has clearly been important. There has been considerable investment in transport and communications networks nationally, which represent a critical part of the equation. In a very real sense, however, it is this, combined with the specific location of Swindon relative to London, relative to Heathrow and the M4 growth corridor and relative to the overall national motorway network and the centre of gravity of potential markets within the UK which has been crucial.

Access, communications and location have been of major significance, moreover, at a number of different levels. Road-based distribution of products and goods to regional and particularly national markets has been a critical factor for many local employers. These include companies which are primarily warehousing and distribution-based organisations, including, for example, Renault's car parts distribution centre, Anchor Butter, WHSmith and Book Club Associates. As one employer put it:

> "... the principle reasons I think for relocating, or for having any site here in Swindon at all, were distribution, were distribution issues and Swindon being quite an established.... I wouldn't want to call it a hub in a sense of sort of Atlanta airport or Chicago or that sort of thing but it is certainly a point where a lot of other organisations have distribution centres, so it makes a lot of sense and that's why I think we moved here originally...."

There is also a much wider range of companies for whom distribution and communications are not so much their raison d'être, but are, nevertheless, key considerations. They include, for example, national headquarters of finance and business services organisations in regular contact with branch networks or customers on a national scale. Road and rail-based access to central London specifically was seen as a key requirement by many employers in terms of contact with other parts of their own organisation, contact with other companies and access to customers and markets.

Access to Heathrow has been an increasingly important factor. This reflects globalisation and the increasing scale of overseas company investment in the town, generating a need for contact with parent companies and other parts of multi-national corporate structures. It also reflects the growth, locally, of organisations which explicitly operate on a European-wide or global scale. The Burmah Group is an early case in point, but the list would also include, for example, Intel, Motorola, Raychem and others. As one company put it:

> "We are ... and always have been a very inter-
> national company so this site services all of
> Europe as well as some other countries and the UK
> probably represents less than a quarter of our
> output, so being able to ship goods abroad, ideally
> not by air but occasionally by air. And in the kind
> of business that we're in, we have unique products
> which are proprietary so we tend to be a sole
> supplier in many cases, which means that you
> have to be extremely reliable. So therefore we do
> ship things by air when it's required. But also
> again it's a very international company so there's
> a lot of movement, customers, people from other
> parts of the corporation need to be able to
> physically come here and meet with people and
> work on things. The R and D centre is a European
> centre so if we didn't have access to a major
> international airport that wouldn't be a location
> that we would entertain."

Several companies observed that ideally they might have liked to be closer to Heathrow – but also observed that access was more reliable than coming out from central London. Summing up, as one employer observed:

> "... transportation is one of the most significant
> benefits. A lot of our business is international;
> Heathrow is one hour away (if you're lucky!).
> We're on an excellent rail connection route, west
> and east; we are on good access roads, north and
> south; we have good communications to the
> Midlands in terms of straight through without any
> congestion, and transportation in terms of
> commuter travel is very easy; you are disappoint-
> ed if you have a three minute or four minute stop
> anywhere on the way in. So I would say every-
> thing to do with transportation is a positive as far
> as this organisation's concerned."

While access at sub-regional and regional scales continue to be seen as excellent, congestion and transportation issues at a local level have increasingly emerged as an issue at the local level. Employers perceived a significant deterioration in journey times and increasing congestion at peak commuting times as a problem:

> *"There has been substantial infrastructure and road development, for example, Great Western Way, a dual carriageway close to the centre of Swindon.   Nevertheless, I'm sure that Thamesdown would be aware that there is severe congestion for people at the peak times coming into and out of work, at office times ... there are very long queue-backs, partly because school hours coincide as well ... it's not just starting, it's severe already and has been over the past recent years, two or three years, so there can be tailbacks for a mile or so, coming in."*

Provision by the Council of bus lanes on a limited number of routes, but without any significant improvement in bus services and prior to the construction of planned park and ride facilities, were seen as exacerbating the problem.   Employers were also, simultaneously, criticising local authority attempts to restrict the growth of car parking in the town centre and to restrict parking provision on new out-of-town developments.   Many companies, including for example, Allied Dunbar in the town centre, have historically aimed to offer their entire workforce free parking.   On the other hand, while congestion may well be worse than in the past, many employers acknowledged that access was still excellent compared with many other urban areas.

It is worth noting, finally, that alongside the obvious elements of physical transport infrastructure, including the motorway network and railway, other aspects of access and communications have reinforced Swindon's nodal location.   Investment by the Post Office and by Royal Mail Parcel Force in major facilities locally has been crucial to the distribution sector locally including, for example, the national book clubs.   There is an important infrastructure of businesses in the transportation and logistics sector meeting the road-based transport needs of local employers. The town is also an important focus for corporate telecommunications and data links, with a range of companies having information technology and data centres locally and dedicated, secure, links into national and international communications networks.

Sites and premises

A second essential factor, in combination with access and communications, has been the availability of a range of sites and premises over an extended period of time, which has been a very positive attraction to companies seeking to invest in or relocate to the local area. Particularly in the 1970s the relative cost of land and premises locally, compared with the City of London, the West End and the South East more generally, was a very major factor. This was reinforced by differences in labour costs and the impacts of high rates of labour turnover in London at the time.

> "Why did we come here – we came here because it was a hell of a lot cheaper to come here, and a lot more flexible to come here than it was to get close to London. And you know what the property prices at the beginning of the 80s were like in London versus here. Or even Reading versus here. We had all that creeping development out of London. And lots of restrictions too. You had to be a local company if you were to be allowed to have a sensible freehold in Reading for example. So flexibility, cost, culture, you know all those things come into it."

> "... office costs were rising, employment costs were rising, I seem to remember labour turnover in central London at the time was about 25-30%, so it was a very difficult market to be in. So it was not surprising that in common with many employers at the time they considered moving out."

Even though the gap narrowed subsequently, Swindon continued to offer considerable savings in terms of rents and land prices in later years. Office rents in Swindon in March 1990, for example, averaged around £15.00 per square foot compared with £23.00 in Reading and Bracknell and £36.50 in Hammersmith (Jones Lang Wooton, 1990).

Not sufficient in itself, the availability of sites and premises was very much a necessary factor in Swindon's attractiveness to industry and employment. Much of the detail in relation to this is set out in Chapter Five. It should be noted, however, that availability has, to a large extent, reflected local planning policy or, more importantly perhaps, the historic commitment of the local authority to securing growth and town expansion, balancing housing growth and growth in employment:

> *"The planning regulations in Swindon were much more flexible at the beginning of the 80's than they were in other parts of the country. They've eased up everywhere now, but they hadn't at that time. I remember going to the Reading Planning Office and saying we're interested in having an office here and we've looked at these and these and these and what about it and so forth and they said 'we hope you are looking at other towns', now do you think they'd say that today? I doubt it, you know. Because they didn't feel they could cope with any more people in the town and they hadn't got the infrastructure to support it."*

Aside from the formal planning framework, there has also been an element of pragmatism, a willingness to treat individual cases on merit. This was the case, for example, with the granting of permission for the Honda development at South Marston, which represented a departure from existing planning policy for that area.

As described in Chapter Five, the local authority has itself also played a key role in terms of its own land ownership and the provision of sites for employment purposes. This has included the Borough's own industrial estates from Cheney Manor and Greenbridge through to Blagrove and the campus-style developments in the western expansion (see Figure 5.1). It also included a willingness on the part of the Council to make available major sites in local authority ownership to key employers. It is notable that Burmah, Intel, Nationwide and most recently Motorola, all now major local employers, are all located on land sold to them freehold by the local authority. As the market for sites and premises for employment purposes expanded, in part, through the efforts of the local authority, the private sector played an increasingly important role, particularly in the western expansion. The supply of sites and premises increasingly responded to market demand, with the private sector identifying and seeking to realise the development potential of sites for industrial and commercial uses. The willingness of the Borough Council to support continued development remained, however, a critical factor – a position over which there is now, as indicated earlier and discussed in more detail in Chapter Five, something of a question mark.

The context of town expansion was itself an important factor historically. According to one employer:

> "... *sports and arts amenities are good, and presumably the northern expansion will bring an increase in facilities there which means other options for people. I remember when it was first identified that Swindon was the fastest growing town in Europe. There was this sort of huge collective pride in that fact alone. You sort of felt you were part of a success story."*

Employers were in some cases able to secure at the outset land in excess of their immediate needs with a view to future expansion. At a more general level, the ready availability of sites and the Borough's commitment to further expansion and ongoing development to the west and later the north of the town did much to convince incoming employers that it was also likely that any future needs for sites, premises and expansion could be met locally without the need for major relocation and disruption to business. As we have seen, this capacity to accommodate local growth and expansion has been critical to a number of the town's major local employers with companies. Burmah, Intel and Honda, for example, expanded on their own original land acquisitions. Raychem and Allied Dunbar have progressively expanded into a range of premises within the town, while Nationwide and Motorola, having first followed this same route, then centralised their operations on a single site – purchased in both cases, as already noted, from the Borough Council.

The Borough Council had generally been experienced by employers as positive and supportive, at least at the level of the major negotiations around site acquisition, planning permissions and related matters:

*"... in terms of the infrastructure, yes, the Borough
have a very good understanding of how to work
with business and on the whole do so effectively as
far as we can see."*

*"The way we were treated, the communication,
the negotiation about the land. We were very
impressed with what they did."*

*"It's been a good relationship ... they're good at
the really crucial things, but the really annoying
things, their kind of bureaucracy takes over. I feel
there's a kind of a level in the local authority at
which there is a vision and then below that,
there's a level at which they're all bureaucrats, it
depends at which level you're operating at."*

What was seen as bureaucratic obstructionism over minor
planning matters had, however, clearly been the source of
considerable irritation. There were also deeper concerns in some
cases as to the overall capacity or commitment of the Borough
Council:

*"I think generally we feel that in terms of the
development of our business and support for our
business then we don't get, even in the tactical
sense, we don't get the value, thought and
consideration from local government in the area ...
in terms of the surrounding infrastructure, even to
small issues like gateways and road adjustments
and consideration of how best we can do that ... I
think there's a competence issue in local
government too, by the way. I don't think they
have the competence."*

*"... they are unhelpful ... they still act in a sense
like a small rural parish council. They love the
old industries and they don't particularly like new
industries ... they've offered us no help whatsoever
and have generally been quite, you know, have on
occasions hindered, have made difficulties where
difficulties did not need to exist on planning issues
and stuff like that ... Honda Works was seen as,
you know, very important because it was bringing*

back the motor industry and all of that. And we were seen as, you know, I think we were seen as intruders ... bringing things here that perhaps they didn't want. And you know it definitely felt as if you were dealing with a parish council rather than, you know, rather than a big Council."

Employment and labour supply

A third key component has been that of employment, skills and labour supply. Needs have changed over time with the changing industrial structure of the town decided earlier this chapter. Early on, in the postwar period, it was the traditions and skills base related to engineering and manufacturing that was important to companies such as Plessey, Vickers and Pressed Steel. As the town grew, the availability of an expanding supply of relatively unskilled labour and, increasingly, female labour, was important to new employers, including those in distribution and other services. Again, the very fact that the town was growing and was committed to further expansion was a positive factor to a number of companies:

> *"Swindon then being a new town ... it gave us room for expansion, a ready, good quality, labour supply, and then whilst it* was *a new town the infrastructure was developed and so you know we felt we would get all the support we needed so that we were pioneers in that sense."*

Increasingly, as well, it was the capacity of employers to draw together a *combination* of different types of employment and skills, including less skilled employment both male and female, together with higher level technical, professional and managerial grades, which was important. This capacity in itself reflected a range of factors including demography and, as noted, town expansion. They also include the attractiveness and image of the town and its environs to different labour market groups.

Continuing town expansion was an important factor, as already observed, in ensuring labour supply at a general level. Swindon certainly had a strong tradition of mainly male, skilled and semi-skilled manufacturing. The expanding supply of new labour with little attachment to existing work cultures and work practices in the locality was also seen as a major attraction by a wide range of employers seeking to assemble new workforces and new work cultures locally. The town itself and town expansion both in the early postwar years and in the 1970s and 1980s provided much of the lower and middle tiers of the workforce: *"the need for junior clerical staff, you know, has always been met from the local community"*. The housing supply, employment opportunities, amenities and social provision offered by the town continued to support market-driven town expansion and growth in the local labour market after the period of formal town expansion.

Critical, however, to the capacity of employers also to attract and to retain high quality staff into higher level, technical, professional and managerial grades was the possibility of living in the surrounding town, villages and rural areas with an easy commute in to Swindon for work. Swindon itself has not generally been seen as attractive to these employment groups. It is seen as lacking much in the way of more up-market housing, in part, for historical reasons.

> *"I don't think its image is great, I mean I don't think people sort of say 'lucky you' if you say that you come from Swindon. And comedians, you know, it's taken over from Wigan or somewhere hasn't it as the place that, if you want to cite somewhere that's seen to be tedious and not particularly inspiring then you would say Swindon more often. It's a bit untrue really, but, let's be honest, it's not that attractive a town."*

It also lacks the sort of amenities, culture and image generally valued by these groups: *"... culturally pretty dead. You have to go somewhere, to Bath or London if you want a bit of culture, music and theatre or what have you."* The surrounding towns, villages and rural areas are, by contrast, however, a very positive attraction:

> *"... the main attraction of Swindon is it's near a lot of nice places but you haven't got to live in Swindon, you can live somewhere, you can go to Oxford or Marlborough or the Cotswolds or Bristol or Bath and enjoy a superb quality of life and it's still commutable within 20 or 30 minutes. I think Swindon itself doesn't hold many attrac-*

*tions to visitors who come here for interview for
the first time."*

This has been important to companies relocating to Swindon in
terms of their ability to hold onto an acceptable proportion of
those employees whom they would consider key workers. It has
also been important in the ability of employers to attract and
retain those with higher level skills in order to meet the need for
expansion or to recruit personnel to replace staff who leave.
Companies positively sell the attractions of living outside of
Swindon when seeking to attract staff to more senior positions, or
sell them the idea of relocation:

> *"... when you first say to people for example based
> in London that we're now planning to move you
> or someone else out, their reaction is usually fairly
> negative. However, once here, once they've got
> over the turmoil of an office and family move ...
> their reaction has been uniformly positive. People
> like the rural environment, they welcome the
> shortened commuting times."*

On the other hand, as a number of employers noted, the rural idyll
was not necessarily attractive to younger staff and those more
attracted to the sort of lifestyle offered by more urban centres, as
opposed to staff at a slightly later stage in the life cycle: *"people
who've got over that now and are much more content with having
their country pile and good schools or quality of life, somewhere for
the dogs to run free."*

The labour market for many of those in higher level
managerial, technical and professional grades can extend
geographically along much of the M4 Corridor. Swindon firms
are particularly well placed to tap into these labour markets. In
terms of financial services, for example, as one local employer saw
the situation:

> *"... in terms of labour supply there are more than
> twenty major financial services organisations'
> headquarters in a sort of thirty mile radius, so it's
> actually the largest and most influential financial
> base outside London."*

Another employer also noted the importance of the regional
labour market:

> *"The ability of people to commute in, or go and work in Reading, or you can live in Swindon and work in Reading, quite easily in fact from here. Or Bristol – quite a few people drive here from Bristol. We always feel on tenterhooks because we feel they might decide that if somebody offers them a job locally that, you know ... so there is that."*

As this suggests, the downside is that this same ease of access puts a considerable range of alternative employment opportunities within reach of a company's existing workforce tending to make the market for certain employment categories very competitive:

> *"... obviously it's a very central location so communication is very good from Swindon, that's a blessing and a curse because it means we're in a much more highly competitive area for people than say, Manchester, and our costs are higher from that point of view ... it's easier to get staff. More difficult to keep them though, because people like the feeling that there is other people around that they can go and work with if the job doesn't work out here, or we have a redundancy or something like that. They like to feel that there are other companies around that they can go to without the hassle of having to move house again."*

While Swindon offers the possibility of combining a range of types of employment, there is very much of an exaggerated split geographically between different components of the overall labour force in many cases:

> *"I have to say there's a definite split between if you like, one level of staff and another. Clerical, customer facing, administrative staff at the bottom end of the business if you like, almost invariably live in Swindon, typically in west Swindon. At another level, managers and I suppose if you look at my immediate colleagues, the directors, they all live out of Swindon and there's only one on the top team of about 100*

> *people that I'm aware actually lives in Swindon*
> *itself which is curious. Everyone chooses to move*
> *out into the rural locations and drive in, which is*
> *sad really. So in terms of physical location, it's a*
> *pity I think that Swindon doesn't offer a more*
> *diverse community if you like, where people could*
> *feel that they could set up families and find*
> *suitable schools and all that sort of thing in the*
> *centre of town, as apparently that option doesn't*
> *seem to exist."*

In overall terms, the labour market locally and the mix of employment that can be assembled in Swindon has been seen as very favourable by major employers. The market is, on the other hand, clearly competitive, and perceived to be increasingly so. This is the case locally, with the build up of employers recruiting within the Swindon labour market itself. It is also the case at a more regional level, with the market for certain categories of technical and professional staff extending along the M4 Corridor west to Bristol and east to Newbury, Reading and London itself. While labour supply or skills shortage had not been seen as a problem area as such, there was concern in relation to particular employment categories as unemployment dropped.

With unemployment in 1989-90 and again in 1996-97 dipping locally well below national rates, employers reliant on low-wage, unskilled labour found the market increasingly difficult. This was particularly the case in relation to temporary and seasonal employment – with tight labour markets, those who might have formed part of this flexible pool of labour which employers could dip into when needed, have, to some extent, been able to move into the more mainstream workforce:

> *"Of late though, I think maybe getting hold of*
> *temporary labour has not been as easy as it used*
> *to be and so you have to be quite quick off the*
> *mark, particularly in distribution, to get people*
> *otherwise they go on to [...] or somewhere else.*
> *And maybe there's less of them."*

> *"... the unemployment level in Swindon isn't*
> *sufficiently high for us to have as much flexibility*
> *as we want that seasonal peaks. I mean literally*
> *we have to take people at Christmas if they're sort*

> *of walking and breathing, they don't even need to be walking, which leads to, some quality control problems.... Therefore it's a real struggle to find, you know, an extra sort of 20 or 30% of staff at Christmas on a temporary basis because there aren't particularly high levels of unemployment and therefore there isn't a pool of labour waiting, especially as most of the other businesses, or a number of the other businesses are also cyclical in nature and therefore have their peak loading at the same time.... It causes a problem now and it is going to ... I do not see how the problem is going to go away because it is the down-side of it being a centre for distribution for a lot of organisations. Especially when you consider that arguably, it's not a skill, so it's not like a TNT setting up next to Motorola so they can take the best digital engineers."*

In relation to unskilled service labour in, for example, distribution and clerical labour at the bottom end of the pay scales engaged in order processing, employers had, since the early 1980s, developed a range of labour market strategies to tap in to different sections of the labour market and new sources of labour. These included different types of shift systems and part-time employment, including twilight shifts, weekends-only contracts, term-time contracts aimed at women with school-age children and annualised hours contracts with longer hours when demand is heaviest.

> *"... we were very early into this, because particular needs we had in the late 80s to find new ways of recruiting staff in a fairly tight labour market led us to develop all sorts of approaches to flexible working. So we have people here working around the clock, we have people on shifts, we have people who work in term-time contracts, we have people who work so called twilight shifts, people who work maybe only one or two days a week, maybe it's Saturdays or Sundays and they're at home during the working week, during what is otherwise everybody else's working week. So those sort of flexible deals are available and I've*

> *always seen that as a deal if you like that we can*
> *offer, that suits employees as much as it suits us."*

Other employers saw the threat of increased competition locally
both for particular employment categories but also more generally:

> *"... unemployment level here is exceptionally low.*
> *It's very hard to get not only trained, experienced*
> *staff but just the ordinary operator because of the*
> *influx of industry it's really dried us up ... we're*
> *almost down to the unemployable. When that*
> *happens it drives up wages, drives up*
> *remuneration packages, and creates employment*
> *problems."*

As this suggests, potential employment problems are more a matter
of cost and quality than labour shortage or skills shortage as such,
but nonetheless a problem. A financial services employer pointed
to the fact that such companies were all, increasingly, going to be
looking to secure staff with the skills and aptitude to offer direct
telephone-based services to customers:

> *"... the financial sector organisations are all*
> *heading the same way in trying to establish more*
> *efficient customer facing functions in central*
> *locations, and we're probably all going to be*
> *looking for much the same sort of enhanced skills,*
> *for those customer interfacing staff. The model*
> *that many people would point to is Direct Line or*
> *First Direct ... I think for the immediate period,*
> *say three or four years, we do need quite large*
> *numbers of those sort of staff and as I say, I*
> *suspect so do most others. A bit beyond that*
> *maybe the need falls away again a little."*

At the other end of the scale, many employers identify particular
professional specialists as difficult to recruit to Swindon, in part
because of national if not international level competition but also
because certain groups in particular tend to be rooted in London
and the metropolitan labour market:

> *"... if you're trying to find lawyers or PR people or*
> *marketing people they tend to want to be in*

> *London and, you know, it's making them make the lifestyle change that's the main problem."*

> *"Swindon is not a location that you can easily attract professionals to. Swindon has no cultural centre, it's a very soul-less town. And if you want to attract world class professionals, technical professionals or whatever, that's a genuine handicap."*

A number of employers had noted an increase in commuting out to Swindon from London by some higher paid professional and managerial employees:

> *"... what's happened is that you pay quite a market premium to get those sorts of people in, typically to the extent that, they're happy to continue living in London and can afford the commitments, so they actually commute from London down to Swindon and back again."*

Locational commitment

As noted earlier in the chapter, a key feature of employment growth in Swindon has been the impact of successive waves of investment by existing employers, both relocating additional functions to Swindon but also concentrating expansion and new investment in the town. There have been firms which have closed down or relocated away from Swindon. Overall, however, there has been a high degree of continuing commitment on the part of the town's key employers. This is not to say that in a number of cases key employers have not considered shifting investment away from Swindon or considered alternatives to investing in expansion and new facilities locally. With unemployment down below 3% in the late 1980s, one of the town's key office-based employers was looking to expand to meet projected market growth. With little capacity on their existing site, and with the clerical labour market in Swindon overheating, the option of establishing a second site outside of the Swindon area, probably South Wales was the likely option.

> *"... five years ago we were seriously considering looking at a second admin centre outside of Swindon because we foresaw enormous growth ...*

> *then we were looking at a second centre*
> *somewhere else, Wales or somewhere.... There*
> *was a fear that Swindon couldn't accommodate*
> *what we then foresaw as our growth."*

As it happened, with rising unemployment and recession in the financial services sector, the need for expansion passed, but the case is symptomatic of the possible impact of serious overheating in the labour market. A second major office-based employer faced the choice of concentrating growth and expansion in one of two corporate centres within the UK, a choice between Swindon and the Midlands. In the end, the decision was relatively clear cut with Swindon offering significant advantages, particularly in terms of the capacity to recruit and retain key staff. A move away from Swindon altogether was, however, a serious option at the time and a decision was only reached after considerable analysis of the alternatives.

A major local manufacturing company looking to make a significant investment in new facilities used property agents to look at a range of possible locations, including South Wales, Scotland and the North East.

> *"At the stage when we were looking at the new*
> *site, yes, we did an exploratory look all over the*
> *country, the advantages and disadvantages of*
> *staying here, going to South Wales, going to*
> *Scotland, North East of England, all the places*
> *where you get substantial grants and support. But*
> *finally we decided to stay here. Essentially the*
> *reason being continuity and the technical aspects*
> *of the kind of people we need. Taking our*
> *development and design engineers who are*
> *effectively local, and I mean local as in the South*
> *rather than necessarily Swindon, and trying to*
> *persuade them to go to Scotland or Wales might*
> *have been a little difficult. That is such a difficult*
> *resource, a scarce resource.... We could not take a*
> *risk of losing say 50% of them, particularly to*
> *competitors who are not that far away from us."*

Again, Swindon won out, with the key consideration being the technical expertise which the company had assembled around its

Swindon facilities and the need to keep research and development functions in close contact with the company's production facilities.

> *"... if a design engineer is going to be innovative and drive the cost of our product down and also try and get technology into the design he's also got to understand exactly how manufacturing works. Or he could design something that's not manufacturable. So you might have the best design in the world, but when we build it doesn't work very well. So those people have to communicate literally like brother and sister, they have to live in each other's offices. It's absolutely critical."*

This outweighed, in the end, the lower costs, the grants and other financial assistance which would have been available elsewhere.

While these, and other cases, have generally seen renewed investment in Swindon, it is significant that at key points in corporate decision making, the location of new investment is put up for serious inspection, with the outcome by no means a foregone conclusion. This can also be precipitated by merger and takeover, with new options and new corporate strategies potentially impacting on existing patterns of investment:

> *"... if we had been taken over, then the business probably would have moved from Swindon, because we would have only been taken over by a company, by an organisation that could have run us more efficiently, and they could only do that by merging us with whatever they had and it would have been unlikely that they would have moved to Swindon."*

It can also be precipitated by the expansion process itself, which can raise the issue of whether Swindon remains suitable – the need to relocate opens a window of opportunity to consider a range of options. It can simply reflect reinvestment in existing plant and machinery in a situation. Where there are already alternative sites within the corporate structure, there may be different options for new investment:

> *"... there was serious discussion just now, even on the investment we've had just now, really serious*

> *discussion of whether that investment should take place in Swindon or not. A massive debate ... that discussion isn't finished yet because, if [the] corporate plan is to be delivered and the growth plan is to be delivered, we still have to put more capacity into the business and it's still a significant debate as to whether that additional capacity should be put in at Swindon or should we put it elsewhere."*

Employers when questioned, indicated that, with a clean sheet, they might not locate their current facilities in Swindon, or even within the UK:

> *"If I was thinking about locating in the UK today I think I would probably locate closer to Birmingham. Some of the areas around there would – it's less congested, and you've got a good international airport so you might choose Birmingham."*

> *"Somewhere a bit closer to the airport would have its attractions. You know with the way Bracknell has developed in the meanwhile for example, maybe it could be Bracknell or even Newbury. Because of course Newbury was quite restricted in planning development at that time but it's been released a lot more."*

> *"If we started the business again it probably wouldn't be in Swindon. If we started from scratch with an instant business, having perfect foresight and knowing exactly what was going to happen, it may well not have been Swindon ... it could well have been somewhere in mainland Europe, for instance in Spain or in France.... It's a hard question to answer but it would have been dependent on a lot of things, access to markets, availability of trained labour and government assistance would help as well."*

The historical circumstances in which the original decisions which brought Swindon's current major employers to the town have, in many cases, changed. Many companies have, nevertheless, put down quite deep roots locally. Investment in property or in specialised plant and machinery is a factor in some cases locally. More significant in others is the embeddedness of employers in local labour markets, and the extent to which their current workforce represents a key asset which would be largely lost through relocation. This, in many cases, ties them quite firmly to their current location:

> *"... when you look at investment cost and opening a new plant, one of the key things people often forget is how much they've really invested in their staff. If you were going to move from, move a facility which is a technology based facility from one place to another, you would not want to have to change staff and that's why we wanted to keep it as close as possible to the current facilities so that we wouldn't lose any staff."*

> *"... we've got here, engineering excellence. Your knowledge base is the intrinsic value here. And therefore essential for the future. So the reason why stay here just now is because of the knowledge base of the technology, the experience and application of that technology, and the ability to apply that technology to get really cost effective high quality components. If you move it somewhere else you've got to recreate that."*

Significantly it is those companies which relied more heavily on lower cost, low-skill labour which were less committed to maintaining their investment locally or which were more certain that they would, in an ideal world, have looked to locate elsewhere. While Swindon continued to benefit from reinvestment and expansion, the investment process and locational decision making remained, however, a dynamic process and one which could seriously alter the pattern of growth and investment over what is, historically, a relatively short time period. Labour costs, labour availability and the overall relationship between labour market supply and employer needs could be a critical factor. So, too, could the pattern of availability of sites and premises both for local employers wishing to expand and for potential new investors. In both respects, local policy with regards to future expansion and physical growth could play a key role. Having looked in some detail here at the patterns and processes of change in the local economy and labour market, the next chapter goes on to look at the role of the Borough Council in particular, in terms of economic strategy and industrial development.

four

Economic strategy and industrial development

Strategies for industrial and economic development have been central to the activities of a wide range of local councils in the postwar period. In many cases this dates from the mid-1970s as a response to rapidly increasing unemployment. In the case of Swindon, the Borough Council was actively involved in industrial development from a much earlier stage. This originated initially from concern particularly in the latter stages of the Second World War at overdependence on rail engineering and the need to diversify the town's narrow economic base. Its strategies in relation to industrial development and employment developed subsequently as an integral component part of planned town expansion and the Borough was very actively involved in promoting economic expansion over many years. By the latter part of the 1980s, with the Borough Council rethinking its role and involvement in active town expansion, the role of economic development and promotion was itself reappraised. Active marketing and promotion was cut back in the 1990s and the Borough Council started to get involved in partnership and joint working arrangements with a range of other organisations in the local area.

Postwar plans: pre-cursors to expansion

Industrial development policy in the immediate postwar years focused on retaining employment and economic activity established through the location of wartime factories in or close to the town. Their conversion to peacetime production was the initial basis for postwar modernisation and expansion. Dangers of dependence on a single major industry had been recognised in the 1930s depression, with the rail engineering works already showing signs of decline. The Council's *Memorandum on the potentialities of Swindon for industrial development* (Swindon Borough Council, 1945a), represented a clear prospectus for industrial expansion. The prime objective was to reduce dependence on the Great Western Railway (GWR) engineering works by diversifying the town's economic base: "To ensure a steady level of employment, Swindon needs to see other industries established in the town." (Swindon Borough Council, 1945b). Also clearly stated was a desire to broaden the social base of the town. It was argued that in the

> ... one-industry town ... social life is correspond-ingly narrowed. Workers rarely meet people engaged in other industries and walks of life, with different ideas and different outlooks and there is a danger of a narrow uniformity of ideas emerging, which will strangle initiative and progress'. (Swindon Borough Council, 1945a)

It was noted that aircraft workers had already been laid off and the Short Brothers wartime factory closed down.

The Council's Memorandum acknowledged the government view

> ... that first attention must be paid to the Development Areas where large-scale unemploy-ment existed before the war. No one will wish to quarrel either on economic or on social grounds with this policy. But one must ask the question whether it must be rigidly interpreted. (Swindon Borough Council, 1945a)

It went on to quote *The Times* commenting on the Distribution of Industry Bill: "And again; 'It is as important to develop fully the industrial potentialities of these prosperous regions as it is to preserve the development areas against a recurrence of depression and unemployment.'" (Swindon Borough Council, 1945a). The Borough Council signalled its intention to establish a trading estate to provide factory space at low rentals to attract further additional industry. Provision of industrial and commercial sites and premises was to be a central component of the Council's expansion strategy over the decades to come. So too, in different forms was the lobbying activity putting the case for Swindon's expansion, exemplified early on by the Memorandum.

Swindon versus the regions

Swindon's plans were frustrated in the immediate postwar years by government regional policy. Tight control of industrial location by the government's Board of Trade by means of Industrial Development Certificates (IDCs) initially prevented much in the way of new industry being attracted in. Clear priority was given to the Development Areas in the peripheral regions of the UK. Wartime factories, including Plessey and Vickers, had, however, expanded and indeed experienced labour shortages which the Council sought to relieve by means of housebuilding and its early commitment to receiving overspill population from London. The Council had established the Cheney Manor industrial estate but much of this remained undeveloped.

The major breakthrough came in 1955 when the Pressed Steel Company was refused permission to build a new car body plant in Oxford to supply the Morris works at Cowley. The Pressed Steel Company persuaded the government to allow them to locate instead at Swindon, within easy reach of Oxford, outside of the South East region and within an official expanding town with supplies of the right kind of labour (Harloe, 1975, p 151). It seemed like the ideal compromise and Pressed Steel purchased the major Parsonage Farm site, outside of the Borough boundary, in what was then Highworth Rural District. Swindon had pressured the Board of Trade to agree the move, and the town development scheme was used to provide both workers and their houses. Meanwhile, Plessey expanded on the Cheney Manor Estate and Vickers expanded their aircraft works at South Marston. Industrial Development Certificates remained relatively easily available until the late 1950s, becoming much more restrictive after 1958, particularly in relation to larger plants. By then, however, almost 800,000 square feet of factory space had been built on the Borough's Cheney Manor estate and additional space was needed elsewhere to secure continuing growth.

The Council had already purchased 48 acres adjacent to the Parsonage Farm site bought by Pressed Steel. It subsequently acquired 84 acres, beyond the Borough boundary to the east, for its new Greenbridge Industrial Estate, which provided much of the employment growth in the town in the 1960s. As economic conditions worsened nationally, however, and incentives to move to the regions were increased, it became increasingly difficult to obtain IDCs in Swindon. Unable to pursue an orderly plan balancing employment growth in relation to housing provision, the Council aimed, more pragmatically, to secure what it could in terms of industrial investment and employment growth when economic conditions and the national policy environment were favourable:

> Swindon soon abandoned the attempt to pursue a pre-planned policy for the attraction of employers to the town ... the town did accept most of the new industry it could get, without too much discrimination. One officer agreed that they had been opportunists, grabbing at almost everything that came their way. But he felt that if they were to succeed in town development, in the circumstances in which the town found itself, such an attitude was both essential and inevitable. (Harloe, 1975, p 148)

The extent to which the town had committed itself to large-scale investment in infrastructure and town centre development in support of expansion reinforced the need to attract industry and people to increase the rateable value and spread the financial burden. This more pragmatic approach was encouraged given the perceived difficulty in obtaining IDCs from the Board of Trade – which made any form of selective policy, picking and choosing preferred employers, impracticable. This was despite Swindon's continued attempts to argue that they should be treated as a special case, in the face of firmly established national policy.

Reinforcing this, Swindon was also less attractive to many of the mobile smaller and medium-sized enterprises seeking to relocate from London than some of the New Towns much closer to London. Most of the New Towns were able to offer what was perceived at the time to be a more pleasant environment and with better access to London, for the sort of white-collar or science-based industries that Swindon might have hoped to attract at that time. Distance, plus the fact that it retained the image, to prove very persistent over time, of an engineering-dominated town counted against it. It was, therefore, competing more directly with the peripheral regions for larger enterprises employing skilled and semi-skilled manual workers and willing to move longer distances or to set up branch plants. The conflict with the Board of Trade and with regional policy was, in this context, understandable. While the really large employers who expressed an interest in coming to the town were generally prevented from doing so, Swindon did, in fact, succeed in getting many of the IDCs that they required and achieved success in their policy of attracting in new industries even through what was perceived as a difficult period (Harloe, 1975, p 153).

As noted in Chapter Two, however, the latter part of the 1960s was a critical time for Swindon's development. With the rail works contracting and new industry unable to offset this to any great degree, town expansion came to a virtual halt. Harloe (1975, p 144) shows that the number of overspill households housed in the local authority stock fell back sharply from the early 1960s. And while new employers had been attracted in, only limited success had been achieved in terms of diversification. In 1966, Pressed Steel and Plessey employed 23% of the economically active population, and the rail works still accounted for significant employment. Employment as a whole thus remained quite strongly concentrated in the engineering and vehicles sector, with a significant concentration in just three companies.

Strategic growth

By the late 1960s and early years of the 1970s, however, warehousing and distribution-based activities were showing in-creasing interest – WHSmith, for example, established its national distribution centre on the Greenbridge Industrial Estate in 1967. From 1965, office development in central London had also been increasingly restricted by the requirement for Office Development Permits (ODPs), designed to relieve development pressures in the capital. Swindon, on the other hand, unlike the case with IDCs, was just outside of the area within which permits were required. The permit system also served to push up the price of office space in central London even further, emphasising the cost advantages of office relocation particularly for companies which were expanding and likely to need additional space. Combined with its locational advantages and the availability of sites for development and labour supply this made Swindon increasingly attractive in the early 1970s to office-based employers.

The Council's strategy in the early 1970s of attracting in major employers across a range of employment sectors achieved a considerable measure of success. Strategically located in the M4 Corridor, the town was well placed to attract in employers in its own right, independent of overspill policies or central government policy. It was able to take advantage of the opportunities created by the restructuring of the regional economy of South East England, and the marked cost differentials which developed in terms of property and labour costs at this time, encouraging decentralisation of economic activity from central London and the rest of the region. Manufacturing companies attracted in included Roussel and Raychem in the expanding pharmaceuticals and plastics sectors. Service sector employers attracted at this time included Allied Dunbar (then Hambro Insurance), and the Nationwide Building Society, both of which located in the central area. Subsequent job growth in these and other inward investors from this period was (as described in Chapter Three) a major contribution to employment growth, and these enterprises remain as major employers in the town in the late 1990s.

Swindon's older established industries in engineering and electronics in particular were, however, far from immune to declining employment and corporate restructuring impacting on these sectors. The rail workshops had already lost around 4,000 jobs in the mid-1960s. There were further job losses from the rail works in the 1970s and major redundancies in Plessey and Garrards. This pushed unemployment, temporarily, above the national average from 1975 to 1980. Local newspaper headlines at the time dubbed it the 'Boom town that ran out of steam' and the Borough Council even lobbied the government in 1975 (unsuccessfully) for regional assistance as an Intermediate Area. In 1978 Garrard (by then part of the Plessey Group) announced the redundancy of 1,250 out of its 1,830 workforce, again prompting the Council and the local Labour MP to call for Assisted Area Status.   Rising unemployment relative to the national picture, albeit temporary, prompted immediate action by the Council in terms of increasing emphasis and expenditure on marketing and promoting the town to potential inwards investors (Bassett and Harloe, 1990). This also coincided with the early phases of the western expansion, threatening an imbalance between population growth prompted by new housing provision and job opportunities. Government assistance was again refused in 1979.   The Department of Trade and Industry took the opportunity to point out that Swindon had, in fact, been supported in a number of respects by government policy in the 1970s: government had adopted a flexible policy with regard to IDCs in the 1970s with none being refused since 1973, clothing manufacturer Triumph's expansion had been assisted by the government's Clothing Industry Scheme and the public sector office decentralisation policy had brought 570 jobs to the town with the Science Research Council and the Natural and Environmental Research Council, precursors to relocation of the Economic and Social Research Council.

The Borough Council's 1976 Corporate Plan had committed it to the ambitious target of creating 3,000 new jobs a year, indicative of an all-out push for economic expansion and job growth via inwards investment. Policy to achieve this combined the launch of a more vigorous marketing strategy, building up a wider portfolio of sites and appointment of a new marketing manager. The Conservatives, who briefly gained control of the Council in 1976, argued the need for someone with a business and marketing background to sell the town and to meet industrialists 'over a gin and tonic in the city' (Bassett and Harloe, 1990, p 48). The post went to a former commercial director of Plessey, who had little sympathy for party politics. He headed up 'Swindon Enterprise', the Council's new marketing unit (established in 1977 to spearhead the campaign and granted a considerable degree of autonomy). It was located, symbolically, not in the Civic Offices, but on the top floor of the Murray John Tower, the one major high rise office block which dominates the central area townscape.

Open for business

The new marketing manager described his priorities at the time (Bassett and Harloe, 1990) as the attraction of hi-tech companies and company headquarters. Advertising and marketing concentrated on promoting Swindon's locational and environmental advantages, described later on, in the marketing manager's own words:

> ... 50 minutes by high speed train from London, one hour from Heathrow, next to the M4 in the golden corridor, but cheaper than rival towns, surrounded by stunning countryside with lots of old rectories for executives to live in. (*Financial Times*, 30 June 1986)

It was an image that significant numbers of mobile enterprises were to buy, whether influenced or not by the Borough's hard sell. Initial emphasis in the campaign was placed on contacting US electronics and pharmaceutical companies and building up contacts with London-based property agents and advisers – profitable concerns which did not need the sort of subsidies or inducements offered by the peripheral problem regions within the UK. 'Swindon Enterprise', under the new marketing manager, developed a considerable degree of autonomy from the Borough Council in terms of its image and the way in which it operated. It worked to an extent at arms length from the Borough, aiming to promote the town and to sell its locational assets to the private sector in order to generate inwards investment and employment. Overall expenditure on industrial promotion more than doubled from £139,000 in 1978/79 to £500,000 by 1986/87. It was little short of this level of spending over the whole five-year period from 1981 through to 1988. Expenditure specifically on actual advertising and promotional activities, excluding staff costs and support services, went up from only £18,000 in 1976/77 to over £300,000 per year over the same five-year period in the second half of the 1980s.

Provision of a wider portfolio of sites to attract new employers was a key component of the overall strategy. Campus-style business park development on the periphery of the town was explicitly encouraged through the planning process. This included both single-user sites, such as that occupied by US-owned semiconductor giant Intel from 1981 (established in temporary accommodation locally in 1979), and high-quality, multi-user sites including Windmill Hill in West Swindon. Private sector interest in industrial and commercial property development had been growing since the 1970s and Windmill Hill, for example, was developed by the Kuwaiti-owned St Martin's Property Corporation on land purchased from the local authority. In general, however, and in spite of pressure from officers, Labour Councillors were unwilling to agree to freehold land sales, insisting on 125-year leases. As land prices escalated the Council, in any case, found itself increasingly priced out of the land market and it was unable to replenish its land holdings.

New employers continued to flow into the town, even during recession in the early 1980s. These included enterprises in electronics, computer software, pharmaceuticals, distribution, office-based administration and financial services (see Chapter Three). Added to this, a number of the more recent inward investors continued to expand employment. Consequently, although traditional manufacturing employers in the town again suffered job losses, manufacturing as a whole grew by around 3% (1981-84), in marked contrast to a drop of 11% nationally. Service sector employment grew even more strongly, by nearly 9% compared with 5% nationally. Swindon's apparent success attracted increasing media attention in the early 1980s, and was dubbed by the *Financial Times* "the fastest growing micro-economy in Europe ... riding a high tech wave" (*Financial Times*, 30 June 1983). Overall, although unemployment rose sharply with the recession, it remained below the national figure. This was significant symbolically and in policy terms compared with the situation in the mid-1970s when it overshot the national trend. Unemployment, in fact, remained below national levels from 1979 onwards (see Figure 3.1). There was a marked upwards blip in 1986 coinciding with final closure of the rail works, but in general terms, unemployment was falling relative to national rates throughout the 1980s.

This in itself is indicative of the strength of the local economy and suggests that Swindon's capacity to generate self-sustaining growth in the face of national recession and massive restructuring was now considerable. The question of how far active policy on the part of the local authority contributed to success over this period is more difficult. Many incoming companies praised the positive and helpful role played by the Borough Council (see Bassett and Harloe, 1990 and Chapter Three above). At the very least it had clearly played an important enabling role. The overall presumption in favour of expansion in West Swindon and elsewhere and, to some extent, its role in terms of the direct provision of sites for industrial and commercial development were clearly important. The town had to compete for mobile investment with locations such as Milton Keynes, Northampton and Peterborough, all heavily into promotion and marketing. Swindon's marketing strategy was, however, working with a powerful tide in terms of factors attractive to firms looking to relocate or to expand their operations a this time, as described in Chapter Three – the excellent road and rail links to London and Heathrow, availability of sites and premises, the pool of skilled and unskilled labour in an expanding labour market and the quality and attractiveness of the surrounding environment. In this context it is very difficult to be precise about the specific impacts of the Borough's marketing and promotional strategies.

A new vision

By the mid-1980s, however, as sketched out in Chapter Two, a combination of factors led to significant policy reappraisal. Promotional marketing and the attraction of inwards investment remained the main thrust of policy into the early 1980s. Concern in relation to rising unemployment led to the launch of supplementary initiatives directed more to small firms and indigenous enterprises. This included 'Swindon Enterprise Trust', established in 1982, a joint council, business, community sector venture to encourage and support small firms. There was some concern expressed by Labour members at the time over some of the marketing director's more flamboyant statements as to the need for expensive housing and up-market entertainment to attract the captains of industry (Bassett and Harloe, 1990, p 50). Concern started to be expressed as to the extent of expansion in West Swindon and the pre-emption of resources which might have been needed for other purposes. Overall, however, the all-party consensus backing a policy of growth and expansion held firm and it was not until the mid-1980s that significant concern started to be expressed in relation to overall policy direction. Articulated in the consultative document, *A new vision for Thamesdown*, this debate developed in an increasingly unfavourable context both in economic terms and in terms of the increasingly constrained financial regime within which local government operated. In overall terms, *A new vision for Thamesdown* recommended growth within the confines of existing plans in the 1990s and consolidation subsequently.

In terms of economic development policy, shifts were evident at this time. Final closure of the railway workshops in 1986, the raison d'être of the town and its economic and cultural heart over so many decades, was highly significant in symbolic terms. Unemployment rose temporarily. Employment growth continued, however, into the mid-1980s, with the expansion of existing employers and further inwards investment. Honda opened a pre-delivery inspection facility at South Marston in 1986, with the prospect of major future investment, which was subsequently realised. The emergence, however, of a stronger left-wing grouping within the local Labour Party and the election of a more left-wing deputy leader prompted, in the context of the '*new vision*' debate, a more fundamental rethink of economic development strategy (Bassett and Harloe, 1990). As noted earlier, there had been growing criticism in the Labour Party of the marketing director's style and approach to economic development and, following a management review, a new Directorate of Economic and Social Development was established in 1986, incorporating the hitherto relatively autonomous economic development unit, Swindon Enterprise. *Thamesdown News*, the Council's own paper, explained that economic policy was to be broadened beyond the attraction of new firms, towards building a partnership with local community groups, the local business community and the labour movement.

Appointment of a new director for this grouping incorporating social as well as economic development functions proved immediately controversial. The director had formerly been economic adviser to the Merseyside Enterprise Board and had been a parliamentary candidate for the Labour Party. In contrast with the cross-party consensus which had previously prevailed in relation to expansion and economic development, his appointment was strongly opposed by the Conservatives on the Council who regarded his appointment as overtly political. Asked to produce for the Council a new economic development strategy for the

1990s, the subsequent consultative document published in 1987 incorporated a range of 'new left' themes and proposals associated with some of the larger, more radical authorities, such as Sheffield and the Greater London Council (GLC). The report pointed out that although the Council's promotional efforts had achieved considerable success, employment generated had been mainly in the service sector and high technology sector. It had not been able to absorb local redundancies in manufacturing due to a mismatch in skills. Far more attention needed to be paid, it argued, both to the quality of jobs created and to access to employment and equality of opportunity. Proposals included in the report included positive support for employment initiatives directed towards women, disabled people and those from ethnic minorities, the setting up of an enterprise board, support for the development of cooperatives, a code of employment practice, and contract compliance procedures for employers assisted by or supplying goods and services to the Council. It also suggested extending the principle of joint planning to include the trades unions and community groups locally.

This debate in terms of employment and economic development policy was being conducted against the background of controversy over the proposed northern expansion where developers had submitted a planning application for 1,500 acres of land in 1986. As described in Chapter Six, the Borough Council were initially, at least, opposed to the northern expansion, lining up alongside the County Council who had traditionally – since the immediate postwar years – opposed Swindon's expansionist thrust. This was largely on the basis that further growth would divert resources for infrastructure and services needed elsewhere in the locality to improve conditions for the existing population of the town. Borough and County finally agreed to the development with considerable reluctance, in the face of an appeal by the developers against refusal of permission. Questioning of established policy direction at a broader level seems to have informed and been reflected in debate around specific issues of economic development.

The sort of ideas set out in the 1987 document were increasingly fashionable, as already noted, among a group of 'new left' authorities at the time, including the GLC under Ken Livingstone, a number of London Boroughs and Sheffield under David Blunkett, and others (Boddy and Fudge, 1984). Rate-capped like Swindon, these authorities were seeking to maintain and develop 'new left' strategies in opposition to the increasing weight of Conservative new right policies under Thatcher. While elements within Swindon Labour Party clearly had some sympathies with the politics and policies of the new left, the Borough Council and the local community had, in other respects, little in common with the mainstream new left authorities at the time in terms of political culture or indeed political strategy and policy direction. Swindon was caught in the net of rate-capping, not because of what was branded at the time the profligate expenditure of 'the loony left' but largely because of the historic interest charges associated with town expansion.

In fact, the 1987 consultative document combined these more radical elements with the continuation of much of established policy (Bassett and Harloe, 1990, p 53). The incoming director supported the continuation of Swindon's promotional policies, albeit in modified form. The need for closer links through partnership with the private sector was also accepted. Publication of the report was, nevertheless, quickly followed by the resignation of the Borough's marketing director. He was quoted in the local paper as saying: "the efforts of Swindon Enterprise have been stultified by policies imposed by the Labour dominated Council who show no understanding of private sector business, and seek to impose their left-wing, doctrinaire ideas on the creation of wealth and jobs." The new strategy, he said, read "more like a left wing manifesto than a business plan" (*Swindon Evening Advertiser*, 13 April 1987). This took place, publicly at least, against the background of bitter political exchanges between the parties. The Conservative leader spoke of "the thin veil of moderate socialism [in Swindon being] blown aside" *Evening Advertiser*, 14 April 1987), although this may have owed something to the upcoming elections. More significant in some ways than the party political rhetoric of the time were the signs that the consensus behind continued expansion was starting to unravel.

In terms of economic development policy, specifically, the debate was around the benefits of continued promotion, marketing and the attraction of inwards investment. It was about the rationale for continued expansion of employment. It was also about the benefits of such growth and expansion, the forms which that growth took and the benefits in terms of different groups within the labour market – growth for whose benefit? Issues in terms of economic development policy were a component of the developing debate at a broader level as to the 'limits to growth' and around expansion versus consolidation which was to continue unabated through the 1990s. Proposals rooted in the rhetoric of the new left, in practice, gained little ground. The possibility of imposing conditions on employers in the face of competition from a wide range of other localities eager to attract employment was recognised as lacking realism. There was some support for the cooperative sector, but on a very modest scale, while the proposed Enterprise Board, with echoes of the larger scale initiatives attempted in Greater London, the West Midlands or Merseyside, did not materialise. Nor did joint planning with the trades unions, which was of declining significance in the face of industrial restructuring. The town continued to advertise itself under the slogan 'Swindon: the profit base', hardly the ringing tones of the new left. Swindon Enterprise as an organisational focus for promotional activities was, however, replaced in 1989 with an Economic Development Team and it was noted that:

> Swindon Economic Development, the newly designated body, signifies a move to a new marketing policy which is geared to not only selling the benefits of Swindon to relocating businesses, but also, importantly, to consolidating the industrial and commercial successes achieved so far. The Borough will continue its jobs-led economic development policy. Key companies will still be encouraged to move to the town to create new job opportunities, but the Economic Development Team will be very much involved in helping existing businesses in the town to develop and grow. (Thamesdown Borough Council, Annual Budget 1990/91)

Increasing attention was, however, paid to the needs of small enterprises and business start-up. There was also increasing involvement, albeit reluctant initially, in partnerships and joint working around economic and employment issues, discussed in more detail below. These shifts originated in the broadening of the debate and the policy agenda in the latter part of the 1980s. The Borough Council's increasing resistance to future expansion on any significant scale also became evident in debates around the statutory planning framework and the emerging conflict between the Borough and County Council as to the volume of future development that was to be accommodated in Swindon (see Chapters Five and Six).

New agendas

From the mid-1980s, therefore, there was a significant shift in the Borough's overall vision for the future of the town. However, it was not until the late 1980s that there was any major shift in economic development activities on the ground. When it happened it was both radical and rapid, involving major cuts in expenditure, an end to high-profile marketing and promotion in pursuit of inwards investment and a major shift in emphasis towards support for existing employers and locally focused initiatives. It also involved new roles and relationships, with an increasing emphasis on joint working arrangements and partnership.

This dramatic shift in the scale of economic development activities and in forms of activity partly reflected the Borough's overall policy shift towards consolidation. It also coincided with significant financial problems for the authority as the government cuts and controls started to bite. Importantly as well, with the Borough's land stocks now depleted, it was the end of an era in terms of development-based economic strategy. This, in turn, had major implications in terms of the economic development function. Up to the late 1980s, as already noted, economic development had been heavily marketing oriented. Partly reflecting a commitment to growth by means of inwards investment, with the Borough a major provider of sites for employment uses, it was also linked to the marketing of the Borough's own land and development portfolio. The scale of marketing activity had been justified by the capital receipts from development which supported what was later described by an officer of the Borough Council interviewed for this study as "primarily a marketing department":

> "It was restructured in the late 1980s because most of the land bank had actually been sold, so the money to support the marketing drive was no

*longer there and the need for it had largely
disappeared. It had achieved what it was set up to
achieve, by and large."*

According to the Borough Council in 1990: "The rapid rate of
expansion of the town over recent years has led to a reappraisal of
the Council's economic development activity and the announce-
ment of a major new approach to its commercial and industrial
promotion" (Thamesdown Borough Council, Annual Budget
1990/91). The Council noted in 1990 that "whilst not completely
abandoning everything that had gone before, there would be a
need for a complete re-appraisal of marketing activity and a fresh
approach to the future" (Thamesdown Borough Council,
Economic Development Marketing Plan, 1990/91).

The recasting of the economic development function also
reflected the shift in emphasis from inwards investment towards
'consolidation'. There had been considerable concern in the late
1980s over the over-heating of the economy and the Borough
Council was under enormous pressure from developers to release
more land – speculative applications were received for sites close
to both motorway junctions and east of the A419, seen by the
Council as the eastern boundary of the developed area (see Figure
5.1). With low unemployment, the labour market was tight and
there was growing concern over perceived problems of traffic
congestion. In this context, the initial policy response was closer
to constraint than the more pragmatic notion of 'consolidation'
adopted subsequently. It was at this time that a senior
representative of the Council (it has been forgotten as to whether
the representative was a member or officer) is reported to have
talked of 'pulling up the drawbridge from the M4' to stem the
flow of inwards investment. Apocryphal or not, the overall
impression created at this time was one of Swindon putting the
shutters up in an abrupt about turn on previous decades. Borough
Council officers reported that this "flung them into headlong
opposition with the private sector locally", much of it channelled
through the Chamber of Commerce. The early 1990s saw a very
difficult period in terms of relations between the Council and the
Chamber of Commerce, with the Council perceived as threatening
the prosperity and success of the town.

Promotion and marketing was cut back dramatically, and the
Council spoke in 1990 of its success in having:

> ... got across the message that the Borough no
> longer has vast resources of green field sites
> available for footloose industry to relocate to
> Swindon.... Further cutting back of the general
> 'above the line' relocation advertising is
> proposed, in favour of more targeted marketing
> aimed at the manufacturing sector in particular,
> and in order to allocate more resources to the
> marketing of locally based economic development
> initiatives'. (Thamesdown Borough Council,
> Economic Development Marketing Plan,
> 1990/91)

In this context, economic development was a ready target for
expenditure cuts. The late 1980s and early 1990s was also a time
of increasing financial pressures on the Borough Council as the
accumulated problems of earlier years and attempts to stave off the
increasingly severe cuts and controls imposed by central
government impacted in a major way, such that serious cuts in
expenditure became imperative. The overall budget and staffing
for economic development were cut back in a major way. The
budget was halved in one year, a major cut given its overall size at
the time and the number of people employed. The budget for
industrial promotion, which had risen to little short of £500,000
per year by 1984, was cut back sharply to around £200,000 by
1989/90. The advertising budget alone, which had been over
£300,000 in 1987/88, was cut back to only £72,000 by 1989/90,
reflecting the move away from general relocation advertising
(Thamesdown Borough Council, Economic and Social Policy
Group Annual Report, 1989/90). Signalling the shift in policy, the
budget for industrial promotion was merged with that for
employment initiatives from 1989/90 under an overall 'economic
development' budget head, and was subsumed within the new
Economic and Social Development Directorate. Similarly,
'Swindon Enterprise' was renamed 'Swindon Economic
Development', signalling the shift in emphasis away from inwards
investment in favour of support for existing local employers:

> Key companies will still be encouraged to move
> to the town to create new job opportunities, but
> the Economic Development Team will also be
> very involved in helping businesses in the town to

> develop and grow. More attention will be given
> to the quality of jobs as well as the quality of the
> environment. (Thamesdown Borough Council,
> Economic and Social Policy Group Annual
> Report, 1989/90).

The Borough continued to advertise to some extent, and other
promotional activities were not altogether eliminated, but they
were very much scaled down. Increasing emphasis was placed on
using staff resources to assist existing companies in the town to
expand and develop locally.

To a certain degree this paralleled national trends. With the
onset of recession and the financial squeeze on the public sector,
spending nationally on marketing as a component of local
authority economic development policy tended to decline. The
cut back in Swindon was, however, very drastic and all the more
so given levels of expenditure in the 1980s. With the recession,
pressures for inwards investment and relocation in any case fell
away, and the Borough noted in 1991 that: "Due largely to the
deterioration in both the national and local economies, as well as
the substantial reduction in direct marketing activity, major
company relocations virtually 'dried up' in 1990/91"
(Thamesdown Borough Council, Economic Development Team,
Annual Report, 1990/91). There were also a considerable number
of closures and redundancies in 1991.

In this context, attitudes in terms of constraint softened
slightly and the more flexible notion of 'consolidation' was
increasingly emphasised. The Borough Council stressed that there
was land in the Structure Plan allocated for employment purposes
which the Council were happy to see developed, and the Council
itself still had some land for industrial purposes. The Borough
also mounted something of a recovery exercise to counter the
more extreme perceptions of its having turned its back on growth.
In its 1991/92 Economic Development Plan, it emphasised that it
would continue to offer a relocation service to companies and staff
and would assist by providing information and advice. In 1992/93
it indicated that:

> Broadly the strategic policy is of pursuing
> 'consolidation and improvement' in the area.
> This involves encouraging business development,
> both of incoming and indigenous firms, in

approved employment areas; whilst at the same time recognising that the infrastructure of the area would inevitably worsen unacceptably if the high growth rates achieved in the past two decades were to continue unabated. (Thames-down Borough Council, Draft Economic Development Plan, 1992/93)

Further closures and redundancies had continued in 1991/92 and unemployment had risen significantly. It was noted that the number of people employed in Swindon even fell slightly, by around 2%. Even service sector employment dropped for the first time in 20 years. The economic development budget, nevertheless, was cut by 64% in 1992/93, reflecting the severe cuts which the Council was forced to implement in the early 1990s. All advertising was cut, as was the "extensive press and public relations activity provided by the Council's external marketing consultants, which had to a certain extent served to offset the decline in awareness through the cutback in corporate advertising." (Thamesdown Borough Council, Draft Economic Development Plan, 1992/93). This left economic development with an annual budget of only £450,000 per year in the 1990s compared with £2.3-£2.6m for community development.

The economic development function was clearly on shifting ground in the 1990s. Prioritised politically and financially and strongly member-driven in the 1980s, the emphasis shifted elsewhere in the 1990s. Following expenditure cuts in the early 1990s, the Director of Economic and Social Policy, controversially appointed in the late 1980s, was himself made redundant. Other personnel changes followed, and after a period marked more by financial and political expediency rather than policy direction, and with the continued existence of the economic development function at times in doubt, it was located within the Council's Development and Project Management Department. Having lost its way in terms of corporate priorities and policy direction in the first part of the 1990s, it took some time for economic development to establish its new role. It started to develop more of an analytical and information gathering function, carrying out a series of studies on topics such as automotive components, the electronics industry and financial services in support of this activity and of policy at a more general level within the Council. There was minimal involvement in marketing and promotional activities as such. The unit did, however, work to support companies already located in Swindon, which had provided much of the job growth over the years. The Council's overall priorities in terms of economic development at this time are set out in Box 4.1. By 1996/97 the total budget was just over £460,000, less than half the budget a decade earlier, for promotion alone. Nearly half of this amount was accounted for internally by staff and support costs (see Table 4.1).

Grants for community-based initiatives made up more than half of the rest supporting training, community businesses and cooperatives, childcare initiatives and initiatives aimed at groups disadvantaged in the labour market. Direct employer-related activity, including inwards investment and aftercare in relation to existing local employers, received a token £20,000. The dramatic scale of cutbacks in economic development activity in general and promotional activity and support for inwards investment compared with less than a decade earlier is very apparent.

Table 4.1: Economic development budget, Thamesdown Borough Council (1996/97)

Activity	1996/97 budget
Employees and support services	227,000
Grants to community-based training and development projects	125,000
European and regional initiatives	20,000
Tourism development and other promotional activities	20,000
Company aftercare and inward investment activity	20,000
Higher education initiative	15,000
Shopmobility	17,000
Economic research and intelligence	7,000
Grants to community enterprises	8,000
Business information and advice	4,000
Other	500
Total	463,500

Source: Thamesdown Borough Council, Economic Development Plan 1996/97, Consultation Draft

Box 4.1: Economic development: priority initiatives

Strategic partnerships
... the Council will seem to establish new partnerships, and strengthen existing ones in order to maximise the opportunities that arise from its new status as a unitary authority.

Building an intelligent local economy
... organisations which are most successful in the new, rapidly changing, global economy are those which have become 'intelligent'. This means that they have the capacity to learn quickly to respond to the new challenges and opportunities which confront them....

Company aftercare and retention services
The Economic Development Team will continue the process which began in 1995/96 of working with relevant partners, especially WEDA, WTEC and SCCI to identify the key needs of local companies, and the means by which these can be addressed....

Higher education
... The enhancement of higher education provision within the Borough is a key element in providing local people with opportunities to access the skills and qualifications they will require to meet the future needs of employers....

Promotion of Swindon
... The economic development team are specifically concerned with the promotion of Swindon to inward investors, and will continue their activities in this field. We will continue to develop the image of Swindon as a city for the 21st century as a profile for the area....

Town centre management
... to produce a comprehensive Town Centre Strategy bringing together the elements necessary to ensure a healthy town centre from economic, social and cultural points of view.

Rural economic development
The economic development team will continue to take account of the needs of the rural areas of the Borough....

Environmental initiatives
The Borough Council is committed to safeguarding the environment which is seen as crucial to the maintenance of the high quality of life that attracts companies and individuals to Swindon....

Source: Thamesdown Borough Council, Economic Development Plan, 1996/97

New roles and relationships

The new agenda for economic development in the 1990s also saw the proliferation of new roles and relationships locally. This, in part, reflected major shifts at the national level. The late 1980s and early 1990s saw a whole range of new players on the economic development scene, including Training and Enterprise Councils (TECs), Business Link and new development agencies. Existing roles were recast and recombined, with an increasing emphasis on partnership and joint working, and increasing emphasis on involvement of the private sector. Much of this was driven by central government initiatives. Training and Enterprise Councils, in particular, took over responsibility for youth and adult training schemes from the Employment Department, together with start-up and business support services, partly from the DTI. They were given responsibility for education/business links and for the national 'Investors in People Initiative' and a key role in a range of other initiatives, including careers guidance and, in partnership with local Chambers of Commerce, the one-stop-shop, business support and advice service, Business Link. Although essentially government-funded, TECs were set up as relatively autonomous, employer-led organisations, encouraged by government to play an increasingly active role in terms of local economic development and the development of strategy at the local level. They were, in themselves, major new players, but they also played a key role in the proliferation of new roles and relationships.

Important as well was the increasing emphasis in government and European initiatives, including City Challenge, the Single Regeneration Budget, the European Social Fund, the Konver Initiative for areas hit by defence cuts and even, more recently, Lottery money, on competition and competitive bidding. Effective joint working and the involvement and commitment of all relevant partners including, in particular, the private sector, was increasingly seen nationally as a pre-requisite for effective initiatives at a local level and evidence of this became, therefore, a prerequisite for successful bids. This in itself, in a very pragmatic sense, was a major driving force behind the rapid growth of partnership and joint working arrangements.

This was paralleled by a similar growth in partnership arrangements and joint working across local authority boundaries on a county-wide, sub-regional or regional scale. Some of these arrangements were essentially local authority-based. Others involved a range of different partners from the public, quasi-public, private and voluntary sectors around promotional activities and inwards investment, and economic development more generally. Again, this was, in part, directed towards securing government or European funding. It also recognised the economies of scale inherent in some of these activities and recognition of the appropriate scale at which to promote and market particular parts of the country. While ostensibly, at one level, about partnership and joint working, the sub-text of this plethora of overlapping organisations and networks was one of competition and struggles for power, influence and resources between different organisations and territorial units (Haughton et al 1997).

These new developments represented a significant shift in economic development policy in Swindon itself. In the course of a decade or so, the Borough went from being the leading player in terms of economic development to playing much more of a support and enabling role in the context of a network of new organisations and new relationships. This also represents an interesting case study of the development of new roles and relationships and partnership in a more prosperous area, dominated more by growth pressures than by the problems of urban regeneration and economic decline, which have provided much of the impetus for new forms of working in many other localities.

The proliferation of new players, new roles and new relationships was very evident at the local level in the 1990s. In Swindon's case, as elsewhere, this partly reflected shifts in the national policy framework and initiatives external to the Borough itself. It also reflected the shift in approach to economic development locally, the cutback in promotional activity, consolidation and an increasing emphasis on existing local employers and locally focused employment initiatives. Paralleling this was the major cutback in resources for economic development. The Borough had to adapt to new players such as the Wiltshire TEC. Partnership working itself became necessary if the Borough was to maintain and develop its role and influence in the changing national and local context for economic development. Recognition of this became evident in 1993, with partnership identified as an explicit objective in the Borough's new 'mission statement' for its Economic Development Strategy, committing it:

> To work in partnership with all relevant agencies to develop Swindon as a balanced, sustainable regional centre and to ensure that the benefits that accrue from this development are enjoyed by all sections of the Borough's Population, safeguard the environment and provide the necessary infrastructure (Thamesdown Borough Council, Draft Economic Development Plan, 1993/94)

The Plan went on to state that the Borough "recognises that partnerships between the public, private and voluntary sector are essential to the effective development of the local economy." The Borough's formal policy statements gave increasing prominence to partnerships and joint working in successive years. Key initiatives derived from the national level included the setting up of the TEC and later Business Link. In the 1990s there was also, however, a proliferation of acronyms, initiatives and partnerships at the local and sub-regional level.

Wiltshire TEC, set up in 1990 as part of the national network of TECs, with responsibility for government training schemes, enterprise support and other government initiatives, covered the area of the administrative county of Wiltshire. Its area of responsibility included, therefore, not only the major Swindon labour market, but the geographically much more extensive rural areas and smaller towns of Wiltshire down as far as Salisbury to the south. As an organisation specifically concerned with labour markets, training and the local economy it was seen, therefore, by the Borough Council in particular, as lacking an appropriate territorial focus and commitment. There was discussion, when the TECs were being set up, of establishing some form of 'M4 Corridor TEC', which the Borough, among others, would have favoured. Relations between the Borough Council and the TEC were very distant early on, reflecting the Borough's perception of the TEC as a quango, strongly identified with the county level, with the Wiltshire chief executive and the county education officer on its Board. The TEC has not been seen locally or regionally as among the more successful TECs. It was relatively small by TEC standards nationally, it suffered from turnover in senior management, and with Wiltshire among the more prosperous counties, its share of TEC funding, much of it linked to government schemes for the unemployed, was less than in other parts of the country. Its performance in national league tables was relatively poor and it struggled to reach the criteria set by the government as a condition for confirmation of its operating licence – in 1996 it was among the last TECs nationally yet to have achieved this. Unlike TECs in some parts of the country, it had not been particularly innovative or taken any very positive role in the development of economic development policy locally, a fact which, in some ways, limited the potential conflict which could have arisen with the Borough Council. The Borough had some involvement with the TEC through membership of its Northern Area Advisory Board, and there was some thawing of relations between the Borough and the TEC subsequently. Thus, by 1995, the Borough was officially supporting the development of greater collaborative working and indicating that it would welcome an invitation to join the TEC Board (Thamesdown, Borough Council, Economic Development Committee, June 1995).

Great Western Commerce and Enterprise represented the somewhat forced marriage of convenience of Swindon-based enterprise agency Great Western Enterprise (GWE) and the Chamber of Commerce, under the pressure from the requirements of the government's Business Link scheme. Forerunner of GWE, the Swindon Enterprise Agency had been established in 1986 with the closure of the rail work. It secured £1.25m from British Rail Engineering Limited, negotiated by the Borough Council, to provide alternative employment opportunities over a three-year period. A board, including senior representatives from the private sector along with British Rail and the Borough, was established and served to bridge the gap between British Rail and what was perceived to be a left of centre Labour Council, which had maintained its outright opposition to the closure to the end. A small amount of money went into grants to ex-rail workers setting up their own businesses and grants to companies creating new jobs, particularly in manufacturing. There were also job premium grants under a national scheme, providing employment subsidies to firms employing ex-rail workers. The Enterprise Agency worked very closely and shared staff with the existing Swindon

Enterprise Trust, which provided business counselling and advice, funded by the Borough Council, and was generally thought to be very effective. Most importantly, however, the Enterprise Agency responded to a perceived gap in the market by providing small, managed, workspace units, available on flexible terms. This proved very successful in meeting the needs of small and start-up businesses, with management support provided by Swindon Enterprise Trust. Importantly as well, the managed workshops also provided the Enterprise Agency with a secure source of rental income for the future. By 1986 it had 370 workspace units accommodating 1,700 people.

When the initial contract with British Rail ended in 1989, the Enterprise Agency merged with the business counselling and support side in the form of the Enterprise Trust to form GWE. Additional funding was raised from local businesses and favourable terms secured from British Rail for part of the old rail works. This was refurbished to provide premises for GWE, for the Borough Council's Economic Development Team (having moved out of the high profile Murray John Tower) and a local base for the DTI – a forerunner of the one-stop-shop. Financial support from the Borough Council ended by mutual consent at this time, with GWE becoming in effect self-sustaining. Part of its funding came from the Enterprise Allowance Scheme, with GWE providing business advice and support under contract from the TEC, but unlike other enterprise agencies, this was by no means critical to its existence. It was also offering courses and training workshops for businesses which generated a further income stream and related increasingly to team-managed businesses with 10-25 employees as well as business start-up.

The government's Business Link scheme, conceived under Michael Heseltine, represented a natural development, offering additional funding over a three-year period to develop a range of activities, most of which GWE was already undertaking with considerable success. There were considerable obstacles in practice, not least the antagonism between the Chamber of Commerce and Industry, required to be a partner under the government's model, and GWE who did not see what was at the time a very traditional and not very active Chamber as an ideal partner. GWE were also concerned to protect their dowry in the form of its property assets and income stream to avoid any subsidy of other elements of Business Link and ultimately, to protect its

future if it all went wrong.   After a difficult 18 months of
negotiation, a workable partnership arrangement did emerge, with
GWE's Advisory Services Division, reborn as Business Link
Swindon and Great Western Properties, as two divisions of an
umbrella organisation, Great Western Commerce and Enterprise,
and the Chamber in a sense a third division but retaining its
governing Council.

There had, in fact, been considerable scepticism within the
Borough as to the value of many of these partnership arrangements proliferating at this time, particularly in the early part of the
1990s.   Other organisations operated at the county, sub-regional
or regional level, with the Borough Council at times a reluctant
player.   The Borough Council tended to doubt the benefit of these
more widely based organisations which it considered of little
specific relevance to the Swindon area, indicating that:

> The energy and resources required to sustain
> successful partnerships can be considerable, and
> we have to be sure that a true synergy will result.
> Partnership working is not always easy and it
> certainly does not offer a quick fix solution to
> resource constraints.   Equally it is not some kind
> of universal panacea that can be applied in all
> situations.   (Thamesdown Borough Council,
> Economic Development Plan, 1996/97)

This was in the overall context of consolidation and opposition to
the County's aims of concentrating further development within the
Borough.   The Borough Council meanwhile saw itself, with some
justification, as among the most successful localities within the
region and tended to think that these partnership organisations
needed it more than it needed them.   In a regional context, it saw
itself more as a part of the M4 Corridor and strongly linked with
if not integral to the South East rather than a part of Wiltshire or
the South West region.   The most immediate exceptions were
where the possibility of funding depended on joint bidding and
working arrangements, as was the case with the Konver Initiative
to secure funding in relation to defence cuts.

In practice, the Borough was involved in a growing catalogue
of partnership arrangements at a variety of scales.   The structural
complexities are illustrated by the county-wide Wiltshire
Economic Partnership, the West of England Economic Partnership

and West of England Development Agency. Wiltshire Economic Partnership was set up, largely on the initiative of the County Council and Wiltshire TEC, bringing together the local authorities, private sector and the TEC (Box 4.2). With the Partnership seen very much as a county-level initiative, supported by the TEC, Thamesdown were reluctant to get involved and certainly opposed to the Partnership having any role in directing or validating bids for 'partnership' money, for example, under the Single Regeneration Budget, or any control over inwards investment and company aftercare. This was not seen as in the best interests of Swindon. On the other hand, the Partnership did provide a structure for partnership with the private sector, albeit at county level, which might be needed in bidding for funds or to support economic development more generally, reinforced by the TEC operating at a county-wide basis. Parallel structures at Swindon level would complicate matters.

The Borough was also sceptical about the West of England Development Agency, set up to attract inwards investment from overseas to the five northern counties of the region, Devon and Cornwall already having their own development agency, as did most other parts of the country. The West of England Development Agency was overlain by and drew its membership from a broader West of England Economic Partnership, incorporating the five county forums. This was not seen as a priority need, particularly from the Swindon perspective of consolidation in the face of pressures from inwards investment-driven expansion. There were also doubts about the effectiveness of this form of promotional activity in terms of measurable returns, and the Borough did not contribute financially to the West of England Development Agency. Again this was an initiative led by the county councils, reinforcing Swindon's reluctance. Here, in particular, the Borough tended to think that the West of England Development Agency needed Swindon more than vice versa in terms of what it had to sell and in terms of experience in handling economic development enquiries, although there were also less sceptical views within the Council. The combination of county-level forums and boards with similar structures at regional level represents an extreme version of the complex multi-layering of institutional structures which developed in the 1990s in different parts of the country. Overall, this was, as Thamesdown saw it, of little relevance, while absorbing time and other resources. It was driven, however, by the external imperative to involve the private sector, and by new organisational structures such as TECs and government-funded development agencies like the West of England Development Agency. Although it was a reluctant player, participation in such networks was a means of accessing certain types of resources and there was therefore some imperative to participate.

Box 4.2: Economic development partnership initiatives

West of England Economic Partnership
An economic forum with public and private representatives from the five counties of Avon (as was), Dorset, Gloucestershire, Somerset and Wiltshire, set up to champion the West of England as a distinct region of the UK and to guide the strategy of the new regional development organisation (West of England Development Agency) to which it provides representatives.

West of England Development Agency
Regional development organisation established in 1995 to attract overseas inwards investment to the region, funded by the DTI, TECs and local authorities. Membership drawn from West of England Economic Partnership.

Wiltshire Economic Partnership
Includes WEO forum which brings together the local authorities, Wiltshire TEC, the private sector and other bodies to discuss economic issues and strategies; Wiltshire Economic Partnership board, with membership drawn from the forum, intended to develop and ensure the delivery of the county's economic development strategy, coordinate programmes and attract resources for the county area as a whole.

West of England Initiative
Launched in 1993 by the Borough Council, Bristol and Gloucester City Councils to develop strategy and initiatives relevant to the three urban authorities within the subregion.

Swindon: city for the 21st century
Partnership between the Borough Council and the private sector led by Swindon Chamber of Commerce and Industry, to facilitate work on initiatives of mutual interest and encourage a positive dialogue.

The West of England Initiative, on the other hand, unlike the West of England Development Agency, was specifically urban led, set up by the Swindon, Bristol and Gloucester Councils to raise the profile of issues relevant to these urban authorities within the predominantly rural South West region. As such it also represented an alliance of what were to be the three main urban unitary authorities in the north of the region. Less significant in terms of economic development as such, it served, however, to strengthen the voice of the urban authorities in terms of regional planning issues, with the setting up of an urban affairs committee linked to the South West Regional Planning Conference. The West of England Initiative organised its annual conference in 1995 on 'Regional government and the South West' in line with its remit to develop and influence policy in a regional and European context. It also responded to an initiative from the Government Office of the South West suggesting in 1996 that urban areas within the region as a whole might come together to discuss the strategies to improve competitiveness in the context of the government's competitiveness White Paper, organising its annual conference around the theme of 'the intelligent region' on behalf of the region. It did so, however, on the basis that this was in line with the West of England Initiative's own long-term aims for the three northern urban areas and would develop its relations with the Government Office.

By 1996 the Borough Council had re-emphasised, officially at least, its firm commitment to pursuing economic development objectives on a partnership basis where they were "sure that this approach will genuinely add value to an initiative" (Thamesdown Borough Council, Economic Development Plan, 1996/97).

> The Borough Council is firmly committed to partnership working and has been involved in a number of partnership initiatives in recent years. This Economic Development Plan contains a number of areas of work where the development of effective partnerships are considered to be critical to the delivery of effective local economic development programmes. (Thamesdown Borough Council, Draft Economic Development Plan, 1996/97)

Moreover, as the Borough moved towards unitary status, it saw itself as better placed in relation to other agencies and partnerships which had become active in economic development, and in relation to the new tier of unitary urban authorities.

> As the move to unitary status alters and strengthens relationships with other agencies, there will be a need for the authority to consider how it wishes to position itself among the agencies and partnerships now active in various aspects of economic development, and the tier of new urban local authorities. (Thamesdown Borough Council, Draft Economic Development Plan, 1996/97)

Unitary status from 1997 shifted the basis for its involvement, putting it on an equal footing in some respects with the County and also reinforcing the basis for alliance with other new unitary urban authorities in the region.

Having also been, to some extent, at loggerheads in the early 1990s with the Chamber of Commerce over its stance in relation to continued expansion, the Borough had started to rebuild bridges. It worked in partnership with the Chamber of Commerce to develop a new marketing initiative for the town. It undertook a programme of work, supported by the private sector, to persuade companies that Swindon was still there and still open for business, under the slogan 'Swindon, in business for the 21st century'. In 1993 it mounted an exhibition in London and used press channels and business intermediaries to put its case across. The improving relationship between the Chamber of Commerce and Initiative and the Borough Council saw the establishment of 'Swindon, city for the 21st century' as a partnership between the two. The aim was specifically "to encourage positive dialogue in which both sides gain a broader understanding of the needs of the other" (Thamesdown Borough Council, Economic Development Plan, 1996/97). By the following year, this had generated support for the idea of achieving formal city status under the banner of 'City for the 21st century'. By this time, the Council was also indicating a rather more positive attitude towards inwards investment:

> Swindon continues to be an excellent location for industry and commerce. The Borough Council is committed to building upon the progress of

> previous decades by attracting new industry
> which will complement the wide range of
> employers already present in the town.
> (Thamesdown Borough Council, Draft Economic
> Development Plan, 1994/95)

This may have reflected its partnership with the Chamber. The Chamber became increasingly active and influential over this period, particularly through the increasing involvement of some of the larger employers in the town as 'patrons' of the Chamber. These companies provided financial support to the Chamber over and above the regular membership fees, representing an initiative to draw in some of the more prominent and influential employers into what had been a vary traditional local Chamber. This met with some considerable success, with the Chamber becoming, increasingly, a focus for private sector interests in the town and increasingly prominent in debates on its future – as in the campaign for city status. Indicative of this, the Chamber was chaired in 1997 by the managing director of the American-owned semiconductor company Intel UK, one of the town's most prominent employers.

The account presented here shows how the Borough Council's high-profile involvement in industrial promotion and economic development operated as a key component of its overall strategy in relation to town expansion. As shown earlier, this represented, initially, a response to the perceived need to diversify the town's economic basis. Swindon represents, however, a particular example of a local authority pursuing economic growth and development in the context of what rapidly became one of the more prosperous parts of the country, dominated increasingly in the postwar period by pressures for growth. Elsewhere, the impetus behind economic and industrial development has more frequently been generated in response to economic decline and strategies for urban regeneration. This chapter has focused in particular on the Borough's role in terms of economic development and industrial promotion. Chapter Five goes on to look at the role of the planning system and the physical development process which underpinned economic expansion and employment growth.

five

Planning and development: industry and employment

As outlined in earlier chapters Swindon provides a case study of
planned development on a major scale. Initially this development
was undertaken in the context of the formal expanded town's
programme and the 1952 Town Development Act. The late 1960s
then saw large-scale, local authority-led expansion of West
Swindon and Swindon's role as a major growth magnet in the
context of the overall strategic planning framework for the South
East. Finally, development of the town's northern sector provides
a model of increasingly market-led development with the local
authority seeking to steer the development process largely by
means of the statutory planning framework. The ongoing
development of the northern sector provides for continuing
growth and expansion through the 1990s and, on current rates of
development, well into the early years of the next millennium.
After successive decades of planned development and growth, the
1990s, however, in a major policy shift, saw the Borough Council
seeking to use the planning framework to secure a period of
consolidation beyond anticipated growth to the north, and to hold
the line against pressures for further expansion on any significant
scale. Swindon thus provides an excellent opportunity to examine
the way in which the planning and development process has
operated in the context of the shifting policy framework of the
postwar period and to examine the way in which different models
of planned growth and development have operated over this
period. After a brief account of the national context in terms of
planning systems and planning policy this chapter focuses in

particular on planning and development in relation to industry and employment. Chapter Six then goes on to focus on housing and housing development.

The national context

Postwar development of the national planning system in the postwar period provided the overall context for managed growth and expansion and for the operation of the planning framework locally. In Britain the early postwar years can be characterised as a period of economic and physical reconstruction, based on a vision of comprehensive planning, which embraced the management of the urban and regional system, housing production and land use. Strategic planning of patterns of employment and population growth at the regional and national level were reinforced by regional planning frameworks established in the 1960s. Much of this overall planning process, moreover, has focused specifically on managing the growth of London as both national capital and, increasingly, global city, generating pressures for growth which extended well beyond the immediate boundaries of the metropolitan area itself. The vision that emerged in the 1940s reflected the philosophy of influential committee reports including Barlow (1940), Scott (1942) and Uthwatt (1942), and by the regional strategies of Abercrombie (1944). These informed the establishment both of regional policy in the form of the 1945 Distribution of Industry Act, and of the 1947 Town and Country Planning Act itself, which established a comprehensive framework for strategic and urban planning. Specific measures included the system of comprehensive development control based on proposals for land development contained in detailed development plans, the designation of green belts around major urban areas, and the New and Expanded Town programmes of the early postwar years. Regional policy measures in the form of controls on industrial location and various forms of regional assistance came later, as did the rather short-lived regional economic planning boards of the 1960s.

The broad features of the approach to urban and regional planning at this time can be characterised as managed decentralisation based on the New and Expanded Towns of the South East and beyond, accompanied by strong 'urban containment' (Hall et al, 1973). There was always a degree of tension, however, between decentralisation to the New Towns and relocation to the Assisted Areas, and a somewhat uneasy relationship between land use planning generally and regional economic planning. This was, to some extent, resolved given growing concern over economic decline and social problems in the largest cities from the late 1960s onwards. In overall terms, many of the strategic policy objectives pursued at this time were, on balance, highly successful, particularly the pursuit of managed decentralisation and containment (Hall et al, 1973). At the more detailed level, however, the system was perceived as failing in a number of respects. Development plans, requiring approval by central government, were slow to come on stream. In many cases plans were failing to keep pace with economic, social and cultural change and were frequently out of date before they were approved. Economic and household growth and increasing car ownership rapidly outstripped the provisions of development plans, which became, therefore, increasingly irrelevant as a basis for decision making on new development. Much new residential development in the period up to the mid-1970s, for example, took place on so-called 'white land' released outside of the development plan process. Pressure consequently built up for reform of the planning system and for a more strategic and flexible system of land-use plans that would prove robust in the face of changing economic and social needs.

The review process resulted in the two-tier system of structure plans and local plans brought in by the 1968 Town and Country Planning Act. This was effectively implemented following local government reorganisation and the introduction of two-tier county and district authorities in 1974. From the mid-1970s onwards, counties such as Wiltshire were preparing structure plans looking forward 15-20 years. Districts, meanwhile, were selectively preparing detailed local plans based on commitments to levels of development for housing, employment and other uses agreed at the strategic or regional level and approved by the Secretary of State. At the same time commitment to the New Towns programme declined and the regional planning framework weakened, with a more explicit switch of emphasis to urban regeneration. Economic crisis and industrial restructuring were also a feature of the 1970s and optimistic growth forecasts of earlier periods were being scaled down. At the local level the new structure plans and local plans themselves took a long time to prepare – it was not until 14 years after the 1968 Act that structure plans achieved national coverage. Conflicts between counties and districts over planning policy in general and levels of growth and development in particular became a recurrent feature of the operation of the planning system, as did challenges to the system by developers, who increasingly turned to the appeal system as a means of securing permission for development.

Planning, as a product of the postwar consensus behind state intervention and seen as necessary to ensure economic growth and social cohesion, started to break down across a wide range of policy arenas following the election of the Thatcher government in 1979. Despite the deregulationist zeal of the 1980s, the planning system itself, however, escaped fundamental reform. The Thatcherite ideology was largely pursued instead by a series of more selective measures, including Urban Development Corporations (UDCs) and Enterprise Zones. These displaced local authority planning control and other powers in designated areas. Regional aid was reduced and more closely targeted to the worst-off areas. Otherwise the system of development plans and development control established in the 1968 Act remained essentially intact. It has, however, been argued that styles of planning in different areas shifted and became increasingly differentiated (Brindley et al, 1989). Moreover, the dominant approaches emerging in this period, including 'trend planning' and 'leverage planning', could be seen as primarily concerned with the facilitation of essentially market-led development.

It has also been argued that the 1980s saw a reorientation of the system away from a concern with social and community need and an increasing emphasis on the interests of business and property development (Ambrose, 1986; Thornley, 1991). Steered by the implementation of the statutory planning system, and operating in practice under the guidance of central government and the Secretary of State, there was an increasing disaggregation of the planning system into different regimes for different areas with an increasing centralisation of power. Central government intervened more directly where it thought necessary, to modify structure plan policies at the local level or to over-ride local policy decisions via the appeals system and to challenge in particular local policies to restrain development. There was also repeated advice and guidance from central government to local authorities to incorporate policies and to operate procedures in a way sensitive to the needs of business and the market. So, while the formal planning framework remained, essentially intact, the peculiar procedural flexibility of the British planning system allowed, as Healey (1992) points out, for considerable flexibility in practice, reflecting shifts in central government agendas. This is reinforced by the status of plans themselves as 'advisory' in the context of the statutory planning framework and the catch-all requirement that authorities take account of 'other material considerations'.

Increasingly, prescriptive guidance to local authorities concerning the release of land for housing (including DoE Circulars 9/80 and 22/80) and requirements to involve the housebuilding industry in decisions on the release of land, via joint housing land studies, had been prominent features of the deregulationist 1980s. Exhortations to local authorities to release more land for housing had, in fact, been issued periodically throughout the postwar period, typically coinciding with periods of housing market boom. By the end of the 1980s, however, several factors seemed to push government policy back towards emphasising the importance of plans. The growing conflict over development, particularly housing development, in the more pressured land and property markets of the south of the country ironically contributed to this move. Government measures to secure additional land for housing were initially introduced in the context of the depressed land and property market of the early 1980s. This was followed in the mid-1980s by economic recovery and a massive inflow of investment into property development. The result was a speculative boom in development followed soon after by severe collapse as boom turned rapidly to slump. By the end of the decade housebuilders were arguing for a system of regional guidance that could provide a strategic agreement on land required for housing and over-ride local political opposition to development, providing greater certainty within the development market. Repeated appeals against the refusal of planning permission by local government intent on maintaining policies of constraint were proving costly for developers and politically difficult for government.

One outcome of these various pressures through the 1990s was the introduction of a comprehensive system of regional planning guidance, prepared by central government on the basis of advice submitted by associations or conferences of planning authorities in the different regions. Government also introduced the 1991 Planning and Compensation Act, under which all districts were required to prepare a district-wide Local Plan, providing for comprehensive plan coverage for the first time since 1968. This ushered in an essentially 'plan-led' system, with advice from central government emphasising the 'primacy' of development plans in development control decision making. It also provided additional incentives for landowners and developers to become much more involved in the process of plan preparation. This was increasingly seen as the first stage in the process of establishing future levels of development and seeking to secure future permissions to develop. Intense lobbying activity and protracted consultations and inquiries are now, therefore, a common feature of plan making, considerably delaying the formal adoption of plans and raising concerns as to whether the system can respond effectively to development needs. Ironically, what was seen as a legislative measure to give more power to plans and planners, may prove the downfall of the planning system if protracted timescales and delays provide the basis for developers to exploit the appeal route once again, issues which are particularly well illustrated in the case of Swindon (as set out both here and in Chapter Six).

Throughout the 1980s environmental interests represented by bodies such as the Council for the Preservation of Rural England, bolstered by support from an increasingly vociferous homeowner lobby in the South East, were also seeking to maintain the long standing objective of the British planning system to protect rural landscapes, and especially green belts. By the 1990s conservation and environmental considerations had broadened to encompass wider concerns of 'sustainability' and 'sustainable urban development', linking local issues with global environmental concerns. The sustainability debate thus gave environmental issues increasing salience at the political level and impacted increasingly on the planning system. The increased political salience of environmental issues has also generated what some have seen as a further shift in national planning policy with a succession of Planning Policy Guidance Notes (PPGs) published since 1990 emphasising sustainability. These argued that the pattern of new development should minimise the need for travel, especially by car, and hence reduce CO_2 emissions and the use of non-renewable resources. This implies the need to balance employment and housing development, to integrate land use and transport planning and to concentrate new development within existing urban areas. The technical arguments, however, become quickly entangled with the political process. The environmental agenda and the language of sustainability has also been adopted increasingly by a broad range of sometimes opposing interests to contest the need for develop-ment, to argue for particular patterns of development, or to emphasise resource conservation and to manage growth. Long standing conflicts over growth and development have thus intensified in the 1990s.

The planning system has also been affected in recent years by the changing financial context of local government. Up until the 1980s it was generally accepted that the costs of infrastructure and other services to support new development should be borne largely by the public sector. Financial cuts and controls impacting on local government in the 1980s, including increasingly stringent controls over the sorts of capital expenditure associated with new development, limited the capacity of local authorities to meet the costs of infrastructure and other development-related costs. Local authorities consequently sought to shift these costs onto developers themselves.

As part of this process, formal planning agreements have been used increasingly to secure financial and other contributions from developers in relation to roads, education, social and health provision and leisure and community facilities. Section 52 of the 1971 Planning Act superseded by Section 106 of the 1991 Planning and Compensation Act provided the legal framework for such agreements. While there are legal constraints on the scope of such planning agreements or 'planning gain' relating to scale and reasonableness, in practice, local authorities have significant discretion to strike deals for developer contributions to a wide range of infrastructure and social and community facilities. Developers have generally acquiesced where this provided the basis for securing planning permission without undermining the overall profitability of development. There has, however, been controversy over the legal and ethical basis of such agreements, illustrated most recently by this being referred in 1996 to the Nolan Committee, and there have been continuing complaints concerning the delay and uncertainty surrounding the use of planning agreements. Major residential developments can involve the negotiation of very substantial financial packages. These may be highly conflictual and extremely protracted, impinging, as they do, on sensitive questions of the distribution of gains arising from development to the wider community. The development of Swindon's northern sector, discussed in Chapter Six, provides a significant example of this process and the issues raised.

Finally, in terms of the actual structure of local government, the 1974 reorganisation separated strategic planning and more detailed local planning functions between county and district tiers. This, as noted in Chapter Two, has been a source of significant conflict. Reorganisation in the 1990s produced a more varied set of reforms with different arrangements in different parts of the country. Larger urban areas, as is the case with Swindon, have generally been given unitary status with responsibility for the strategic planning function. In theory, this might have reduced the scope for conflict. In practice, however, strategic planning issues generally transcend the geographical boundaries of the new unitary authorities, necessitating joint arrangements for strategic planning policy. Conflicts between authorities, particularly over the sensitive issue of allocating growth and development, could well, therefore, increase.

Industrial development and employment

Having set out some of the broader shifts in the nature of the planning system over recent years, the rest of this chapter focuses in particular on planning and the development process in relation to industrial and economic development as an integral component of town expansion and physical development. It looks first at the local authority's key role in the provision of industrial estates and sites for employment uses in the early postwar expansion, and in the subsequent planned expansion of West Swindon. This also shows the increasingly prominent role of private sector development alongside that of the Borough Council, as demand for sites from industrial and office-based employers took off in the 1970s and 1980s. It then looks in more detail at planning issues in relation to employment uses in the 1990s in the context of the Borough Council's strategy of consolidation and constraint.

Figure 5.1: Employment areas in Swindon

Estate development and town expansion

The Borough Council was actively involved in the provision of employment land and sites for major employers from the early 1950s, with the development of the Cheney Manor Estate (see Figure 5.1). Developed as a municipally owned industrial estate on land owned by the Council, this was the first planned, postwar estate, with sites leased to occupiers. Initiated in 1953, Plessey expanded their operations in premises on the estate early on, with other companies following through the 1950s. Refurbished and redeveloped to some extent, Cheney Manor Estate remains a significant concentration of industry and employment with what is now GEC Plessey Semiconductors still a major occupier. Pressed Steel purchased their Parsonage Farm site in the 1950s, where operations now continue as Rover Group. The Borough Council, meanwhile, took the lead in terms of employment land provision, initially purchasing around 48 acres adjacent to Pressed Steel.

As described in Chapter Two, by the late 1950s there was renewed pressure for housing expansion locally. The Borough Council initially sought planning permission for 400 acres of land beyond its then eastern boundary and undertook a complex process of land acquisition. As part of this new phase of physical growth of the town, it developed on part of this area the Greenbridge Industrial Estate (started in 1961), the first estate provided specifically as an integral component of town expansion. WHSmith was a key occupier here, setting up its national distribution centre in 1967. The following year, Pharmaceuticals company, Roussel, established a major facility on a site of its own at Covingham, on the edge of the eastern expansion, and other sites were developed for traditional industrial and warehousing adjacent to Pressed Steel around 1970.

Development of the first mixed-use employment development occurred in 1970, at the Dorcan Estate on the eastern fringe of the Borough. With the M4 due to open in 1971, there was increasing interest in Swindon as a location for warehousing and distribution and for office-based activities, as well as some continuing demand from manufacturing activities. The Dorcan Estate, on the main access road to Junction 15 of the M4, was developed by the Borough Council in 1970 to accommodate future employment growth. Major occupiers included the American-owned hi-tech plastics manufacturer, Raychem, which also had premises at Cheney Manor Estate.

A significant landmark, completed in 1973, was Burmah House, the first major campus-style office headquarters site to locate in the town following completion of the M4. As the administrative headquarters for Burmah Oil, and employing over 1,100 people at the time, this was an impressive, architect-designed complex on a major, prestigious, green field site on the edge of the built-up area and overlooking the valley to the south of the town and to the Downs beyond. The Groundwell Estate adjacent to the A419, a major feeder to the M4, on the east of the Borough, was developed from 1977 to meet the continuing demand for standard warehouse and industrial space. This was, again, a Borough Council development on land which it had acquired and where it remains as the overall landlord. North Star, on the other hand, developed immediately north of the railway station on former railway sidings, was designated specifically for office-based employment. Built up at a relatively slow rate it now provides a location for the various government research councils, including the Economic and Social Research Council, and British Telecom's administrative headquarters.

Western expansion

With the push for jobs initiated by the Council in the late 1970s, the focus in terms of employment and industrial development shifted to West Swindon. The development process included both local authority and private sector schemes and also mixed, public–private sector partnership development. As with housing development in the western expansion (see Chapter Six), much of the land had been acquired either by the Borough itself or by the development company Bradley. The period 1979 through to around 1984 saw a wide range of new, green field developments initiated, which provided the basis for the major expansion of employment and economic activity in the 1980s and 1990s. The first major development was undertaken by the Borough Council at Blagrove, on land it had acquired adjacent to Junction 16 of the M4. This was a fairly standard, motorway-oriented, mixed industrial, warehouse, administrative development with a number of major occupiers, including Anchor Foods UK storage, processing and distribution facility, and an initial Swindon base for Motorola. It was later extended by the adjoining Euroway development, a private development by Abbey Life Assurance, again, providing larger sites and speculative premises for motorway-oriented users.

Later on, the western expansion provided an increasing diversity of environments, including high quality 'business parks', smaller scale premises and individually designed facilities for specific users. The Borough Council sought to secure this partly through the planning process and partly through more direct involvement in the development process itself. The 'use class' orders were used under the planning acts to steer different types of development to different sites, with more of an emphasis on B1 'office uses' on some sites, B2 'general industrial' and B8 'warehousing' on others. It similarly sought to steer other uses, such as retail, and car showrooms, to particular sites while limiting them on others. Planning agreements and other negotiations over the giving of planning permission to developers were used to reinforce the 'use class' orders, while the capacity to create and maintain a variety of types of environment, attracted to different types of development, was reinforced where the Council could shape or influence the nature of the development by virtue of its ownership of land.

The Borough Council itself undertook a number of these developments, including Westmead, started in 1979, and Hillmead, developed later, from 1986 (Figure 5.1). Kembrey Park, a high density, Civic Trust award-winning business park, was a redevelopment on the site of obsolete Second World War factory buildings, undertaken initially by property developers British Land, later acquired by Sun Alliance. As with later business park developments, this has its own on-site management and management agreements to ensure the quality of the development as a whole. Both Kembrey Park and the Windmill Hill Estate (described below) are examples of high quality developments, managed by private developers on behalf of institutional investors.

The Rivermead Estate, started in 1981 and developed on land part-owned by the Borough Council, part by Bradley, includes architect Norman Foster's famous Renault Building, housing the company's UK parts warehouse and distribution centre. The Delta Estate was a high quality, well-landscaped partnership development, between the Borough Council and Taylor Woodrow, with permission for B1 office uses on Council-owned land. As a Borough planning officer put it: *"that was part of the Western Development area where the Borough Council did have very substantial landholdings and therefore dictated terms to a considerable extent..."*. Windmill Hill, started in 1984 and adjacent to Junction 16 of the M4, is similarly a well-landscaped prestigious business park. Windmill Hill was developed by the St Martin's Property Corporation, with the Borough Council acting simply as planning authority. Originally intended for a mix of B1 and B8 uses, offices and warehousing, it was all developed for office-based uses. It includes individually designed properties built for and leased to specific users, including National Power and airline reservation system operator, Galileo.

Lydiard Fields, a major 92-acre site immediately adjacent to Junction 16 of the M4, but actually over the Borough boundary into North Wiltshire District, was originally designated for development on appeal in 1990, granted by central government against the opposition of both Thamesdown and North Wiltshire. The Borough Council had seen Windmill Hill as a prestigious development, marking the boundary of the Borough, and was opposed to further extension of the developed area into North Wiltshire. The application had come from BMW who wanted the site for a headquarters building with offices, warehousing and training facilities. In the event, BMW pulled out within a week of the planning permission being granted by the Secretary of State, reputedly on the basis that it was BMW. However, since the permission was not specific to BMW, it remained in effect. Delay, shifts in the world car market and the opening up of Eastern Europe with the fall of the Berlin Wall were possible explanations for BMW's withdrawal – ironic, given BMW's subsequent acquisition of Rover Group, including the Swindon factory. The site was subsequently acquired by developers ISIS Properties on behalf of institutional investor, Equitable Life Assurance, who secured permission for a mix of offices, warehousing and industrial development together with a hotel. Development was slow to get off the ground, with a hotel being completed in 1994 and initial warehouse development starting in 1996. Having opposed the development in the first place, largely on environ-mental grounds, the Borough was later to use it as part of the argument that sufficient land had been allocated for employment purposes to meet the County's purposes in terms of the Structure Plan.

Major sites and major employers

Other significant developments related to the former Vickers site at South Marston, most notably the Honda development on the old wartime airfield and adjacent site. Outline planning permission was granted on the 148-hectare site in early 1985 to establish an operational centre for the Honda Motor Company UK. This represented a departure from the established planning framework due to the special importance of the case. With successive stages of development subject to detailed planning permission, development started with a pre-delivery inspection building and warehouse in 1985, followed by the engine manufacturing plant in 1987 and permission for the car manufacturing plant in 1989. At the Local Plan Inquiry Honda argued that the restriction of development under the Plan to a specific envelope within the site as a whole, identified in the initial outline permission as a 'major commitment', was unacceptable. Honda indicated their intention to increase capacity on the site by 50% by the year 2000, with employment rising to around 2,500. The Borough Council response indicated that it was trying simply to retain some control over the detail of new development and to ensure that it could secure payment from Honda for road improvements if traffic volumes generated by the development exceeded given levels – commitment to support Honda's continued growth clearly remained strong. The draft Local Plan also reserved land between the Honda plant and the main railway line for a rail freight terminal and link to be provided. Although not formally agreed, it was hoped that Honda would be a major user, thus cutting down on the heavy volume of car transporter and other traffic related to the works. Outline planning permission was granted for the link in 1995, subject to there being a legal agreement tying the site specifically to the intended use. The Council were anxious to avoid its possible use as another major site for general employment uses, in the event of the rail and freight terminal not going ahead, and for this reason, the site was also not identified for employment purposes in the Local Plan.

Adjacent to the Honda site was a further major area of land which had formed part of the Vickers aircraft works in the war, used, among other things, for assembling Spitfires. It largely remained in the ownership of what was now Vickers Properties, who had sold a major part of the site as a whole to Honda in 1994. Development for employment purposes had, in fact, started in the 1970s, with these early units largely occupied by the Royal Mail. The Honda development stimulated greater interest in development in this general area, and planning permissions were granted for further developments starting in 1986. The site has been gradually built up with a variety of schemes, some built for specific users, others built speculatively. Various conditions were imposed on the continuing development of the site to ensure that the capacity of the local road network kept pace with activity on the site. The Borough later sought to provide for a possible bus-lane and park-and-ride scheme associated with further development on the site. With a considerable area still remaining to be developed, however, it represented a significant component of the total volume of land, argued by the Borough Council to be available to meet structure plan requirements. There were objections, however, around the time of the Local Plan Public Inquiry and the debate around the replacement Structure Plan as to its real availability as employment land. The conditions relating to road capacity and public transport provision attached to development of the site amounted, it was argued, to an additional development cost. Up to around 14 hectares was, nevertheless, still capable of development without the requirement of financial contributions towards infrastructure.

The former GWR (subsequently British Rail Engineering Ltd) rail engineering works and sidings had been acquired by Tarmac subsidiary, Tarmac Swindon, established for the purpose following final closure of the works in 1986. This provided a massive redevelopment opportunity in the heart of the town and the opportunity for considerable employment generation. Outline permission was granted for a mixed development scheme providing 41 acres for employment uses, 90,000ft^2 of retail space, and housing development. The site included a conservation area, with a number of listed buildings identified for refurbishment for employment, retail and leisure uses. Employment uses within the development as a whole included an Iceland Cold store and distribution centre on part of the site, adjacent to a Sainsbury supermarket and Homebase store. A considerable area of around 8 hectares adjacent to this was identified in the Local Plan for a mixture of industrial, office, storage and distribution uses and awaited development in 1996. The stated policy indicated a preference for jobs to compensate for the loss of engineering employment on the site, although detailed planning permissions granted in 1995 included a car showroom as well as speculative industrial units. A further 6.6 hectares in the conservation area close to the existing railway station was identified for employment uses. Very appropriately, in 1996, the Royal Commission for Historic Monuments relocated to accommodation redeveloped within the shell of one of the former GWR buildings on this part of the site. Planned uses for the conservation area also included factory-outlet shopping and a railway heritage centre (see below).

Elsewhere in the town, further prestigious, campus-style development followed Burmah's early lead. American-owned Intel Corporation UK moved into its own, purpose-built accommodation close to the Burmah site in 1983. By 1996 the site included the company's European distribution centre, together with sales and marketing and other functions relating to the UK and Europe. The site which it initially acquired in 1980 provided for staged growth, with a second building added in 1985 and a third in 1989. Employment grew from around 200 in 1983 to 700 by 1996. Thamesdown Council were considered by Intel to have been flexible in terms of planning regulations at the time compared with some other localities which were looked at. Originally, this site was also leased by the Borough Council to Intel in line with what was then Council policy. Later, however, the Council sold the freehold to Intel.

Nationwide Building Society later developed an architecturally striking office development close to Burmah and Intel, on a site overlooking the valley south of Swindon. Nationwide, had in fact, first set up a technology centre and related administrative functions in Swindon as early as 1974. Nationwide expanded in central Swindon, to a point where it had staff in some seven different office blocks within five minutes walk of each other, until the opportunity came to acquire their current site in 1989. Nationwide merged with the Northampton-based Anglia Building Society in 1987 and, with the weight of management and key functions in Swindon, it was decided to consolidate in Swindon itself.

By 1996 Nationwide employed some 2,200 people in the new development, compared with 300-350 in the 1970s. The site had been identified by the Council as early as 1981 for a prestigious, campus-style office development, and it had drawn up a development brief for the site and deemed itself outline planning permission in 1992 in order to market the site. Outline permission was granted to Nationwide in 1989 for 46,000m^2 of office space and full permission for the first major phase of 35,000ft^2. Permission for a further 11,000m^2 was given by the Council in 1996. Although there does not appear to have been much likelihood of Nationwide Anglia significantly reducing employment or pulling out of Swindon, this was a striking example of the Borough Council enabling the consolidation onto a single site and further expansion of an employer which had originally relocated part of its operations to the town in the 1970s and subsequently expanded its operations to a major extent. Nationwide also established a new computer centre, or 'data centre', on the

Borough Council's Hillmead Estate on the town's north-east fringe, away from its main campus and with an emphasis on security. The Woolwich Building Society, with no other significant employment locally, also selected Swindon as a location for a high security data centre, developed on an old hospital site in the Borough.

A similar case was that of Motorola, although, by way of contrast, it is a major high technology and manufacturing concern, as opposed to office-based employment. American-owned cellular phone manufacturer, Motorola, established in Swindon in 1989 with 45 people, had expanded by 1996 to a point where it employed around 1,400, in five separate leased premises. These included premises on the Council-developed Blagrove Estate and Kembrey Park Estate mentioned earlier in this chapter. In 1996 Motorola bought from the Council a 66-acre site designated for employment use in the northern expansion. The site was originally acquired by the Council in the early 1970s and was identified in the northern expansion Master Plan and in the draft Local Plan for employment uses. It already had outline planning permission. The Council had been negotiating with the Cranfield Institute of Technology to develop a science park on the site, representing a high quality development of business and industrial uses with related research and development and possibly hotel and conference facilities. The Institute was intending to develop as Cranfield University on an adjoining site and the development was intended to relate to the academic and research skills of the University. These plans did not come to fruition and by October of 1995, the site was described by the Council as "available to the market" (Thamesdown Borough Council, 1995c). Motorola approached the Council and secured the site on which to construct a 510,000ft^2, £116m development for the European headquarters of the company's Cellular Infrastructure division. Completion was scheduled for the end of 1998.

As with Nationwide Anglia, the site allowed a major local employer, which had undergone major expansion since its initial move to the town, to centralise and further expand its operations in a single, purpose-built prestigious development. This was very much in line with Council policy of meeting the needs of expanding local employers, particularly so in the case of Motorola as a manufacturing concern. Council Leader Sue Bates commented at the time:

"I am delighted that Motorola ECID sees its
European future as continuing to be based in
Swindon. Nurturing this kind of growth in our
local economy is a very important aim within the
Council's economic development strategy.
Motorola has clearly decided its proposed move
will be good for the company and its people, and
I believe this will be an excellent development for
the site concerned, and for Swindon." (*Motorola
Matters*, 11, Spring 1996)

Again, as with Nationwide, it was a Council-owned site that
facilitated the development, identified for employment purposes in
planning terms and integral to the planned northern expansion. It
was, as described above, fortuitous, however, that the site actually
became available to Motorola, given that the Borough had been
pursuing the science park strategy with Cranfield as part of its
plans for a new university in the town. The site was not part of
any specific plan as such to meet the needs of local employers,
such as Motorola, wishing to expand. On the other hand, when
the original plans fell through, with deft pragmatism it was quickly
put to this use and claimed as a success in terms of economic
development strategy. Appropriately, as well, Motorola also
represented high technology activity, although the science park
concept with multiple users, linked to university-based research
skills was not realised.

Retail development

Retail development represented both an integral component of
town expansion and also a major generator of employment in its
own right, accounting for 10,000 jobs locally by 1993 – over 12%
of all employment. Retail development was planned as an integral
component of earlier phases of town expansion. This saw
considerable investment in the town centre, together with district
centres and a lower tier of neighbourhood convenience shopping.
Development of West Swindon included a district centre adjacent
to the Link Centre leisure complex, and smaller 'village centres'.
The northern expansion also includes proposals for a district
centre and village centres along similar lines. A hierarchy of
provision in this form had been envisaged in the original *Silver
Book*, much of it serving the local population. However, it also

saw Swindon developing as a key sub-regional, if not regional, shopping centre, generating additional employment locally.

By the 1990s, however, it was widely recognised that the town centre was in need of significant investment and improvement. More generally, as the 1994 draft Local Plan observed:

> In the 1980s, a number of major trends emerged that have had a significant effect, in general, on retailing in the UK; these have included the development of 'out-of-town' and 'out of centre' shopping centres particularly catering for the car-borne shopper, supermarkets and superstores based on bulk food shopping, retail warehousing and retail parks, enclosed shopping malls and concepts of 'leisure' and 'discount' shopping.
> (Thamesdown Borough Council, 1994a, p 101)

Added to this, while out-of-town or edge-of-town developments boomed in the 1980s, government policy guidance by the early 1990s emphasised the need to consider the viability and vitality of town centres. This was reinforced by concern over sustainability and energy conservation, which implied the need to focus retail growth in centres which operate as public transport nodes.

Much of the existing provision in Swindon town centre had been developed in the 1970s, including the Brunel Centre, owned and managed by the Council. This represented a significant revenue earner for the Council, generating over £6m in rental income by the early 1990s and a 'profit' of £2.5m underpinning service provision and general expenditure by the Council. By the early 1990s, however, it was recognised that the Brunel Centre was in need of major refurbishment if rental levels were to be maintained and if the looked for improvement in the quality and quantity of retail provision and in the quality of the town centre more generally were to be achieved. But Swindon had never achieved the broader sub-regional or regional status, envisaged originally in the *Silver Book*. This had implications in terms of the range and quality of retail provision in itself, but also in terms of the scale of employment generation within the sector. Retail development was widely acknowledged to have lagged behind other aspects of town expansion in terms of both quality and scale of provision:

> Despite the growth of the town over the past two decades, the one area which has fallen behind in terms of provision is retail space in the Central Area. (Thamesdown Borough Council, 1991a)

Competing centres including Bath, Newbury, Oxford and Cheltenham limited the growth of Swindon as a retail attraction, while smaller towns such as Cirencester and Chippenham, with significant developments of their own, proved attractive to shoppers. This was reinforced by the lifestyle and residential location choice of a significant proportion of managers and professionals in particular who chose to live outside of Swindon in the smaller towns and villages or larger, more historic urban centres. Studies carried out for the Council by consultants CNN Marketing demonstrated the limited catchment area of Swindon town centre: 72% of shoppers using the Brunel Centre had travelled less than 2 miles and almost 93% came from within 10 miles of the town centre. Profiles of those using the Centre, moreover, indicated that lower and moderately well-off income groups were over-represented. Higher income, higher spending groups typically seeking a more up-market and broader range of goods and services tended to be under-represented.

The Council's efforts to redevelop the Brunel Centre illustrate the changing role of the local authority and the changing capacity of local government to play an active role in economic and social provision. Refurbishment was seen as essential and the Council as the major landowner and landlord clearly had a central part to play. Originally, the Council had acted as developer, acquiring the land, funding the development and, as noted earlier, generating significant rental income on its investment to the benefit of the local community and local ratepayers. Built between 1972 and 1978, the Centre included over 500,000ft^2 of shops, and 40,000ft^2 of office space and flats in the high-rise Murray John Tower, named after the former town clerk who had played such a key role in the town's early development (Harloe, 1975). The Centre was seen as a key asset for the town in the context of rapid expansion in the early 1970s. The Council at the time was investing heavily in the future of the town and over this same period it also developed the Oasis Leisure Centre and Wyvern Theatre, and it made major land purchases, including 568 acres for £4.2m in 1972 in the western expansion, and Groundwell Farm in what was to become the northern expansion purchased for £4.3m in 1974.

Built at a cost by 1978 of £27.5m, the Centre was initially in deficit, with loan charges exceeding rental income. By the late 1980s, the Centre was contributing a surplus to the Council's finances at a time when government 'rate-capping' had limited its capacity to raise revenue via local taxation. By 1993 rental growth was such that the Centre was generating rental income to the Council's finances – after loan charges on the outstanding debt of £30m – of £3.5m. This represented some 18% of the total cost of providing local authority services in the town. By the early 1990s, however, the Council was faced with the cost of major refurbishment if rental levels were to be maintained and the broader objectives of upgrading the town centre realised. The Council commissioned Chapman Taylor Partners, architects of major retail developments including Meadowhall in Sheffield and Lakeside in Essex, to undertake design work. Their proposals included provision for a major anchor store, and House of Fraser, who had previously shown interest, were seen as a likely candidate. Government restrictions on local authority capital expenditure were such, however, that the Council could not raise the money itself to fund the refurbishment. Freehold disposal, even if the Council saw this as acceptable, was not a viable option in financial terms. The capital sum required to make it feasible for the Council to forego the rental income it currently received would have put the value of the Centre way above what the market would pay. The Council was therefore forced to seek joint funding arrangements.

The Council therefore structured a deal involving leasing the Centre to a private sector funder. The funder was to refurbish the Centre on a basis agreed with the Council and would be paid for this out of the rental income. The remainder of the rental income would then pass to the Council. The refurbishment and ongoing management of the Centre would be undertaken by a private sector management company. The viability of the deal turned on the legal interpretation of local government legislation. It also took advantage of an incentive established by the Chancellor of the Exchequer in 1992-93 to encourage joint ventures between the public and private sector by easing, temporarily, the capacity of local authorities to benefit from capital receipts. Thus, in the 1970s, the local authority was free to use its resources and to undertake development on commercial grounds and in line with its overall objectives for the development of the town. In the 1990s, however, its capacity to act was dependent on complex financial and legal constraints and dependent on exploiting a government measure which was apparently intended to encourage local authorities to dispose of their capital assets to the private sector.

With work on the Brunel Centre largely complete by early 1997, plans for adjacent areas of the town centre remained more dependent on private sector investment decisions within the overall planning context which supports further enhancement. Other developments locally reflected national trends in shopping as identified in the Local Plan. There was a considerable increase in retail warehousing and superstores from the late 1980s – over 800,000ft^2 of space out-of centre, compared with 1.4m ft^2 in the town centre overall. This included a significant concentration of retail warehouses in the Mannington area to the west of the town centre. The Council had encouraged the redevelopment of part of the Greenbridge Industrial Estate in East Swindon as a retail warehouse park and leisure complex – lacking any land ownership in the area it could only express its support in terms of the planning framework and in overall policy terms. The hope was to catch up with developments in West Swindon where earlier provision by the Council had been complemented by private sector investment in a multi-screen cinema, bowling, restaurants and nightclub, hotel and leisure facilities.

Finally, 'concept shopping', combining leisure and discount shopping, came to Swindon as a component of the Churchward development. American developers McArthur Glenn and airports operator BAA, with expertise in airport shopping malls, combined to develop the Great Western Designer Outlet Village. The idea was developed in the US, with a number of UK examples, including Clark's development at Street and BAA McArthur Glenn's earlier Cheshire Oaks development outside of Chester. The principle is based on offering goods at 'sale' prices on a permanent basis, including up-market designs, unsold and end-of-season stock from mainstream retailers. Main retailers in more expensive prime sites, meanwhile, maintain prime prices for their stock for longer, disposing of the surplus through 'outlets'. Successful outlet developments have become important attractions combining shopping, leisure activities and tourism. As one feature article put it, describing Swindon as "the former railway town cashing in on the latest leisure craze":

> Swindon's centre is about more than shopping. It
> is part of 'Heritage Britain'. Outlet centres offer
> not just a place to buy a new dress or a pair of
> trainers, but somewhere to go for the day – an
> alternative to the theme park or the stately home.
> (*Guardian*, 20 April 1996)

The Great Western Designer Outlet Village at Swindon, opened in
March 1997, includes 178,000ft^2 of lettable floorspace, representing around 100 units, of which some 80% were occupied soon
after opening. Individual units are restricted in size, with no major
'anchor' store. The terms under which units are leased specify the
prices at which its goods are to be sold relative to normal high
street prices in order to ensure the 'discount' element. The Village
incorporates a food hall, with outlets offering a range of fast food
from fish and chips and pizzas to Italian crepes, ice cream and
cappuccino.

In design terms, the development itself has been built into and
around part of the original structure of the railway engineering
works. It makes a feature of the original structure building on and
extending the railway heritage and memorabilia, including the
Swindon-built City of Truro locomotive, which sits in the centre
of the food hall. In a wider sense, cultural commentators refer to
post-modernism in terms of irony, playfulness and pastiche. The
irony of cut-price designer wear, railway memorabilia and carefully staged displays of heritage on the site of Brunel's once great
engineering works is particularly marked. Design standards,
however, are high, and it represents a high quality development of
its type without any sense of a cut-price feel to it. It represents, in
a sense, an instant 'concept mall' for the town, adding a whole
new dimension to retailing.

The expected catchment area based on previous developments
is 1.5 to 2 hours, taking in a population of around 10 million. It
has parking for 2,000 and plans to rent a further 600 spaces for
weekend overflow. Emphasising its role as a major visitor
attraction it aims to generate coach-borne visitors on a major scale.
Cheshire Oaks, the Chester development, generates 2,000 coach
trips per year bringing visitors to the centre. Swindon is expecting
1,500 in its first year and by mid-April had played host to the first
coachloads of Taiwanese and Swedish visitors. The company is
heavily involved in the active promotion of the Village as a
tourism destination and, with publicity material, including

information on Swindon more generally and Wiltshire's tourism attractions, sees significant benefits for the area. Locally it is also hoped that the new development will complement rather than compete with existing town centre retailing. Its economic impact includes significant employment generation, initially estimated at around 800 in all. Reinforcing the leisure theme, in 1997, the Council secured National Lottery Heritage Fund money for a railway heritage centre as part of the complex.

The Borough Council role

To summarise, the Borough Council played a key role in the provision of sites for employment throughout the postwar period, not only in terms of planning but also, to a major degree, as a landowner and developer in its own right. This extended to the Cheney Manor Estate in the early postwar years and Greenbridge and Dorcan in the early eastern expansion. It also included the Borough's major role in the provision of employment land in the western expansion from the late 1970s onwards, and its role in retail development. Earlier developments, such as Cheney Manor and Greenbridge were, in a sense, traditional industrial estates developed with services and access roads, leased as relatively large plots and with little in the way of landscaping or design. Dorcan and Groundwell were similar, but with more in the way of warehouse and office uses, reflecting the shift in the pattern of inwards investment in the 1970s. Blagrove, the Borough's first development for industrial and warehouse uses in the western expansion, was similar again, with basic infrastructure provided and relatively large plots leased to individual occupiers or for speculative development. Reflecting changes in the market, it was, however, more imaginative in design terms, starting to reflect the 'hi-tech', M4 Corridor image.

Subsequent development of the western expansion saw a mix of local authority and private sector development and, in some cases, joint partnership development between the two. This partly reflected the pattern of land ownership which had been established in the area following land purchases by the Borough Council and private developers such as Bradley. It also reflected the increasing attractiveness to the private property sector of industrial and commercial development in this period, particularly in a high-growth area such as Swindon, with considerable demand for sites and premises both from inwards investors and from established employers seeking to expand. Whereas the Borough Council had undertaken the bulk of earlier provision of employment sites in east Swindon, the Council-sponsored western expansion increasingly provided a vehicle for private sector property development and investment.

The Borough Council, both in its role as planning authority and landowner and developer in its own right, sought to ensure, in combination with the private sector, provision of the appropriate scale and mix of types of developments for employment uses. Working alongside the private sector and responding to some extent to changing market demands, it sought to differentiate different types of uses and to ensure the creation of a variety of environments for employment development. This resulted in a mix including high quality business parks, smaller industrial units, sites for specific individual enterprises and more standard serviced sites for industry, warehousing and distribution.

The Council also played a very significant role from the early 1970s in providing individual sites for prestigious headquarters premises, including Burmah, Intel, Nationwide Anglia and Motorola, all developed as noted earlier, on Council-owned sites. All took the form of major, single-user campus-style developments, on the fringe of the urban area. This generated, increasingly, privatised, relatively self-contained enclaves within the area of the town, a theme to be revisited in Chapter Eight. All four companies initially represented inwards investment to the locality and all generated major employment growth subsequently employing between them over 5,000 people by 1996. The Council also facilitated, through its operation of the planning system, other major single-user developments, most notably Honda, granted planning permission at South Marston as a departure from the existing planning policy.

The Borough Council's policy in terms of land disposal was generally to retain the freehold interest. It was very resistant, particularly early on, to selling the freehold of any land which it owned, believing that land should stay in the ownership of the local authority for the benefit of the community. With the early estates, it would typically service the sites with roads and sewers, provide a layout for the site as a whole, and sell individual sites on a leasehold basis. From about the mid-1980s, while this remained the official policy position of the Council, they had been forced to relax this in a number of cases in order to secure particular employers who would not accept a particular site on a leasehold basis. It sold Intel the freehold of its site which it had previously held on a leasehold basis and sites sold, later on, to Nationwide Anglia and Motorola were sold freehold.

Planning and employment growth in the 1990s

Postwar town expansion had seen the Borough Council pushing for development and physical expansion, frequently against the opposition of the County in terms of both boundary extension and the formal planning framework. In the mid-1970s, for example, the Borough appealed against the County's refusal of planning permission in the western expansion and was granted permission by the Secretary of State in 1977 against the County's wishes. The Borough was also highly critical of the County's draft North East Wiltshire Structure Plan when it appeared in 1980 (Bassett and Harloe, 1990). Conservative members of the Council and the Conservative MP joined with the Labour majority in opposing the County. The Secretary of State again supported Thamesdown, approving increased targets for population, housing and employment and confirming central government support for Swindon's strategy of planned growth and physical expansion.

The mid-1980s, however, saw a turning point in the town's postwar history, marked by policy reappraisal in the context of the *A new vision* (see Chapter Two). In 1986 the Borough lined up with the County Council in opposition to development proposals submitted for the northern expansion. This was tactical to some extent, seeking to secure the maximum contribution from the consortium of developers to community facilities and to the cost of infrastructure. The debate around the alterations to the Structure Plan in the late 1980s, however, saw the Borough starting to question the scale of land allocated by the County both for employment and for housing purposes. By the time the Local Plan and the replacement Structure Plan were being prepared, the Borough's new commitment to consolidation and constraint was clearly expressed. This section examines the changing process of planning and development over this period.

Planned restraint

In the absence of major policy statements in the period after *A new vision for Thamesdown*, the Borough Council's de facto policy of consolidation and constraint can be traced through its stance in relation to the evolving statutory planning framework. This included in particular the draft Thamesdown Local Plan in 1994 and related statements and, running almost concurrently, the emerging Wiltshire Structure Plan. The contrast with the earlier periods, with the Borough Council pushing for expansion, boundary extensions and the release of land for development, against the opposition of the County Council and at times, central government, became very evident. This was particularly the case in relation to the draft Wiltshire Structure Plan in 1996, which, in a complete reversal of earlier positions, saw the Borough Council firmly resisting the County Council's strategy to concentrate growth on Swindon. This was very much the case in terms of housing (see Chapter Six). It was also closely paralleled in terms of employment land and economic development, with the Borough Council strongly resisting the idea that it should accommodate the economic development pressures of the M4 Corridor and realise the full potential of the area for expansion and inwards investment. Employment and housing were, indeed, seen as closely linked with any 'excessive' build up of jobs and inwards investment likely, in turn, to generate pressure for additional housing.

Thamesdown's 1994 Local Plan

The strategic planning framework in the 1980s included three separate structure plans for the County, including that for North East Wiltshire (which covered Thamesdown, and the adjoining districts of North Wiltshire and Kennet). This was approved in 1981 and reviewed and updated subsequently. The Local Plan drawn up by the Borough Council (Thamesdown Borough Council, 1994a), aimed to identify and set out in detail how the overall level of provision of employment land identified by the North East Wiltshire Structure Plan would be met, in the period up to 2001. Drawn up some 13 years after the approval of the Structure Plan – and still in 1994 only in draft form – the context for the Local Plan had clearly altered substantially in the intervening years. The planning horizon for the existing Structure

Plan, moreover, only extended as far as 2001. Much of the period covered by the Structure Plan was history by the time the Local Plan was drawn up. Indeed, the planning process for the new, County-wide Wiltshire Structure Plan was already in progress and this was itself published in draft form soon after the Public Inquiry on the Local Plan. Given this timing, the Local Plan and the arguments developed by the Borough around its proposals could be seen as a holding operation pending the new Structure Plan. They could also, however, be seen as a specific intervention in the ongoing debate, which was unfolding with the new Wiltshire Structure Plan and the timescale for this, which extended well into the next millennium.

The Local Plan (Thamesdown Borough Council, 1994a) itself noted that, despite the closure of the rail works in 1986, there had been substantial growth in employment in the period 1984 to 1989. This had included both manufacturing industry and services. In carefully chosen words it noted that:

> The local economy generally has prospered at a rate enabling the expansion of existing firms and the birth of new firms to service the needs of the commercial sector and the expanding local population. As pressure continues for the movement of firms along the M4 Corridor the plan will need to try to balance the demands of new businesses with the needs of existing local companies. (Thamesdown Borough Council, 1994a, p 47)

Elaborating later for the Local Inquiry, the Borough referred rather more explicitly to "the need for some further investment to stimulate the local economy" (Thamesdown Borough Council, 1995b, p 5). Overall, however, one can detect an increasing emphasis on the requirements of the local area rather than on meeting the demand created by growth pressures within the M4 Corridor, an emphasis on existing local companies, local business start-up, the commercial sector and the local population. The Borough was resistant to the idea of any further land being allocated for employment purposes, arguing in the plan that: "Existing commitments together with new proposals contained in the Plan are capable of providing a range of sites in terms of size, type and location." (Thamesdown Borough Council, 1994a, p 47).

Explaining its strategy, the Borough noted that earlier technical argument in relation to the revision of the Structure Plan had suggested that exploitation of the economic growth of the M4 Corridor "could bring heavy pressures for employment and housing development and a much increased level of inward migration resulting in pressure to open up new areas for town expansion in the 1990s in addition to the proposed Northern Development Area and bring environmental and infrastructure problems" (Thamesdown Borough Council, 1995b, p 4, referring to Explanatory Memorandum [1991] of Structure Plan Alteration 2, Wiltshire County Council, 1991). This second alteration to the Structure Plan shifted the balance away from exploitation of the growth potential of the area, and the Borough noted in support of its own view the revised strategy:

> The Strategy for the 1990s of the North East Wiltshire Structure Plan is to recognise and accommodate development opportunities in the M4 corridor, where compatible with the environment and infrastructure. Rather than exploiting the full potential for employment growth, the strategy seeks to maintain the existing growth momentum through the development of the Northern Development Area and to protect the rural environment elsewhere as the countryside surrounding Swindon plays a major role in the town's attractiveness.   (Thamesdown Borough Council, 1995b, p 2)

To understand the argument, it is necessary to examine, briefly, the process whereby the future need for employment land is estimated and how this is compared with land already allocated for this purpose. The discussion gets somewhat detailed but it goes to the heart of the debate around consolidation and around the future role of Swindon in the context of growth pressures along the M4 Corridor. It also has wider relevance in terms of managing growth pressures more generally, rippling out from London and the South East region.

The technical argument, set out in relation to the Structure Plan (Wiltshire County Council, 1991) compared growth in the local workforce (those needing jobs locally) with projected growth in the number of jobs available. The calculations allowed for a reduction in unemployment and for continued increase in commuting, both of which would push up the demand for jobs locally. It was also noted that employment land allocations related only to strategic sites for offices, industry and warehousing covered by 'Class B' of the Town and Country Planning Order (1987) – other jobs would be created in retailing, hotels, and leisure, and in services related to the local population. It was further acknowledged that a significant proportion of the new jobs created would be on existing employment land or in town centre offices and retailing. This would limit the need for new land to be allocated for employment purposes. The County calculated that locally only around half of all new jobs in recent years had been on sites newly developed for employment purposes as opposed to sites previously or already used for employment purposes. The Borough Council had been arguing this point for some time, maintaining that the amount of land identified in the Structure Plan for employment had a capacity for jobs well in excess of the likely future supply of labour.

This process generated an estimate of the growth in employment that would have to be accommodated in future years. This could then be compared with the capacity of land already allocated in planning terms for employment purposes – using an estimate as to the number of workers that could be accommodated per hectare of available land, based on past experience. On this basis, referring to the Structure Plan calculations, the Borough Council argued that:

> Comparisons of projections for jobs and work-force growth for Thamesdown ... reveal that the capacity of the existing commitments in terms of potential job creation could far outstrip the job needs of the local expanding population, even when allowing for a reduction in unemployment and a continuing increase in inward commuting. Thus the Structure Plan strategy, which aims to concentrate growth in Swindon and minimise its effects in the smaller settlements and rural areas, also enables Swindon to serve the job needs of a wider population including such settlements as Wootton Bassett, Cricklade and Marlborough.
> (Thamesdown Borough Council, 1994a, p 48)

In other words, the Borough was arguing that employment land already identified (sites with planning permission or identified in the draft Local Plan) was more than adequate for future needs – defined in terms of the local population and including nearby villages and small towns. Emphasising the case based on local needs, it went on to state that the study of existing commitments undertaken for the Structure Plan "when compared with predicted requirements was found to be able to provide more than enough scope for local needs and thus no additional development was proposed." (Thamesdown Borough Council, 1994a, p 48).

For the period 1990 to 2001, the Structure Plan (as revised) identified the need for around 220 hectares of employment land. Developments completed since 1990, developments still to be completed and with sites still available and, finally, sites which already had planning permission for employment use amounted to around 178 hectares. This left a further 42 hectares or so to be identified. Major sites identified in the Local Plan included 29 hectares in the Northern Development Area outlined in the Master Plan for the area and on which outline planning permission had been granted in 1992. The other major site identified in the Local Plan itself was a further 27 hectares at South Marston Industrial Estate, part of the old airfield, adjacent to the Honda site and owned by Vickers Properties. Other smaller sites were identified in the urban area of Swindon.

The Borough reiterated this case at the Public Inquiry, with some minor revisions to the figures. It was argued that the total land available, including completed development, existing commitments and proposals identified in the Local Plan, amounted to some 255.5 hectares compared with the identified need of 220 hectares (Thamesdown Borough Council, 1995b, Appendix 1). The balance of some 35.5 hectares was intended, it was argued, to allow for possible restricted availability. At this stage the Borough also made the case that 37 hectares at Lydiard Fields at Junction 16 of the M4, adjacent to the Swindon urban area, but in fact within North Wiltshire District, represented additional capacity within what it termed the 'Swindon Sector'.

In short, the Borough Council thus argued that employment land provision was more than adequate for local needs. It had clearly turned its back as far as the formal planning framework was concerned, on any major commitment to future expansion based on inwards investment and in-migration. Future job growth was seen primarily in terms of the employment needs of the local population rather than accommodating – let alone embracing, as in previous periods – regional or national growth pressures within the M4 Corridor. This approach reflected fairly clearly the thinking set out in *A new vision for Thamesdown* and debate as to the 'limits to growth'. Clearly absent was any reference to strategic expansion or a future for Swindon as a new city. At this stage, the Borough was largely in agreement with the County Council, and basing its own case on the technical argument put by the County. This, in itself, is significant seen in the historical context of the Borough pushing for expansion against the opposition of the County.

The Borough's policy in terms of employment land as set out in the Local Plan was scrutinised in the course of the Public Inquiry in October 1995. This provided the opportunity to respond to formal objections. The process, as in such inquiries, was, in part, one of responding to individual objections, many concerned with purely local issues and concerns. Other objections were intended as a more fundamental challenge to the basis of the Plan and the strategy which lay behind it. In this context, the Borough took the opportunity, particularly in its Employment Land Topic Paper (Thamesdown Borough Council, 1995b) to reiterate and to develop the case set out in the draft Local Plan. It restated its commitment to 'consolidation', and made explicit reference to the danger of economic growth pressures fuelling demands for further housebuilding:

> If employment developments are allowed much in excess of Structure Plan requirements there is a danger that economic pressures could fuel demands for further housebuilding over and above that already planned for, or result in increased inward commuting and further traffic congestion. (Thamesdown Borough Council, 1995b, pp 1-2)

It quoted in support of its case Regional Planning Guidance for the South West (RPG10), published after the draft Local Plan and intended to provide the context for strategic planning up to 2011, well beyond the current Local Plan period. In particular, it noted the statement in this, that Swindon would no longer be expected to grow at the rate which characterised previous years, that plans should encourage greater use of public transport to counter the effects of increasing traffic congestion and that the surrounding rural area should be protected.

When it came to the Public Inquiry, the Borough Council also took the opportunity to link its case for restraint explicitly to environmental issues and issues of sustainability which had emerged into the policy arena in the intervening period, mainly by way of the government's Planning Policy Guidance (PPG). The Borough made explicit reference to PPG4, which emphasised the need for continued economic growth to be compatible with environmental objectives, and to PPG12, which highlighted the contribution that development plans can make to ensuring that development and growth were 'sustainable' (Thamesdown Borough Council, 1995b, p 1). The Borough was clearly attempting to appropriate the green agenda, the discourse or language of environmentalism and sustainability, to support the case for constraint which it had earlier built into the draft Local Plan – a tactic which the County itself was soon to adopt in the new structure plan process in putting its own case for concentrating development in the Swindon urban area.

Holding the line

When it came to the Local Public Inquiry there were a number of skirmishes challenging the Borough's overall policy of consolidation and resistance to further expansion on any significant scale. These included tactical objections, arguing that specific sites should not be counted as land available for development and that the overall allocation of employment land by the Borough was therefore inadequate. There were also objections that specific additional sites should have been included, to compensate for this shortfall. Property agents King Sturge objected that the allocations did not include sufficient larger sites or sites for the expansion of local companies on the edge of Swindon. The Department of the Environment (DoE) raised the objection that there was insufficient land allocated for the anticipated economic development of the area, raising doubts as to the genuine availability of land identified, and that the choice and quality of the available land was limited. King Sturge, however, withdrew their objection and the DoE did not back up their own case. Swindon Chamber of Commerce objected that the Plan failed to provide sites of the right quality to attract new business and put the case that: "Additional land should be allocated, including releases suitable for 'campus style' development to make up the shortfall and allow for the continuation of development after 2001." (Thamesdown Borough Council, 1995a). Property agents objected that the Borough Council's land in the northern sector was not actually available for employment purposes because warehousing was excluded, and it formed part of plans then linked to the Cranfield University development. The Council pointed out that the land was now available, the Cranfield development having fallen through. They also observed that: "the objector is seeking to have this site, in addition to a number of others, deleted from the Council's allocated employment land supply simply to promote an additional major site within the Borough for his client." (Thamesdown Borough Council, 1995c). Similarly, in relation to the Chamber of Commerce, the Borough Council observed that "This and other objections seek the deletion of a number of proposals in order to reduce the overall level of employment land provision, in an attempt to justify major new site allocations outside the present Swindon Urban Area and its new town expansion area." (Thamesdown Borough Council, 1995a, p 5).

As this suggests, agents and development consultants acting on behalf of landowners and potential developers also sought to have specific individual sites added in to the overall allocation. These included sites east of the A419 dual carriageway on the east of the built-up area. Agents acting for developers wanting to develop a 'food park' on 39 hectares of farmland east of the A419 argued that the draft Local Plan "provided insufficient land that is truly available for employment development, in particular sites of the right size, location and price for incoming firms" (Thamesdown Borough Council, 1995d). The site in question, it argued, should therefore be allocated for employment uses. Similarly, Swindon-based consultants DPDS and Chapman Warren argued on behalf of various landowners and developers that a site of nearly 40 acres, known locally as 'the triangle site', should be allocated in the Local Plan for employment uses on the basis that the Plan: "fails to meet the employment land requirement in the Borough" and "does not provide a sufficient range of sites in terms of choice and location of size. There is a need for a larger site to accommodate employment uses requiring good access to the M4 and A419 and also to serve the existing motor industry in the next decade." (Thamesdown Borough Council, 1995e). This site was, in fact, something of a long-running saga, illustrating the tactics of landowners and their representatives. There had been attempts to get the site allocated for employment uses earlier on, in relation to the alterations to the North East Wiltshire Structure Plan, with a planning application submitted for the site in 1988 and further attempts to have it included at the time of the Public Inquiry.

These speculative applications, trying to break through the existing planning framework and the assumptions on which it was based, paralleled similar moves in relation to housing land, discussed in Chapter Six. There were other cases where approaches were made to the Borough Council, in effect, to see which way the land lay, but which were not pursued to the point of formal objections. Similar kites had been flown around the time of the alterations to the old Structure Plan, including a speculative application for a massive development of around two million square feet of office space in the area of open landscape between the town and the M4 adjacent to Coate Water Park. This early attack on the 'front garden' went to an appeal and Public Inquiry before being finally rejected by the Secretary of State for the Environment.

The Borough Council, for its part, was seeking to hold the line at the A419, seeing this as the natural boundary for expansion at least up to the end of the existing planing period of 2001. The Borough maintained that the major South Marston Industrial Area and the Honda site, both east of the A419, did not breach this in policy terms, as some objectors had argued, since these developments were located on the former Vickers site and the wartime airfield, and had not therefore constituted new development. The Honda development, moreover, had been permitted as a departure from this policy "due to the national significance of the project and the unique operational potential afforded by the airfield site including the use of old runways for car testing and storage and the possibility of a rail connection to the site." (Thamesdown Borough Council, 1995d). Permission granted for a rail terminal, which it was hoped Honda among others would use, was subject to a legal agreement and conditions tying permission solely to this use. It was also in line with the environmental objectives of Planning Guidance Note 13 encouraging a switch of freight from road to rail.

The Borough Council argued in relation to the 'food park' and 'triangle site' objections respectively, for example, that:

> There is no shortfall of employment land as the Plan does make sufficient provision to met Structure Plan requirements and, taking existing commitments together with new allocations, provides a range in terms of size, location and type of site. (Thamesdown Borough Council, 1995d)

and that:

> The Local Plan provides for a range of sites in terms of size, location, quality and potential uses. The largest areas to be identified, some of which already have outline planning permission and others which are allocated in the Plan, are within the Northern Development Area and at South Marston Park. Both of these areas are close to the A419. In addition, these are supplemented by further sites which are within the Swindon employment area but lie outside the Thamesdown Borough boundary, such as Lydiard Fields. (Thamesdown Borough Council, 1995e)

The Borough argued that any additional allocations would extend the built area of the town well into open countryside and increase what it already considered to be the overprovision of employment land in the Local Plan. To provide for employment uses beyond 2001 would also, it argued, pre-empt the replacement Structure Plan covering the period up to 2011 and the next Local Plan which would identify specific sites in relation to the new Structure Plan. Against the Chamber of Commerce, for example, it argued that:

> ... although the Chamber has not specified any particular location. The sites that have been suggested are so large as to be considerably in excess of the perceived shortfall which would take the Local Plan out of conformity with the Structure Plan. The safeguarding of these as for the period beyond 2001 would pre-empt and restrict choices to be made in the light of the Replacement Structure Plan to 2011, which will

be a matter for the following Local Plan.
(Thamesdown Borough Council, 1995a)

Similar arguments were put in relation to the other objections.
The Borough further argued that there was no reason why existing
sites could not be used for campus-style development, and that the
northern development, South Marston and Lydiard Fields offered
scope for 'prestige' development. It also argued in relation,
specifically, to land for motor industry developments, that existing
provision was adequate and that demand for such sites, linked to
the Honda development, had not been as great as anticipated.
Overall, the Borough maintained that:

> ... to increase the provisions of the Local Plan, as
> suggested by a number of objectors, will take the
> employment land provisions far in excess of, and
> out of conformity with, the Structure Plan quan-
> tum, leading to additional traffic congestion and
> pressure for additional residential development.
> Furthermore it would limit choices that are to be
> made regarding further employment allocations at
> Swindon in the next Local Plan. (Thamesdown
> Borough Council, 1995a)

It therefore urged the Inquiry not to make any changes in response
to these various objections. It was a view, interestingly, that
Berkshire County Council (adjoining Wiltshire down the M4
Corridor to the east) shared. Berkshire submitting a formal
objection to the Inquiry, argued that excess allocation of
employment land in Swindon would encourage increased
commuting from Berkshire and pressure, therefore, for an
increasing allocation of land for housing within the County.

Having been out of phase with the existing Structure Plan, the
Borough also at this point in time (October 1995) signalled its
intention of commencing preparation of the new Local Plan as
soon as the Inquiry for the present Local Plan was over, that is, in
parallel with the replacement structure plan process. In order to
put its case effectively at the consultation phase of the new
Structure Plan regarding the amount of additional development
that the Borough would be able to accommodate, it would not be
waiting for the replacement Structure Plan to be approved before
it started to prepare the next Local Plan (Thamesdown Borough
Council, 1995a, p 6). Many of the same issues – and may of the

same sites – would resurface in the course of the structure plan process, the early stages of which are described below.

Planning for the next millennium

At the time of the Local Plan Inquiry, the Borough Council and the County Council were roughly in agreement in relation to plans for economic growth and the allocation of land for employment processes. As the debate rolled forward with preparation of the new Wiltshire Structure Plan, however, significant differences started to emerge. Particularly in relation to housing but also in terms of employment land, the Borough found itself at odds with the County, opposing the extent to which Wiltshire was seeking to concentrate development in the Swindon urban area. Interestingly, as well, the County was itself now using arguments regarding the environment and sustainability to support its own case against the Borough, grounds on which the Borough had earlier based its own case for *limiting* growth and town expansion. By this phase of the debate, then, there had been a complete reversal of the historical situation in much of the postwar period, which had seen the Borough pushing for expansion and fighting for planning permissions on appeal against the attempts of the County to contain Swindon's growth.

The draft Wiltshire County Structure Plan, published in revised form in August 1996, following public consultation, set out a strategy for the County as a whole up to the year 2011, replacing the three existing separate structure plans. In common with structure plans in general, its purpose was two-fold: first, to provide a framework for local plans and development control decisions; second, to ensure consistency with national and regional policy. The situation was complicated by the fact that from April 1997, with Swindon gaining unitary status, the strategic planning framework was the joint responsibility of the two authorities. In theory, the County and the newly autonomous Borough Council would agree jointly on the new Structure Plan. The new Swindon Borough Council was also required to prepare a new district-wide Local Plan consistent with the Structure Plan.

The new Structure Plan aimed to reflect the regional and national planning context, which had itself changed. As the draft Plan itself noted, this has increasingly reflected European perspectives particularly in relation to environmental issues. The requirement to contribute to sustainable development was especially relevant, and had been a key feature in the government's Planning Policy Guidance Notes, not least PPG13 on Transport. At the regional level, and reflecting the input of the South West Regional Planning Conference, Regional Planning Guidance for the South West, RPG10, stated the need for development plans to secure a sustainable level of growth and distribution of development. Thus, as the Structure Plan saw it, "while seeking to safeguard and enhance the distinctiveness and diversity of the South West's environment, the plans should encourage and maintain a healthy economy" (Wiltshire County Council, 1996, 1.14). As described in Chapter Six, RPG10 set out figures for overall growth in new dwellings over the Structure Plan period, 1991-2011. These were to be tested via the structure plan process, with the location of household growth and new housebuilding the key issue for the Plan.

While the overall context was set in terms of household growth and hence dwelling requirements, closely bound up with this was the link with growth in the workforce, economic growth and hence issues of employment land. By way of context, the Structure Plan noted that:

> Parts of the South East Region, including the M4 Corridor have been subject to development pressures in recent years. Increasingly during the 1970s and 1980s these pressures have expanded into adjoining areas. Consequently Wiltshire is one of the ten fastest growing counties in the country. (Wiltshire County Council, 1996, 2.2)

Swindon, it noted, was the largest and fastest growing urban area in the County in the 1980s, while outside of Swindon the county is generally rural in character with an outstanding landscape:

> Swindon, which has a strategic location on the M4 and the Inter-City rail corridor between London and Bristol, has been well placed to accommodate much of this pressure in Wiltshire. Development has secured a wider and sounder base for the town's economy and its position as a regional centre has been confirmed. The Northern Development Area, the last of the major areas accepted for town expansion, will accommodate some 10,000 houses and is likely to be completed

before 2011. (Wiltshire County Council, 1996, 2.5)

It was also noted that Regional Planning Guidance had earlier suggested some slowing down in Swindon's rate of growth:

> Swindon will no longer be expected to grow at the rate which characterised previous years, although its location in relation to the rail and motorway networks means that it will continue to be a major regional centre for the South West. Plans should encourage greater use of public transport in order to counter effects of increasing traffic congestion, and should protect the surrounding rural area. Land to the south west and north of the town is designated as a rural buffer zone in the Structure Plan and this should continue to be protected from inappropriate development. (DoE, 1994)

The concentration of employment growth in Thamesdown was recognised as a key feature of the 1980s. In the districts of North and West Wiltshire between 1981 and 1991 jobs increased by around 10,000, whereas resident workers increased by some 16,000, considerably more than job growth. In the case of Thamesdown, employment went up by over 24,000, compared with an increase of only 18,000 in locally resident workers. This reflected to a major extent the fact that the net balance of in-commuting into Thamesdown more than doubled over this period.

The structure plan process identified a set of objectives covering a wide range of issues, with environmental concerns and sustainability a common theme, It then set out to evaluate a range of development options in terms of how well they were likely to perform against these objectives. Initial work narrowed the field to five main options:

A. Major development at Swindon
B. Major development in the Western M4 Corridor
C. Continued development of towns
D. Major development in West Wiltshire
E. Dispersed development including villages

Appraisal indicated that options A and C, which included a high
concentration of development in the urban areas, performed best,
suggesting development should be concentrated in the towns,
broadly according to size, with a particular focus on Swindon.
Under Option A, a variation was considered with a new or much
expanded settlement close to the town.   Data from the 1991
Census showed that Swindon had the highest proportion of people
living and working in its urban area (around 90%): "This indicated
a relatively sustainable pattern of land use and transport, because
most journeys would be relatively short.   Also, the current and
possible future scope for changing from use of the car to making
journeys by foot, bicycle or public transport was highest."
(Wiltshire County Council, 1996, 3.11)   The County's detailed
transport appraisal was strongly in favour of urban development at
Swindon itself and costs of water supply and sewage similarly
favoured concentration.   Combined with forecasts of potential
additional employment, this was taken to support the case that
"new development should be predominantly urban and largely at
Swindon itself" (Wiltshire County Council, 1996, 3.13):

> ... development should be concentrated at
> Swindon, where the economic momentum needed
> to attract new jobs is largely to be found.   The
> alternatives involving development of new settle-
> ments close to urban areas would not perform so
> well against some of the Objectives.... (Wiltshire
> County Council, 1996, 3.18)

Although some modifications were made, Option A, Major
development at Swindon, was therefore the starting point for the
new County strategy.

The link between estimates of new housebuilding and jobs was
a key element of the strategy.   The County Council's testing of the
level of new dwellings proposed for Wiltshire by the region
indicated that:

> ... the 69,000 dwellings proposed for Wiltshire in
> Regional Planning Guidance could be supported
> by growth in the economy and jobs, but only if
> the forecast economic growth potential of
> Swindon was realised.   County Council forecasts
> of job growth show that the greatest potential for
> employment growth lay at Swindon, which is

> expected to be the location of 70 per cent of
> forecast new jobs.... The need for further major
> development in this area was supported by the
> appraisal of strategy options. (Wiltshire County
> Council, 1996, 3.20)

The strategy which emerged revised the estimate for new dwellings
down slightly to 65,000, reflecting in part the fall-off in the level
of housebuilding which had actually been achieved in Swindon in
the early 1990s (see Chapter Six). The overall policy to locate
major development on Swindon, however, remained. This was
justified partly on environmental grounds: "progress towards
sustainable development is more likely to be secured by urban
concentration than by dispersed development, with Swindon
continuing to play a major role" (Wiltshire County Council, 1996,
3.31). The possibility of attracting significant employment growth
to smaller centres within the County, in contrast with the evident
potential of Swindon, was also thought to be limited. This, in
turn, was seen as limiting the possibilities for relatively self-
contained growth in smaller centres and to be, therefore, less
desirable on sustainability grounds.

Future employment needs

The County strategy proposed that 260 hectares of employment
land was required in Thamesdown, 1991-2011, some 15 hectares
more than the estimated area of sites built on or already
committed for development. It also noted that allocation of land
is seldom sufficient to achieve development. In arriving at this
proposal, the County used a similar methodology to that described
earlier (pp 162ff), relating workforce growth generated by
demographic factors to the likely growth in jobs. It was forecast
that the County's workforce would grow by over 38,000 between
1991 and 2001, almost half of this in Swindon. The County's
analysis, however, made the point that its strong economic
performance had encouraged significant inwards migration – the
County's workforce as a whole had expanded by around 30% in
the period 1971 to 1991, compared with less than 7% nationally.

Forecasts of job growth were also carried out. These took
account of the continuing impact of inwards investment and
nationally based forecasts of job growth for each industrial sector.
While acknowledging the problems of predicting economic

fortunes at county level, Wiltshire's analysis assumed there was little doubt that it would continue to perform relatively well compared to national trends. Swindon, together with Reading, Milton Keynes, Northampton, Peterborough and Cambridge, had attracted inwards investment and been a major focus for growth within the broad band of prosperous counties stretching north and west of London, from Wiltshire to Suffolk. The analysis noted that:

> ... these favoured locations, including Swindon, will continue to attract inward-investment. Local conditions will need to remain attractive to employers, who will expect employment land to be available and the labour market to be favourable. For Swindon, the prospect of a direct link to Heathrow from the west, relative ease of access to London and links to the Continental rail network may enhance its attraction. (Wiltshire County Council, 1996, 2.49)

The remainder of the County, it was noted, was unlikely to attract inwards investment on anything like the same scale. Overall forecasts of job growth saw an increase in jobs of around 42,500 for the County as a whole, with about 30,000 in Thamesdown. This suggested job growth in Swindon well ahead of growth in the workforce. Around 75% of this increase, it was estimated, would result from inward investment. Part of this gap between the resident workforce and the increase in employment locally, was likely to be filled by increased inwards commuting to the Borough – net in-commuting had increased from around 4,300 in 1981 to some 10,200 by 1991. Estimates of job growth were then translated into employment land requirements. For Swindon, this produced the figure of 260 hectares over the period 1991-2011. This was somewhat higher than the volume of land already developed over this period, plus additional sites identified for development in planning terms.

Proposals for employment land thus took account of the level of housebuilding and hence growth in the workforce proposed by the Structure Plan. Other factors taken into consideration, however, meant that there was "an increase in land provision to a level significantly higher than that required by the local workforce." (Wiltshire County Council, 1996, 4.24). Here the County's strategy parted company with the Borough perspective. The County was clearly intending to accommodate employment growth generated by inwards investment: "the expected level of economic growth includes an allowance for a continuing substantial rate of inward investment." (Wiltshire County Council, 1996). Job growth at this level was also likely to result in increased inwards commuting to Swindon. This strategy was also likely to generate in-migration and to generate the pressures for additional housebuilding, which the Borough was keen to resist. In the case of Swindon at least, the County's proposals for employment land were demand-led, that is, related to job growth rather than to estimated growth in the existing supply of labour. Projected growth in jobs exceeded the highest workforce-based estimate by around 10%. Thus: "In Thamesdown, the figure is determined by the projected increase in jobs" (Wiltshire County Council, 1996, 4.32). Elsewhere in the County, estimates of land volumes needed for employment based on the size of the likely future workforce were little different from those based on projected future employment.

Workforce-based estimates of employment land needed in Swindon for the period 1991-2011 came out at only 155 hectares. This was well short of the highest estimate of need based on estimated job growth, of some 290 hectares. The final proposal actually came out at 260 hectares – allowing for the contribution of Lydiard Fields to Swindon's needs. In fact, 245 hectares was already claimed to be accounted for by completed developments and land already committed for development for employment purposes. In practice, this was the terrain over which the battles over 'real availability' and pressures for additional land to be allocated for development would be fought at the Public Inquiry. The shortfall of 15 hectares itself, moreover, led the County to conclude that the employment proposals, like those for housing "will necessitate the identification of strategically significant new development areas, over and above commitments." (Wiltshire County Council, 1996, 4.46) – an open invitation, it would seem, for pressure to be brought for further sites to be identified for employment purposes. This was likely to generate robust opposition from the Borough. As one Borough planning officer commented in late 1996: *"the line we are taking now is that ... the development of Thamesdown or Swindon ought to slow down dramatically and, you know, you can't see a time when you are going to need to make any massive additions to the employment capacity at present."*

Conclusions

The mid-1990s, then, saw the debate over economic growth and physical expansion shift into the arena of the statutory planning framework.   Both the local plan process, in theory, at least, fleshing out the earlier North East Wiltshire Structure Plan, and the replacement Wiltshire Structure Plan, provided a framework for debate.   In practice, both were part of an evolving process through which the Borough Council, the County Council and other   interests   including   representatives   of   local   business, developers and landowners all sought to establish their positions.

It was a process which saw the Borough Council increasingly hardening its opposition to growth and physical expansion, particularly in relation to housing, but also in terms of employment land.   Excessive allocation of employment land could potentially generate inwards investment and employment growth at a scale which would generate increased inwards migration and even greater pressure for increased housebuilding.   The contrast with earlier phases of Swindon's development is very clear.   The immediate   postwar   years   and   the   battle   over   Industrial Development Certificates (IDCs), town development, the New City proposals and the western expansion in the late 1960s and the 1970s, had all in turn seen the Borough Council pushing for expansion against the constraints and frequently downright opposition of the County Council and central government.

Environmental issues and arguments around sustainability became increasingly central to the debate, driven by the international and national policy agenda and translated down to regional and sub-regional level in a formal sense, as noted earlier, via Planning Policy Guidance Notes.   In the 1980s and early 1990s there was clearly concern with preservation and conservation in relation to the countryside, 'areas of outstanding natural beauty' and the 'rural buffer'.   The sustainability debate, which gained momentum in the early 1990s, however, provided a new language and a new discourse for debate.   It was a discourse, in the sense of a structure through which power might be mobilised, which different interests attempted to appropriate.   As we have seen, the

Borough, by the time it came to the Local Plan Public Inquiry, was making explicit reference to environmental objectives and sustainability, as contained in Planning Policy Guidance Notes, in support of its case to limit economic growth. The County, on the other hand, when it came to the replacement Structure Plan, appropriated the sustainability argument to support its case for concentrating major growth on Swindon.

By the time of the deposit draft of the replacement Structure Plan, Thamesdown was arguing, essentially, for a policy of containment, based on existing commitments of housing and employment land. In terms of employment land, however, the County strategy aimed to accommodate a significant volume of inwards investment, basing its estimates of land needed for employment purposes in Swindon on forecast job growth and employment demand, rather than workforce estimates based on the employment needs of the local population. Forecast job growth was itself based on some fairly heroic assumptions in terms of the proportion of job growth that would generate demand for new employment sites compared with that which would be accommodated on existing sites or other land not identified for strategic employment purposes, such as town centre office sites. It was also based on assumptions regarding rates of job growth in different industrial sectors, notoriously difficult to forecast at the sub-regional or local level. Forecasts were based on national forecasts. Swindon's history, on the other hand, has been characterised in this sense by the extent to which it has *not* tracked national patterns of growth and decline. The contrasting implications of supply-led versus demand-led approaches to strategic planning are particularly evident in the context of an area such as Swindon, subject to considerable external pressure for growth and development.

In terms of the planning system, development in the wake of the 1990 Town and Country Planning Act was supposed to be 'plan-led', that is, in accordance with development plans. As we have seen, however, the formal planning system increasingly represented, in effect, a forum through which the competing aims of the Borough, the County and other interests could be contested. The conflict of perspective between the Borough and County Councils, particularly around the revised Structure Plan, was likely, as suggested earlier, to invite pressure for additional development land to be allocated. The Structure Plan itself saw the need to identify further strategic sites to meet its estimate of overall need in relation to job growth and inwards investment. The commitment to accommodating inwards investment was, in itself, a challenge to the Borough Council's position, which essentially remained that of consolidation and meeting local needs. Again, in the context of pressures for growth and the potential at least for further expansion, the shift in the nature of the planning system is very evident.

It is important to remember, by way of context, that the Borough's policy of 'consolidation', although initiated in the 1980s, was confirmed in the 1990s against a background of deepening recession and a slump in development pressures. Economic forecasts were increasingly optimistic from the mid-1990s. Unemployment fell, but pressures in terms of economic growth, the housing market and development pressures even in the M4 Corridor were slow to build up. There had, therefore, been little in the way of immediate and material challenge to the Borough strategy. Moreover, the Council had maintained its policy of catering for the needs of existing employers throughout this period, policy which remained central to its future approach. Motorola's development in the northern sector on land sold for this purpose by the Borough Council was the most outstanding example of this. Economic recovery and increasing pressures for economic growth and inwards investment in the late 1990s would, however, put the policy of consolidation under increasing strain. The links between economic development, demographic change and household growth are also very evident. Having focused here on issues around employment and economic development, Chapter Six, therefore, goes on to look more closely at issues around housing and the housing market.

six

Planning and development: housing and urban growth

This chapter focuses on planning and development issues relating to housing development and urban growth in the postwar period. It also provides a brief account focused more specifically on housing provision and the housing market. The overall context for housing development and housing growth at the local level has, to a significant extent, been provided by the planning and housing policy framework at the national level. The account presented here is therefore very much one of the interaction between policy and action at the local level, and the changing planning framework as a whole. In this, the management of pressures for growth and development on the fringes of the South East region and around London as both national capital and global city, has been a key feature. Government forecasts in 1996 were predicting household growth of 4.4 million nationally in the period 1991-2016 (DoE, 1996). Growth pressures will clearly intensify as we move into the next millennium. Swindon's recent history is clearly very relevant to any discussion as to how such pressures are to be managed. With Swindon now, however, intent on consolidation and resistant to further planned expansion on any major scale, the potential for conflict between policy at the local scale, and planning frameworks and policy at regional and national levels is clearly considerable. Issues raised in looking at the case of Swindon, therefore, go to the very heart of the national debate around managing future growth and the challenge this poses for the planning system and planning policy at regional and national levels.

The strategic framework: laying the basis for growth (1953-74)

As outlined in Chapter Two, planned postwar growth in Swindon was prefigured by wartime production and relocation, with the case for economic expansion and diversification in the town outlined in the published document *Planning for Swindon* (Swindon Borough Council, 1945b), and implemented via the Borough's enthusiastic response to the 1952 Town Development Act. The initial eastern expansion was largely carried out by the Borough Council on land acquired through a mix of compulsory purchase and negotiation, and given planning permission by the minister in the face of resistance from a range of interests opposed to urban expansion into rural areas. Opposition included that of Wiltshire County Council, then the planning authority for Swindon. By the early 1960s, this phase of development was drawing to a close and the Borough Council commissioned a report (Vincent and Gorbing, 1963) to advise on where further growth should take place, with the aim that population in the town should grow to about 230,000. This essentially local initiative was, however, overtaken by developments at national level in terms of regional and strategic planning, which laid the basis for Swindon's expansion in subsequent years.

The broader policy context for the second major wave of expansion, to the west of the Swindon, was effectively set by the publication in 1964 of the government's strategy document *The South East study* (Ministry of Housing and Local Government, 1964), discussed more fully in Chapter Two. Predicting that the population of the South East region would grow by 3.5 million between 1961 and 1981, this proposed a series of counter-magnets beyond the first generation of New Towns to accommodate forecast growth. In 1965 consultants Llewelyn-Davies, Weeks and Partners were commissioned to examine the options for growth in the area west of London and in the 1966 report, *A new city*, recommended significant growth at Swindon (Llewelyn-Davies et al, 1966) with a target population of 400,000 (see Table 6.1). This recommendation was made in the face of considerable opposition from Wiltshire County Council, concerned at the scale and pace of growth, and the likely resource implications for the County Council.

The report suggested that the GLC, Wiltshire County Council and Swindon Borough should consult with a view to carrying out

The Rail engineering works, 1946, immediately after the last war, dominating the town physically and still its economic raison d'être. Seen here looking east with the massive 'A Shop' in the foreground, Brunel's older buildings beyond in the junction of the Gloucester and Bristol lines, the three carriage shops and the railway village to the south of the junction.

Postwar manufacturing: the former British Leyland car body plant pictured in 1975, set up originally as Pressed Steel Fisher in the late 1950s. The plant now operates as part of the BMW-owned Rover Group.

© SBC, 1975 Taken by W. Bawden

Warehousing and distribution: WHSmith's national distribution centre first established in 1966, pictured here in 1980.

The Brunel shopping centre, echoing railway station architecture, with Brunel's statue and, in the background, the tower named after David Murray John, former town clerk and driving force behind Swindon's postwar expansion.

Western expansion: West Swindon seen here in 1986, looking south towards the M4 on the top margin of the photo. The Renault Building and Rivermead industrial development is in the foreground with residential development at Shaw, the last of the urban villages, beyond this. Toothill and Freshbrook, the first urban villages, are top left, beyond the Link building and West Swindon Centre.

Campus development: Burmah House, headquarters for Burmah Oil, set up locally in 1973, one of a number of purpose-built, campus-style developments by major employers. Intel and Nationwide Building Society occupy adjacent sites.

The Link Centre, a major sports and recreation facility financed and developed by Thamesdown Borough Council as part of West Swindon Centre in the western expansion.

Windmill Hill business park, a private sector development by St Martin's Property Corporation adjacent to Junction 16 of the M4. Occupiers include National Power's administrative headquarters, and airline reservation system operator, Galileo, in custom-designed premises.

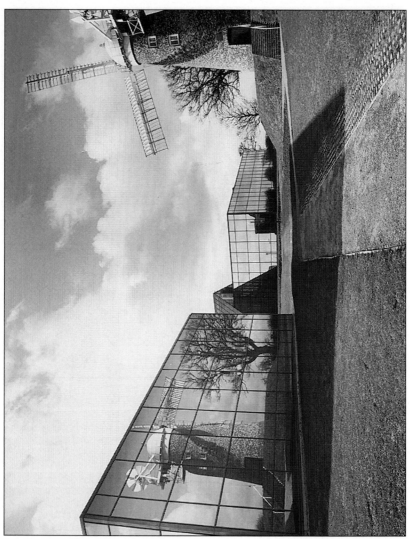

the development under the 1952 Town Development Act. The resulting report, *Swindon: a study for further expansion* (Swindon Borough Council et al, 1968), the *Silver Book*, was to be the key document in terms of the town's subsequent development, effectively up to the end of the century. The *Silver Book* envisaged population growth to 240,000 by 1986, approaching 300,000 by 2001. It also indicated the broad area within which development should occur (Figure 6.1). This consisted mainly of the area to the west and north of the town – in parts of which the western expansion later occurred, and where the new northern development is now underway. In addition it included two smaller areas to the east, including South Marston, and the South Dorcan area. Altogether some 13,000 acres were identified as available for development, accommodating an additional 175,000 people. The *Silver Book* also established the principle that further expansion should take place in the form of urban villages, with integrated housing, social provision and services, and a mix of tenures to achieve 'social balance' (discussed further in Chapter Seven). Alongside housing growth, the existing central area would be redeveloped as a regional shopping and commercial centre.

Despite the fact that the report was a joint exercise with Wiltshire County and the GLC, the County continued to express objections. There was unease about the scale of the planned intake of Londoners (75,000) and concern that population growth would exceed the targets set, due to the additional spontaneous voluntary migration that the development was likely to stimulate, over and above the planned relocation of households under the town expansion scheme. Above all, the County expressed concern about the financial impact of expansion on the County rate. There was also disagreement about how the development should be implemented. Swindon wanted to carry out the development itself under the powers of the Town Development Act, but Wiltshire also wanted participation so that it could influence the pace of development and the allocation of its own resources.

Ministerial approval for the scheme came in 1970, but on a reduced scale – a planned population of 200,000 by 1986 – compared to the *Silver Book* proposals of 240,000 (see Table 6.1).

Figure 6.1: Policy proposals for town expansion as set out in *Swindon: a study for further expansion*

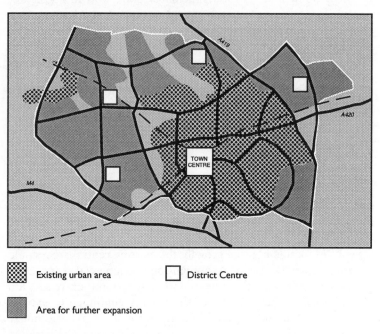

▨ Existing urban area   ☐ District Centre

▧ Area for further expansion

Source: Swindon Borough Council et al (1968)

Table 6.1: Population proposals for Swindon

1966	A new city	400,000 by 2001
1968	Silver Book	240,000 by 1986
1970	Revised Silver Book	200,000 by 1986
1978	Appeal decision (western expansion)	200,000 by 1986
1997	Estimated population	182,000
2004	Projected population	200,012

In the meantime the Borough went ahead with further development to the east at South Dorcan, applying the urban village design principles and exercising powers under the Town Development Act to acquire land and secure overspill agreements with the GLC. The Eldene and Liden Estates built in this area were the first explicitly mixed tenure developments in the town (see Figure 6.2). However, the strategic planning framework established by *The South East study* and subsequent reports provided the basis for Swindon's development over the next two decades with formal town development powers linked to overspill increasingly irrelevant.

Figure 6.2: The main housing estates, residential areas and retail centres in Swindon

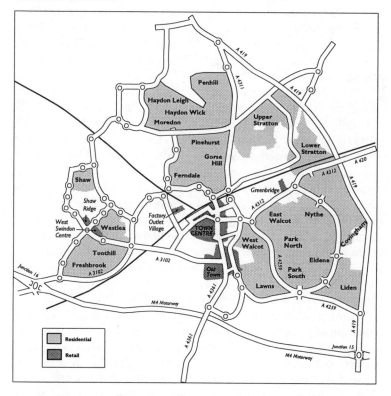

Western expansion (1971-80)

In January 1971 a joint team of officers from the County and Borough Councils, advised by Llewelyn-Davies et al, produced a follow-up to the *Silver Book* – the so-called '*Gold Book*' (Wiltshire County Council et al, 1971) – which set out strategies for Toothill, the first area to be developed in West Swindon (housing developments referred to in this chapter are identified in Figure

6.2).   This made it clear that the adopted strategy was employment-led, the starting point being estimated changes in (male) labour demand from existing and relocating firms. It was anticipated that this initial development would accommodate a population increase of almost 7,000 people by 1975. Compared to earlier developments the proposed tenure mix placed more emphasis on private housing. Around half the new houses would be built by private developers for owner-occupation with the remainder either built-for-sale by the local authority or local authority housing for rent. Plans were unveiled in 1975 for a further three urban villages (Freshbrook, Westlea and Shaw), with a planned completion rate of 1,500 houses each year over a 10-year period.

The Borough Council moved ahead with land acquisition to make the development possible. In 1972, 580 acres of land at Toothill were bought from the County, and by 1975 Harloe (1987b) reported that the Borough had assembled 1,000 acres of land in the western expansion and a further 250 acres at Groundwell Farm for employment. As the planned western expansion proceeded, however, it took in areas where much of the land was already in the hands of private sector developers. They included, in particular, Bradley, the main local housebuilding company, which, recognising the likelihood of further development in the west, bought up extensive tracts of land between 1964 and 1975. This was largely 'white land', undeveloped, agricultural land which had not yet been identified in planning terms for development and which could be acquired for well below its value as housing land or for other purposes. The Borough Council consequently had to consider partnership development, relinquishing some of the control it had previously exercised in earlier rounds of expansion. The master plan for Westlea was carried out jointly by the Borough Council and Bradley Planning Services. Harloe (1987b), in fact, suggests that by the end of the 1970s Bradley were effectively coordinating the development, selling on land to other housebuilders, and funding infrastructure from the proceeds of land sales – the role previously played by the Borough Council. In Shaw, the fourth area in West Swindon to be developed, much of the land was owned by Wimpey, who again undertook partnership development with the Borough.

One consequence of this increasing private sector influence was a shift in the balance of tenures as the western expansion proceeded. While Toothill, the first area to be developed, contained around 35% council housing for rent, subsequent phases consisted primarily of owner-occupied housing. As the Borough Council's land ownership powers, and hence control of the development process diminished, there was also growing concern over the phasing of social and community facilities to support the new housing in the western expansion. Private sector developers were reluctant to provide such facilities 'up-front' and there was concern that provision would therefore lag behind housing provision and the build up of new households.

Progress in the western expansion was also to prove slower than initially planned, with development extending well into the 1990s. The slow take-off partly reflected the falling birth rate and slower population growth in the early 1970s. It also, however, reflected planning difficulties arising from the continuing opposition of the County Council to growth and expansion on the scale envisaged. County planners recommended refusal of the first planning application for Toothill made in 1971 on the grounds that the development was 'premature'. The DoE put significant pressure on the County to overturn this decision in a wider context where house prices were escalating and there was growing pressure on local authorities to release more land for housing, specifically urging Wiltshire to release enough land for 7,500 houses to be built by 1976. Construction at Toothill was significantly delayed, commencing in 1974 and only reaching 1,200 houses by mid-1979.

Towards the end of 1974 a series of major planning applications were made for later phases of the western expansion on sites to the west and north of Toothill, submitted jointly by the Borough Council and Bradley. By late 1976, however, the County had failed to 'determine' or make a decision on these applications, leading to appeals by the applicants. The County, clearly worried about the impact of the recession, public expenditure cuts and the declining commitment of the GLC to overspill, wanted to complete a planning review as a precursor to the production of a structure plan for the area. It put forward the view that growth targets for Swindon should be scaled down to around 150,000 by 1991, that town expansion be abandoned and plans made to accommodate natural growth only. The Borough were requested to withdraw their appeal, but refused, contesting the pessimism of the County over growth forecasts for the town.

The inquiry into the four linked planning applications made by the Borough Council and Bradley opened in May 1977. The Borough's case was supported by a consortium of builders – Bradley, Costain, Wimpey and Barrett – all of whom wanted to develop in the western expansion. This was the first major development in Swindon for each of the three national housebuilders. The County, backed by North Wiltshire and the Parish Councils in the area of the western expansion, argued that the development was premature, pre-empting the conclusions of the planning review, due later in the year. In January 1978, however, the DoE granted all four planning appeals brought by the Borough and the housebuilders. The DoE, in the Inquiry report, was strongly critical of the County, asserting that decisions could not be put off until the Structure Plan was approved, as this was still some years off. While the "changed circumstances and policies of recent years" were noted there was "no evidence of any kind to indicate that Swindon's growth should be slowed down, let alone stopped". Fears over the resource implications of further expansion were exaggerated, as developers would now be expected to meet most of the additional costs. The Inspector accepted Swindon's estimates of the need for a housebuilding programme of about 1,500 houses a year up to 1981, confirming the revised *Silver Book* estimates of future growth (Table 6.1, above) and stated that a 7- to 10-year supply of land was necessary to avoid a slowing down of growth. In referring to the objections from residents of the rural areas the Inspector considered their numbers small compared to the numbers who needed homes and jobs in the western expansion. Housing completions continued at a rate of 1,100 to 1,800 over the whole of the 10 years 1979-88 with West Swindon contributing a major share, particularly in the first part of this period (Figure 6.3).

Over and above the opposition of the County and surrounding rural areas, there had, up until this point, been little sign of concern within the town over Swindon's continued growth. By the late 1970s, however, signs of anxiety started to emerge. A working party of community organisations were arguing that the balance of tenure in the new developments should be shifted in favour of more public housing and that standards of educational and social provision should be improved. There was also concern at the blighting effect of uncertainty regarding central area redevelopment on housing areas in the town centre, and more general concern with central area housing conditions. In 1978 the Community Planning Committee, in an early precursor to the *A new vision* debate, argued that profits from the western development should be used to improve community facilities elsewhere in the town. There were other complaints that the western expansion was receiving favourable treatment in the allocation of resources. On the other hand, as development in the western expansion got underway, there was growing unease about the failure to provide social and community facilities locally at the same rate that housing was developed and there was press coverage of social problems on the new estates. Blame for the lack of infrastructure was variously attributed to Bradley as the developer, the Borough Council and the County Council. The chair of the Planning Committee, responding to resident complaints, reflected on the changing role of the local authority in relation to the form of development, stating *"when you don't own the land you do not have the control"*.

Figure 6.3: Housing completions, Thamesdown and West Swindon (1979-96)

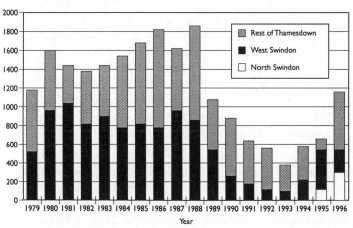

By this point, also, the financial position of local authorities in general was deteriorating with the first rounds of public expenditure cuts (see Chapter Two). In Swindon's case the problems were exacerbated because the western expansion was actually outside the Borough boundary, which had the effect of reducing the amount it got in terms of its Rate Support Grant from central government. On reorganisation in 1974, when the new Thamesdown Borough came into existence, it included the old Swindon Borough and Highworth Rural District (see Figure 2.1, Chapter Two). Areas to the west, including the proposed western expansion, were, however, excluded at this stage. The Boundary Commission agreed to review the western boundary of Thamesdown when planning permission for the expansion was secured. But this did not happen until 1981, when boundary extensions to include the four urban villages were agreed.

Despite these difficulties, western expansion is generally perceived to have represented a successful phase of town development, with the urban village concept providing a design and planning framework that avoided the monotony of many similar large-scale residential developments taking place in the late 1970s and early 1980s. Moreover, the sales of Borough Council-owned land provided the basis for expansion of recreation and leisure opportunities in the town, broadly sustaining the growth consensus. As a senior officer of the Borough Council put it:

> *"Over a period of twenty odd years we were very successful ... the profit we made from that [the western expansion] we were able to plough back into the community and provide the facilities. Places like the Oasis Leisure Centre, the Wyvern Theatre, the Broome Manor Golf Course and many of the country parks, and so on – all funded by the land transactions we were involved in. So we were getting jobs, we were getting leisure facilities, it was all paying for itself.... Success breeds consensus."*

As discussed in Chapter Two, it is evident that decisions made at national level in terms of road and rail infrastructure were crucial in terms of Swindon's development during the 1970s. Also crucial, as this account makes clear, was the direct intervention of central government in the planning arena, reinforcing the position of the Borough Council and over-riding objections from the County. The granting of planning permission on appeal for all of the development in the western expansion was the prime example. The continuing support of government for growth at Swindon was to prove significant in subsequent controversies over the strategic planning framework for Wiltshire County, to which we now turn.

The Wiltshire Structure Plan

In early 1980 the draft North East Wiltshire Structure Plan was published, Wiltshire having chosen a strategy of preparing three separate structure plans for the whole County. This put the case that after the first three urban villages were completed in the western expansion, no more should be built. 750 acres of land were to be allocated over 10 years for industry, some 300 acres below the assessments of the Borough Council. The Borough Council expressed their disagreement with the strategy, threatening to apply for planning permission and to appeal when this was refused by the County. Soon after this the Borough and Wimpey applied for permission to develop Shaw, the fourth 'urban village' in the western expansion. Explicit moves were also being made at this time to open up the northern sector for development. Bradley, on behalf of a national housebuilding consortium, were proposing a massive 1,000-acre development for housing and industry on land north of Haydon Wick, and put in a planning application in advance of the Structure Plan Examination in Public (EIP).

The Structure Plan EIP began in September 1980, although the Secretary of State had already exercised his powers to 'call in' the Bradley application and that from the Borough Council and Wimpey, so that decisions might be made centrally by the DoE. The now familiar arguments were played out, with the Borough Council accusing the County of being too pessimistic in its forward projections of growth and of land allocations. Thamesdown specifically wanted housing land allocations increased to meet the needs of key workers, over and above forecasts of local demand and in-migration. In the end, the Structure Plan modifications, confirmed by the Secretary of State in November 1981, supported the case for continued growth in line with the Borough's views. Provision was to be made for 20,500 houses, 6,000 more than proposed by the County. Industrial land and office provision was increased. Various road proposals to open up access to the western expansion were added. The policy of 'incremental development of land contiguous to that which is already developed' was to be continued, and attempts to argue for further land release to the north were rejected.

The Secretary of State specifically noted that: "the Structure Plan should correctly interpret national policies including those of promoting national economic recovery, improving industrial performance and increasing productive potential". This reflected the views of the Department of Industry at the EIP, together with those of two local MPs at the time (one Conservative and one Labour). Throughout the statement the implication was that Swindon was seen as a growth area of national significance whose ability to expand should not be hindered. At the same time the Borough Council/Wimpey application for development of the fourth (Shaw) urban village was granted. The Bradley application for the proposed northern expansion area, however, was at this point rejected. Bradley continued to pursue this via a high court challenge to the Structure Plan, but were not to be successful at this time. Development pressures, meanwhile, had intensified, with high rates of employment growth and inwards investment driving the increasingly market-led growth of the M4 Corridor. Crest Homes, later to become a key player in the northern sector development, carried out an M4 Corridor study, which identified Swindon as a likely area in which they could expand their operations beyond their traditional home counties base.

Development in the western expansion area continued, reaching more than 1,000 completions in a single year in 1981 (Figure 6.3). Outline plans were agreed for the fourth, Shaw, urban village; the largest part of the residential land here was owned by Wimpey. Speculation was also continuing around the potential northern expansion. However, further signs of anxiety about more development emerged from residents of areas west of Swindon. In neighbouring North Wiltshire there were calls for a green belt on the western boundary of Swindon to restrict development. Within the Borough boundary residents, forming the Northern Action Group opposed to further development, were calling for further consultation before any more permissions were given. The western development was effectively going ahead on a pragmatic basis under the provisions of the modified Structure Plan and an agreed programme of master plans, with Thamesdown arguing that preparation of a more formal local plan would be a waste of resources.

A new vision

As discussed earlier (Chapters Two and Five), the Borough Council's consultation document *A new vision for Thamesdown* (Thamesdown Borough Council, 1984) represented the first official sign of a shift in the policy stance of the authority, with significant implications for housing development and urban growth. The need for a reappraisal was motivated by the general context of recession and public expenditure restrictions. There was agreement that continuing growth was required to meet the natural increase in the population arising from earlier development, but this, it was argued, had to be balanced against the needs of existing communities and other parts of the town. There was a need for considerable urban renewal, for intervention to meet the shortcomings of private development and to enhance the quality of life throughout the Borough and to control the pace of development to avoid pressure on restricted public resources and facilities. The changing role of the local authority was reflected in the adoption of a strategy of "selective intervention in future development, leaving the rest to private enterprise to be controlled through the planning system" (Thamesdown Borough Council, 1984).

Likely scenarios for further development in the town were explored, acknowledging the now increased reliance on market forces. While demand for private sector housing in the town was likely to continue at a high level into the 1990s, there was much greater uncertainty on employment. Swindon, as elsewhere, was hit badly by recession in the early 1980s (see Chapter Three), and this seems to have dented confidence in the town about continued expansion. All-out policies for employment growth would, in any case, undoubtedly, when recovery came, attract further in-migrants to the town which was already attractive due to its relatively low house prices in a surrounding area of restraint. The dilemmas raised by this included the pressure on social and community infrastructure and growing hostility to further development on the urban fringes. In the next likely area for development, the northern sector, the Council owned little land so its influence was limited. As *A new Vision* noted, many of the factors that underpinned the previous rounds of expansion – a publicly stated set of long-term aims, strong local support, Council land ownership, low rate levels, financial support from central government and minimal competition for jobs from people living outside the area – were now changing. The benefits of growth for existing residents and companies were 'increasingly hard to grasp'.

The Council's room for manoeuvre was also increasingly restricted. Central government were taking a laissez-faire stance on development, the town was increasingly subject to housing demand pressures originating beyond its boundaries, there was increasing uncertainty about employment growth and the County, through the Structure Plan, were now attempting, in effect, to determine population levels. The chief executive, in a speech in 1984 (quoted in Harloe, 1987b) made some telling points:

> In the past the Council would have bought most of the land in the Haydon sector, obtained planning permission and controlled land release with the profits paying for infrastructure and any surplus invested in community facilities. But housing land was now at £90,000 per acre and industrial land at £130,000 per acre, so to buy all the land at Haydon would cost £130 million. (Harloe, 1987b)

The Council seems to have had two choices. It could resist planning applications for development in the north pending the rolling forward of the Structure Plan and leave the making of future policy in central government hands. Alternatively, it could agree a local plan in which the private developers would be expected to finance most of the infrastructure and maintain good environmental standards. This would, of course, have been a departure from the Structure Plan, and would have needed the compliance of the County to make the agreements stick. The beginnings of a shift in attitudes in adjoining areas also began to emerge. Kennett District Council expressed the fear that reduced growth at Swindon would increase the development pressures in neighbouring rural areas. In subsequent Structure Plan reviews, this reversal of attitudes to growth in Swindon became a strong feature.

Following consultation on *A new Vision* Thamesdown issued a strategy statement which incorporated the conclusions of the policy reappraisal and also defined the Council's stance with respect to the Structure Plan. Further development to the north was inevitable, but the rate of growth needed to be reduced. In the subsequent plan the area of growth was outlined, stretching from the A419 in the east to the western boundary of the district. It was expected to contain 10,000 houses, 30,000 people, a district centre and 150 acres of industrial land. Most of the land was already in the hands of private developers. Bradley, by then taken over by English China Clay and Crest, were the largest land-owners, with significant holdings by a number of other national housebuilders, together forming the Haydon Development Group.

Clearly throughout these early negotiations over the northern sector, Thamesdown were treading a fine line. On the one hand, development seemed inevitable, but there was a need to find a mechanism to slow the rate of growth and also to secure agreement from the developers for a substantial contribution towards infrastructure. On the other hand, if pressed too hard the developers would appeal to the Secretary of State, whose recent announcements had stressed the need for the planning system to respond to market forces. In 1985 the housing market in the south was booming. It was reported that housing shortage and rising prices were encouraging many from Berkshire to look for housing in the Swindon area (Harloe, 1987a). House prices in the town, while still low by South East standards, were by 1985, however, increasing at rates well above the national average. Housing land prices were also increasing rapidly. There must therefore have been considerable pressure for the developers to get on with the development, but also a perception locally that there were potentially rich pickings from such development at that time.

The northern development area (1986-96)

In October 1986, the Haydon Development Group submitted an application for 1,500 acres of land in the northern development sector. The consortium included Crest, now the major landowner with over 580 acres, and English China Clay, which had taken over Bradley, Prowting, McLeans, Costain and Wimpey. All had been buying up land in the northern sector in the period 1982-84, with the exception of Bradley, whose land holdings went back to the 1960s. The scheme was put together by locally based planning consultants, Chapman Warren, whose principal partners worked for Bradley in the 1970s and were involved in earlier attempts to secure release of this land. The outline application was for around

10,000 dwellings, expected to house 24,000 people, 120 acres of employment land, a district centre, three local centres and a substantial amount of open space, to be developed over a 12-year period. Supporting the application Chapman Warren produced a comprehensive master plan (Figure 6.4). This detailed a scheme based on a series of urban villages, reproducing to some extent the development model used in the western expansion and taking forward the framework set out by the Council in their earlier outline plan for the area. At the same time, and as a counter to the Haydon Development Group application, the Borough Council submitted an application for employment, residential and retail uses on 150 acres which it owned at Groundwell Farm at the eastern end of the site (acquired back in the early 1970s). The intention here was to protect the Council's interests, and in particular, to influence the distribution of land uses on the whole site. The Haydon Group application also included this land.

Figure 6.4: Original master plan for northern expansion area

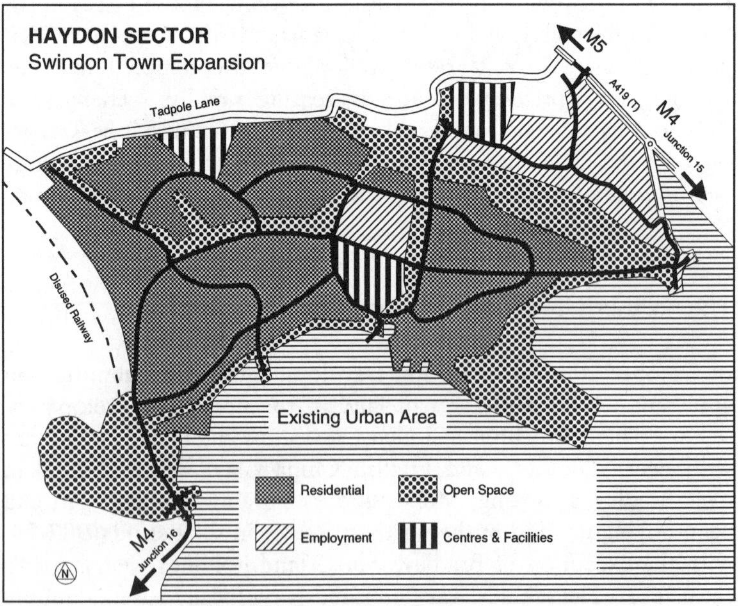

Source: Redrawn from Harloe and Boddy (1988); original by Chapman Warren, Planning Consultants

Both applications were clearly in contravention to the approved Structure Plan running to 1991 and both were called in by the Secretary of State as a departure from the approved planning framework. Draft alterations to take the Structure Plan up to 1996, published in 1986, provided for between 12,500 and 13,700 additional houses in Swindon from 1985 to 1989, including 3,500 in the northern development area, though indicating that this would be the first phase of a much larger development. The major problem with this from the point of view of the developers was the lack of any long-term commitment to development beyond 1996. Thamesdown wanted to secure a comprehensive scheme for the whole site, reproducing what they saw as the best qualities of the western expansion. The infrastructure requirements were substantial, including completion of the northern orbital road linking the M4 to the A419, well ahead of much of the return. From the developers' point of view the financial implications of such a package required a firm commitment to the whole scheme. As Harloe and Boddy (1988) note, the particular model of private sector-led planning being promoted here raised difficult issues for the planning system:

> ... there is a clear conflict between the economics of speculative development and the Structure Plan process. The planning framework fails to provide the certainty which represents a key component of the operating environment for private speculative development. This is exacerbated by the scale of development and the attempt on the part of the consortium to demonstrate the ability of the private sector to plan and implement development on a comprehensive basis. (Harloe and Boddy, 1988)

From the local authorities' point of view, a formal commitment would have ruled out future flexibility should the economic or demographic basis of current plans have changed significantly. Both County and District were by this time in agreement that the scale and pace of growth should be reduced and were seeking a mechanism that guaranteed both a self-financing development and future flexibility. The speculative wave of development taking place across South East England at that time no doubt contributed to fears that development could easily run out of control. There was, however, acknowledgement by the local authorities that the northern sector development would now go ahead, completing the pattern of expansion envisaged back in the *Silver Book*. To a certain extent, the apparent resistance represented a bargaining position. But it also reflected caution with the District moving into unknown territory in terms of the way in which development would now be managed. As a senior planner with Thamesdown commented:

> "The Borough Council objected to the Northern Sector at the time, but I don't know that it was so much in principle as the way it was being done and the timing. Our only control was through our planning function ... that required a fairly radical shift on the part of the Council, because hitherto they tended to regard planning as perhaps little more than a formality because of the control conferred by [land] ownership".

Negotiations continued, but failed to resolve the infrastructure contributions, and an inquiry into the planning applications submitted by the consortium and by the Borough Council opened in November 1987. By this point the County had, in fact, reached agreement on an indexed contribution from the developers to highway costs (approaching £20m) together with land and contributions (£850,000) to the provision of educational and social facilities. Negotiations between Thamesdown and the developers were, however, only concluded after the inquiry had started. As a result of this agreement the Council withdrew its own planning application. The Inspector's report, following the inquiry, recommended that planning permission be granted subject to conditions and the conclusion of legal agreements. It was noted that the offers made by the developers for contributions to the costs of infrastructure were "quite exceptional". The Secretary of State agreed with the Inspector and in the decision letter in September 1988 gave the go-ahead in principle, allowing a period of six months for the conclusion of negotiations and the completion of legal agreements.

The Inspector's report recognised that the development raised difficult issues concerning the strategic planning framework for Swindon, and indeed wider regional planning issues. However, the existing Structure Plan continued to propose housing and employment growth on a substantial scale in the town, and the current proposals were consistent with the historic role of Swindon as a regional growth centre. The proposed development of a further 10,000 houses thus carried forward the principle of continued growth up to 1996 and beyond. As far as central government was concerned there was no reason to depart from the overall policy of strategic growth, which previous plans had provided for.

In the meantime the EIP into the first alteration to the North East Wiltshire Structure Plan had taken place, though the Secretary of State's modifications were not issued until April 1990. In marked contrast with previous years, Thamesdown and Wiltshire were at this point, at least, in broad agreement about the scale of growth planned. The Secretary of State on the other hand, recognising the strong demand for housing and the possibility of exploiting the economic growth potential of the M4 Corridor, considered that both housing and employment land provisions should be increased. In Swindon the housing target was increased from between 12,500 and 13,700 to 14,250, with Swindon taking the bulk of the proposed 1,800 increase. But it was recognised that delay in starting the northern sector development made the more optimistic assessments of the housebuilders unrealistic, and the target for housing construction here remained at 3,500 in the period to 1996. This, it was accepted, implied a reduction in the rate of development compared with recent years. The Secretary of State also held back from including a reference to the ultimate total of 10,000 houses in the northern sector.

The Structure Plan alterations had also proposed the intro-duction of a 'rural buffer' to the north, west and south of Swindon within which development would be strongly resisted. There were strong representations from environmental bodies and Parish Councils that the more formal and better understood, statutory green belt designation should be applied. The Secretary of State's report, however, considered that "until strategic decisions had been made on the longer term growth beyond 1996, permanent boundaries for a Green Belt, as required by government policy, could not be drawn up". The rural buffer policy, potentially more open to challenge, was thus retained, but with some extension to include land to the south east of Swindon. The Inspector was not persuaded that extension to the east was necessary.

The master plan for the northern sector development was subject to public consultation in late 1988 and agreed with the local authority by the beginning of 1989. Finalising the legal agreements was proving, however, far more complex. Failure to agree reflected in part the fast deteriorating housing market conditions. In 1988, when the Secretary of State gave approval in principle to the development, housing demand in the town was still buoyant: 1,800 houses were completed in Thamesdown in 1987/88 and housing land prices were up to £600,000 per acre. By 1990/91 completions had collapsed to 630 and land prices were down to no more than £280,000 per acre. This was significant because a number of the housebuilders had based their participation in the consortium on a strategy of disposing of part of their land holdings as a means of funding infrastructure contributions. The rapid fall in land values threatened this strategy. Furthermore, the original infrastructure offers were based on a target of 900 completions per year. By 1991 the consortium considered that 400-500 completions a year was the best it could expect, which was insufficient to produce the income necessary to support the original proposals. These problems were compounded in June 1991 by the withdrawal of English China Clay from housebuilding and from participation in the northern sector development. Their land holding was crucial to the implementation of the whole scheme as the major road through the development crossed this land.

With the collapse of the consortium there was a real possibility that the land holdings in the northern sector would fragment and that individual housebuilders would pursue piecemeal development. Chapman Warren were therefore asked by Crest to come up with a scheme that could rescue at least part of the development. In 1991 Crest approached Thamesdown with a scheme known as 'Haydon 2'. This included land in the east and west of the site, including the Borough Council's land holding, but not the English China Clay land in the middle of the site. Both the Borough and the County Councils were concerned that a more piecemeal approach to the northern sector development would threaten the level of infrastructure contributions previously agreed as part of the comprehensive scheme. Indeed, a commitment to comprehensive development of the scheme as a whole had always been fundamental to the developers' agreement that substantial contributions were required from them. The Council were now concerned that developers of early parts of the scheme could avoid contributing a share of the overall infrastructure costs that would be necessary to open up later stages of the development. At the same time, the legal status of planning agreements between developers and local councils, 'Section 106' agreements, was changed in the 1991 Planning and Compensation Act. Developers could now make unilateral undertakings, in the absence of agreement with planning authorities, and these would be taken into account at any appeal. In addition, the Act gave developers the right to appeal to the Secretary of State to overturn or modify such 'planning obligations', as this form of agreement was now known, after a period of five years. The position of landowners and developers in negotiations over planning was therefore enhanced and agreements potentially time-limited. From Thamesdown's point of view this added to their concerns that contributions agreed at the start of the development might be subsequently rescinded.

Later in 1991, the developers submitted two planning applications for land owned by Crest and Prowtings, and also for that owned by the Borough Council for Haydon 2 – a strategy allowed for within the planning system. These covered around 600 acres and 3,300 houses. Both of these applications were 'twin tracked'. This was a device that became common in the late 1980s, allowing one application to proceed on the basis of negotiation with the local authorities, while the other could be taken to appeal in the event of refusal, or more typically 'non-determination' or failure to make a decision. This happened and an inquiry into the appeal was set for July 1992. In the meantime English China Clay made their own planning application for the remainder of the northern sector area, known as 'Haydon 3'.

From the Borough's point of view, the status of their land holdings was crucial. Not only were they seeking the best value possible for this site, they were also aware that as the gateway to the whole development it carried certain negotiation value. Once access across the land was provided, however, the Borough's negotiating position would be weakened. For the developers there remained a strong incentive to reach agreement with the Borough as the results of the inquiry were not likely for some considerable time. While the total package of infrastructure contributions remained as agreed under the original 1987 comprehensive scheme, the problems now revolved around finding a mechanism that ensured they could be enforced in the context of a piecemeal scheme. The negotiations were complex and no agreement was reached by the start of the inquiry. The inquiry opened and was then adjourned in order for negotiations to continue.

In this somewhat heated atmosphere agreement was eventually reached. The essential elements of this were that the schedule of infrastructure contributions remained as before, with contributions being triggered by housing completions, but with mechanisms to ensure that each phase of development met its obligations. The complete schedule of contributions for the whole site was to be made part of the planning approval for Haydon 2; developers of Haydon 3 would be bound by this and would know the requirements in advance. To provide further guarantees that development could not proceed without the necessary contributions being made, the developers were required to convey ownership of 3-metre wide 'performance strips' of land to the Borough Council. The location of these was flexible in that they would move to the margins of development as it proceeded. Development would not, then, be allowed to proceed beyond these boundary strips unless the terms of the planning agreements were met. Therefore, the Council would maintain a strategic controlling interest in the area through its ownership of the performance strips even after its original land at Groundwell had been crossed by the main access road. While clearly unhappy about the imposition of this requirement, termed 'ransom strips' by Crest, the developers agreed, and planning permission was granted for Haydon 2. The inquiry closed. English China Clay at this point also withdrew the Haydon 3 application.

Development of the whole of the northern sector is being further controlled by a division into eight framework plans, which develop the proposals of the master plan and provide detailed guidance on lay-out, design, landscaping and infrastructure. Construction of the first phase of the northern orbital road was completed by early 1995 and by 1996 three framework plans had been agreed by the Council. Crest, operating in much the same way as Bradley had done earlier in relation to the later phases of western expansion, is disposing of land to other developers to fund the infrastructure.

By 1996 most of the major national housebuilders had an interest in part of the scheme. Construction had started in 1995 and by the end of 1996 nearly 400 houses had been completed (see Figure 6.3) and the developers were forecasting 450 completions each year thereafter. As noted in Chapter Five, in 1996 Thamesdown also concluded negotiations with Motorola for a major industrial development on the Groundwell Farm site.

The northern sector now provided the basis for housing development in Swindon well into the next century, although there was continuing uncertainty about the status of the English China Clay land holdings. These, as we have seen, were acquired originally by Bradley during the 1960s when land prices were much lower. The holding costs were therefore minimal, and there could be a strong incentive for English China Clay to hold back from developing or disposing of their interest until housing land prices recover significantly from the early 1990s recession. This illustrates the difficulty in a heavy reliance on the private sector to manage the implementation of major, phased town expansion and to balance housing provision against other elements of the equation, including social and community provision and employ-ment. The process as a whole also illustrates very clearly the complexity of bringing forward such large sites for development and reaching agreement with private sector developers about substantial infrastructure contributions, particularly in the context of a volatile property market. The scheme had taken four years from the initial agreement in principle to the granting of outline planning approval in July 1992; it was a further two years before any detailed planning consents were issued. It also provides a stark contrast to the way in which western expansion was managed. Here the Borough Council's land ownership provided the basis for arguably a more effective (and certainly more speedily resolved) partnership.

Structure Plan review and replacement: conflicts over growth

Looking beyond the northern sector, policy debate around the pattern and scale of any future development of the town shifted back into the formal planning arena, including review and replacement of the existing Structure Plan and preparation of the Swindon-wide Local Plan. On the basis of the existing planning policy framework, population estimates saw the town's population expanding beyond 200,000, the revised *Silver Book* proposal, by the year 2004, up to around 211,000 by 2011 (Figure 6.5). This in itself posed major issues in terms of housing, population pressures and housing development. Any change in the policy framework for the latter part of this period would, however impact on projected growth.

Figure 6.5: Population projections, Swindon (1991-2011)[1]

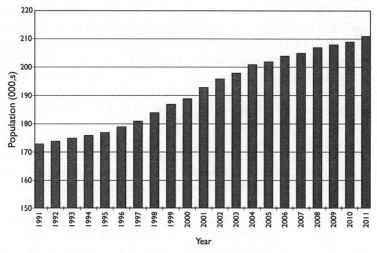

[1] Area of modern Swindon borough, mid-year estimates.
Source: WCC estimates (Thamesdown Borough Council, 1995)

A draft second alteration to the North East Wiltshire Structure Plan has been published in November 1990, taking the Plan forward to 2001.   On the basis of lobbying by the Borough Council, and reflecting the higher political salience of environmental concerns generally, a change of County strategy was flagged up.   While previous structure plans, in line with national strategy, had   talked about "exploiting the growth potential of the M4 corridor by development at Swindon and Chippenham in order to encourage the maximum number of jobs to be created in those areas where firms are likely to invest" (Wiltshire County Council, 1981), the new plan stated the need for "recognising and accommodating development opportunities in the M4 corridor where compatible with the environment and infrastructure" (Wiltshire County Council, 1991).   The Secretary of State's modifications, published in April 1993, accepted this change of strategy, making only minor amendments to the housing and employment land allocations for the plan area. During the Structure Plan consultations the Borough had also pushed for the extension of the 'rural buffer' to include the area east of Swindon, concerned that failure to do this "could encourage the assumption that this area is expendable" (Wiltshire County Council, 1991). This was turned down. The House Builders Federation, on the other hand, recognising the delays over the northern sector, had tried to argue for additional land allocations in the rural area beyond the Swindon boundaries. This was resisted in the face of opposition from the rural districts and environmental interests.

In the meantime, there were changes in the regional planning framework with potential implications for Swindon. In the South East region there were growing disputes over the allocation of projected regional growth in household numbers between counties within the region (Breheny, 1993). Growth pressures in London and the surrounding area reflected its role as both national capital and global city. Counties to the west and south of London pursuing policies of restraint had successfully shifted a high proportion of the growth pressure on to London and the East Thames Corridor. There remained, however, great uncertainty about the capacity of the capital to absorb such levels of development. Even so, a number of counties, including Berkshire, were arguing through their own structure plan reviews that they could not accommodate even this reduced level of growth. The Berkshire Structure Plan, submitted to the Secretary of State in 1992, was proposing a level of housing provision 3,000 less than the Regional Guidance figure. Thamesdown responded that "any action to ameliorate these difficulties should not impose additional strain on Swindon". Clearly there were fears that political opposition to development in the South East in areas from which the government drew support would result in development pressures being pushed further down the M4 Corridor.

In the South West region, preparation of Regional Planning Guidance was also underway. In the strategic advice submitted to the Secretary of State by the South West Regional Planning Conference (1993) the assumption was that the South East should "consume its own smoke" in the sense of absorbing growth within its own boundaries. On Swindon the advice noted a need to review the role of Swindon in the longer term. It advocated "consolidation, with significantly reduced rates of development ... needed to provide a better balance of social facilities, improvements in infrastructure ... and protection of the surrounding countryside" (South West Regional Planning Conference, 1993). While Swindon would continue as a regional employment and service centre, it should no longer, according to the South West Regional Planning Conference at least, be regarded as having a national growth role. In Regional Guidance published in 1994 (DoE, 1994), the general thrust of this was carried forward and it was acknowledged that "Swindon will no longer be expected to grow at the rate which characterised previous years". Although without a formal place on the Regional Conference, Thamesdown had successfully argued for the inclusion of this statement, a tactical move perhaps to distance itself from the political issues surrounding growth in the South East, and align itself more firmly in the South West. This belies the fact, however, that Swindon's development remains inextricably linked to the wider South East region. It has long been acknowledged locally that the regional boundary is arbitrary in planning terms, as the sphere of influence of the South East has expanded. Wiltshire remains a key destination for in-migration from the South East; net inward migration, mainly from the South East, averaged 2,000 people per year during the 1980s, with a peak of over 5,000 in 1987 (see Figure 6.6) and the County gained almost 8,000 jobs from the relocation of major employers in the period 1987-91.

Figure 6.6: Net in-migration to Wiltshire (1984-95)

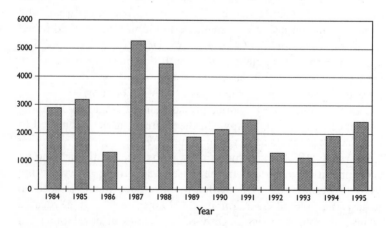

Conflicts over growth and development came to a head with the preparation of a replacement structure plan for Wiltshire during 1995. This was to take the Structure Plan, now for the whole County, forward to 2011. Regional Guidance for the South West specified a need for an additional 69,000 houses in the County in the 20 years 1991-2011. After further consideration, the County accepted this figure and went through a process of environmental appraisal to allocate these additional housing requirements to the districts in the County. The testing of various options against a range of criteria revealed a preferred strategy of concentrating development in the County's main towns, with a particular concentration in Swindon, where most new employment growth was expected to occur. The possibility of attracting significant employment growth to other towns was thought to be limited. Census data on changing commuting patterns during the 1980s confirmed that commuting out from the rural districts had increased.

The total inflow to Thamesdown, meanwhile, had increased by over 60% in the 10 years to 1991 (see Table 6.2). A key part of the County strategy was to counter the trend in commuting, in part, on environmental grounds.

Table 6.2: Change in commuting flows into and out of Swindon (1981-91)

Workforce	1981	1991	Change 1981-91	Change 1981-91 (%)
Commuting in	10,410	17,060	+6,650	+64
Commuting out	5,950	9,680	+3,730	+63
Living and working in Swindon	61,360	75,445	+14,085	+23
Total working in Swindon	71,770	92,505	+20,735	+29

Source: Thamesdown Borough Council (1994b) from Census of Population OPCS

At this stage of the process it was estimated that around 27,000 additional houses would be required in Swindon, at least 10,000 above current commitments for housing development, including the northern sector. This provoked outrage in the Borough

Council, who were appalled at the prospect of a further round of town expansion on a scale similar to the northern sector, then barely underway. The County was accused of dumping all of its growth pressures on to Swindon, paying scant regard to the local policy of reduced growth and consolidation. Following further consideration the County strategy was amended to take some account of this response. The County acknowledged Regional Guidance that Swindon should no longer be expected to grow at the rate which characterised previous years, together with the impacts of recession and collapse in housebuilding in the town in the early 1990s, the start of the new structure plan period. Accordingly, it reduced the total housing requirement in Swindon by 4,000 to 23,000. This figure was included in the 'deposit draft' of the Structure Plan published in August 1996. However, in order to reduce the housing requirement in Thamesdown, the County argued that it would be necessary to reduce the overall County provision to 65,000 new houses – leaving a shortfall in relation to the total allocation in terms of new housing growth which the South West region was expected to absorb by central government. The lower figure of 23,000 for Swindon in any case implied finding sites for around 6,000 new houses beyond the successful completion of the northern sector by 2011. The required rate of development over the plan period as a whole would be reduced, but given the slow start, reduced only marginally in that part of the period left to run. The Borough Council, according to a senior planning officer, remained convinced that this was unacceptable:

> *"There is a strong feeling in the area amongst members, when is all this going to end ... we're taking all this growth and we need a period to stop and think, or at least be able to cope more easily with a more modest growth level."*

The Wiltshire Structure Plan EIP took place in February 1997, when the issues surrounding growth and its distribution were debated. Adding to the Borough Council's concerns was the shortfall at the level of the County as a whole in relation to Regional Guidance figures noted above. Experience elsewhere was that the Secretary of State was unwilling to accept any challenge to Regional Guidance figures. The prospect was that the

County would be forced to accept higher levels of growth with additional pressures, therefore, on Swindon.

At the heart of this dispute, as discussed in Chapter Five, was the meaning and operationalising of the concept of sustainability. From the County's perspective, its strategy was to minimise travel, especially journeys to work, by focusing housing growth in locations where economic and job prospects are best. All of the economic indicators point to Swindon as an area with continuing good prospects because of its locational attractions. Politically, also, there was resistance to growth in the rest of the County. From the Borough's point of view, growth on the scale proposed by the County was seen as incompatible with the sustainability of the town, especially the need to conserve the rural fringe and deal with the emerging problems of traffic congestion. The suspicion was that the interests of Swindon were being politically marginalised in a County dominated by rural interests.

Notwithstanding the merits (and politics) of these positions the developers, at least, appeared convinced in terms of the next phase of Swindon's expansion. As part of the structure plan consultation exercise a series of proposals emerged proposing significant new strategic land allocations for housing to the south and east of the town. There were at least three competing and overlapping schemes being promoted on land east of the A419 and a further scheme to the south. National housebuilders had been buying up options on land to the east for some time, seeing the area as the 'natural' location for a new phase of growth. This was the area that was crucially excluded from protection by the rural buffer, though until recently, little development interest had been shown here, beyond the Honda development at South Marston.

Significantly, however, representations to the EIP on the Structure Plan second alteration had raised the possibility of opening up a 'second housing front' to compensate for the lack of progress in the northern development area. A further major area of land to the south, between the built-up area of the town and the M4 and known locally as 'the front garden', was owned by the Goddard Estate and the County Council. While in many ways better located in terms of transport links to the town centre, the land was environmentally sensitive and regarded locally in many ways as sacrosanct. Throughout 1996 the local Swindon newspaper was running a 'Save Our Front Garden' campaign. Many of the same key players were involved in promoting these schemes. Planning consultants Chapman Warren were representing clients in the east. Local consultants DPDS, whose senior partner was a Bradley's employee in the 1970s, meanwhile, were promoting the 'front garden' on behalf of the Goddard Estate who owned around 185 acres. The need for these schemes was the subject of debate in the arena of the Structure Plan EIP in 1997. Officially, the Borough Council remained implacably opposed to further major development east or south. A further twist to the story was provided by the fact that following the granting of unitary status to Thamesdown in April 1997, some 700 acres of land owned by the County in the 'front garden' which lay within the Borough boundary came into the ownership of the new Swindon Council.

The Thamesdown Local Plan

The structure plan process, intended within the national planning framework to take a more strategic perspective, focused in relatively broad terms on the overall scale of future development. It was the role of a local plan to translate the broad parameters for housing development onto the ground in terms of individual sites. The Thamesdown Local Plan, published in draft form in 1994, replaced Local Plans for Swindon central area (1983) and the rural areas (1988) and a variety of informal plans for the west Swindon area. It was, in fact, prepared in accordance with the earlier North East Wiltshire Structure Plan second alteration and therefore covered the period 1991-2001. It was, however, being prepared in parallel with the work on the replacement Structure Plan discussed in the previous section. As the introduction to the Local Plan noted, the plan was a response to the new requirement introduced in the 1991 Act to prepare a local plan covering the whole of the Borough. In fact, commitments already created by the granting of major planning applications left little to be resolved in terms of new land allocations in order to meet Structure Plan housing and employment targets to 2001. The Plan could therefore be seen as something of a holding operation pending the taking forward of the broader strategic framework as discussed above.

Despite this, the Borough used the Local Plan as a vehicle through which to restate its new philosophy of consolidation, based on a review of the *A new vision* carried out in 1991. While it was recognised that growth pressures from London and the South East were likely to continue, those pressures, it was argued, had to be tempered by local interests. Expansion continued to be an important feature of the plan, but that was "coming into increasing conflict with local concerns about rural protection, the capacity of the Borough's infrastructure and the quality of the environment generally. External pressure should only be accommodated within defined limits" (Thamesdown Borough Council, 1994a, p 8). New development needs were primarily to be met by the northern development area. The plan aimed to give equal importance to conservation, urban renewal and sustainable growth. In order to give some additional protection to areas vulnerable to development pressure 'areas of local landscape importance' were defined, including land to the east of the A419 and 'the front garden', where only very limited development would be permitted. Beyond commitments carried forward from the central area Local Plan, further office development was to be restrained.

In relation to housing, the Local Plan argued that the provisions of the Structure Plan would essentially be met in the northern development area, the final phases of western expansion and on a number of smaller sites in the existing built-up area. The northern sector, it was estimated, would contribute about 8,500 of the total 15,000 Structure Plan total in the period 1991-2001 (Table 6.3). It is evident that the Borough Council were making an extremely optimistic assessment of the likely progress on this site. By the end of 1995 only around 80 houses had been built and 300 were estimated for 1996. Halfway through the plan period only 700 of the required 8,500 houses would have actually been completed. To achieve the Local Plan target, completions in excess of 1,500 houses a year would have been required in the remainder of the plan period, a fairly heroic assumption.

Private sector development interests, on the other hand, saw a much slower rate of progress in the northern area. They put estimated completions by the year 2,000 at 2,788, so at that point the existing permission for Haydon 2 would still have been 500 houses short of completion. As already noted, permission for Haydon 3 had yet to be granted, and although there was agreement in principle to this going ahead, English China Clay as a major land owner in Haydon 3, was unwilling to agree to the

Table 6.3: Housing land requirements, Swindon (1991-2001)

Area	Structure Plan allocation for 1990-2001	Housing completions 1990-94	Balance of Structure Plan allocation	Houses under construction or with planning permission	Balance still to be provided for
Northern sector	8,500	18	8,482	3,782	4,700
Rest of Swindon	6,600	2,363	4,237	2,664	1,573
Total	15,100	2,381	12,719	6,446	6,273

Source: Thamesdown Borough Council, 1991(b)

financial commitment implied by the schedule of infrastructure contributions which had been negotiated, without a firm buyer for the land. For any prospective buyer the problem was that the return on investment would come well into the future; the developers were estimating three or four years before outline planning consent was agreed and a further two years for construction of the next phase of the northern orbital route. Therefore, Haydon 3 was unlikely to come on stream before the year 2002. All of this was, of course, subject to housing market conditions over the period. Thamesdown argued that there was no reason why completions should not build up to mirror the earlier rates achieved in the western expansion which peaked at over 1,000 houses a year during the 1980s. However, there was a high degree of scepticism that the boom conditions of the 1980s would return.

At the Public Local Inquiry on the Thamesdown Local Plan starting in October 1995 there was intense pressure for additional housing sites to be brought forward to compensate for the difficulties in the northern development area. It was hard to imagine, however, that any major new phase of expansion could be brought forward within the remaining period of the Local Plan. Moreover, the strategic framework confirmed the northern development area as the main focus for new development in the period to 2001. The panel report of the EIP referred specifically to the undesirability of opening up a 'second housing front'. Further major land release was therefore more likely to be considered in the context of the emerging Structure Plan. The Inspector's report of the Public Local Inquiry was not expected until well into 1997, but in the meantime the real battle had shifted once more into the structure plan arena. At least some of the major development interests in the town, in fact, made a tactical decision to hold back new growth proposals until the structure plan consultation period in 1996.

The impasse over strategic growth policy

As we have seen, this situation represented a complete reversal of the earlier positions of the County and the Borough in relation to strategic policy. While in earlier periods the Borough was arguing for growth and expansion in the face of significant resistance on the part of the County, the Borough was now attempting to resist the County's strategy to concentrate growth pressures in Swindon. These issues were debated in the Structure Plan EIP, which started in February 1997. The panel report of the EIP was not expected until some months later, but in April 1997, following reorganisation of local government in Wiltshire, Thamesdown became a unitary authority. From this point the new Swindon Borough Council was a separate Structure Plan authority responsible for adopting its own strategic planning framework. Clearly the intention was that Wiltshire and Swindon should jointly adopt the new Wiltshire Structure Plan. The ongoing dispute suggested, however, that agreement was unlikely. In addition, there remained the 4,000 shortfall in the Structure Plan housing figure compared to Regional Guidance, and it was not certain that central government would accept the County's case for this.

Legal complications surrounding the 1992 Local Government Act added to this increasingly confused situation. The Act specified that where new unitary authorities were set up, the Secretary of State had the power to require joint preparation of a structure plan, together with powers to step in if the authorities failed to agree (Section 21 of the 1992 Act). This was the case, for example, in the new unitary authorities established to replace the County of Avon. However, in the case of a new hybrid structure, where the two-tier structure continued in part of a County and there are one or more unitary authorities, the Local Government Commission considered that no such powers under the 1992 Act existed. There was still uncertainty about the precise legal position on this, but it was possible that because the hybrid model emerged during the process of local government review, the legislation was defective. Any joint arrangements would therefore be entirely voluntary, each authority having the right to prepare and adopt its own structure plan. At least two possible scenarios could develop from this.

Under the first scenario, assuming broad support for the new Wiltshire Structure Plan strategy following the EIP, the County and the new Swindon Council fail to agree. Wiltshire adopts the Structure Plan for its part of the County and Thamesdown moves ahead with the preparation of its own Structure Plan. In the likely event that these strategies are incompatible, the Secretary of State has the power under planning legislation to direct modifications to one or both Structure Plans. The second, and possibly more likely scenario, is failure of the County and Thamesdown to agree. This would result in delay in adopting the Structure Plan. In the absence of an agreed strategic framework for the County, it would be impossible to roll forward the Thamesdown Local Plan which only ran up to 2001.

In either case there was likely to be an extended period of uncertainty, in the context of increasing pressures to deal with housing land shortfalls in the County. Developers would then have a fairly strong case for arguing that the statutory planning system was failing, and might be confident that, not withstanding the 'plan-led' system, planning appeals stand a good chance of success. In adopting these tactics, reference back to the earlier history of major land release in the western and northern development would support the view that it is only central government intervention that has resolved interauthority conflict. Planning consultants in the town clearly saw this as a possibility:

> "*Will the next phase of development in Swindon be resolved through a development plan, or is it going to be settled by a planning application? Now, I don't know the answer to that, but I think the situation in terms of land supply is becoming a little precarious.... The housebuilding industry will take the view that you can't bring the Northern Sector forward in a way that will deliver the scope, range and choice, and there will be a strong lobby for additional land release.... I suspect we will see a number of proposals come forward and be called in ... one thing's for certain ... there's going to be more major inquiries on all the major controversial planning issues.*"

If a further round of town expansion were to occur (and this remains uncertain) then the process would probably be driven to an even greater extent by speculative pressure from the house-building industry. The indications are that this would be most likely on the eastern side of the town. The future protected status of land to the south is not entirely cut and dried, however, particularly given the transfer in 1997 of land from the County to the new Swindon authority. Exhaustion of its historic land stocks was a key factor behind consolidation and the shift in the Borough Council's role and strategy in relation to town expansion in the wake of *A new vision*. Now it had 'inherited' major landholdings, albeit in a location where there had been a strong presumption against development and in the context of a planning policy framework based around consolidation. Given the inevitable pressures for growth from outside of the Borough, this presented the temptation to realise the value of its inheritance. The possibility existed, in theory at least, of planned development with the Borough Council playing a key role as a major landowner. As one senior Labour Councillor observed:

> "*I think we'll have to face up to the responsibility and if we have to then I suspect we will. We as a new Authority will have to say right, well there's no sacred cows. There's no areas that are no goes for development, whereas previously there were. And the front garden is the only area I think along the line of the M4 ... you know, that's prime development land. It's where people want to be, it's visual, they haven't got to spend millions of pounds in advertising, they just build their factory there and make sure that their name's up there. So that's prime development land. And the likelihood is that land will be developed. But other land will have to be developed as well. Well I don't believe we can win the argument about not developing more areas for housing because the houses are being taken up. But it's not just about building houses for people coming any more, it is about building houses for those people already here.*"

Consolidation, he maintained, slowing down the rate of growth and opposing any major development proposals until infra-structure provision had caught up, remained the Council's strategy. Further expansion seemed, at some point however, inevitable:

> "*What we'll endeavour to do is to push it back and push it back for as long as we can. And what we do want is to ensure that whatever we do agree to, or we do plan, it's planned well and that we don't have at the end of the day the Secretary of State saying, right, well you know, there's been a*

speculative application and we're going to allow that developer to develop there.... If the pressures, development pressures are going to be repeated like that, then I think the lessons that we've learnt, and the expertise that we've learnt from that exercise will be put to good use again. It does mean though that we have to swallow hard and acknowledge that there's going to be development somewhere where previously, where now there isn't any development. And that will be contrary to what people have wanted. Where you see green fields now."

Planning in the 1990s

The latest period sharply illustrates the shifting attitudes to growth and expansion in the 1990s. The reversal in the stances of the County and the Borough, with respect to continued town expansion, can be attributed in part to the different pressures which they now face. In the past the County's opposition was motivated by concerns over the resource implications of growth in Swindon, together with a more generalised concern that growth pressures originating beyond its boundaries threatened the character of an essentially rural County. Swindon's amoeba-like expansion threatened the rural interests which lay at the political heart of the County. These concerns have been tempered in the new context where developers are being required to meet the supporting costs of development, and where from 1997 the County would cease to have any financial responsibility for the town.   There would also seem to be some acceptance that Wiltshire has effectively been brought within the social and economic sphere of influence of the South East in general and of London as national capital and global city. Growth may therefore be unstoppable, particularly in the context of a more globally integrated economy where foreign inward investment is accounting for much of the new growth pressure. In the face of hardening opposition to development from rural constituencies, however, it was thought that much of these pressures could conveniently, from the County's perspective at least, be contained within areas such as Swindon. The town, in any case, continues to possess locational attractions not available in the rest of the County.

Thamesdown Council (now Swindon) had itself shifted from a position where growth was seen as offering unequivocal benefits, including the opportunity to diversify economically and expand social, cultural and leisure provision in the town on the back of development. Politically the Borough had been able to shape the form of development to meet its own conception of local needs, essentially through its powers of land ownership in the early phases of expansion. From the mid-1980s, however, this strategy has been increasingly questioned; while the pressures for growth if anything intensified, the powers of the local authority to control and shape development have decreased. Several factors contributed to this: the financial pressures on the Council; its inability to manage new development through control of land; increasing dominance of housing production by national developers who took control of the development process; and increasing speculative pressures for new housebuilding emanating as much from wider regional forces as from local pressures. All of these factors, together with the changing nature of the authority, have contributed to a major shift in the local politics of development that makes long-term strategic thinking more difficult. One officer commented in 1996 that:

> "The long-term strategy that was produced 25 years ago was produced when there was a strong chief executive in post. The relationship now is different between officers and members and this is a more politically driven organisation ... the members are more reflective of the views of their constituents.... But the fact remains that it is more difficult to get an acceptance of the need for a long-term strategic vision. Politicians prefer shorter term thinking. So it is probably impractical now to produce a 20-year vision of where Swindon should be going."

As the Council discovered, however, it was not easy to restrain the growth it had worked so hard for many years to promote. Within this conflict considerations of the environment and the contested meanings of sustainability have become particularly significant. This can perhaps be seen at least partly as a new language for debating older long-standing conflicts over development. More broadly, the issues surrounding whether Swindon should continue to expand, or be allowed the breathing space for the consolidation it seeks, illustrate a tension in central government policy in terms of urban and regional development between economic competitiveness and support for inwards investment, on the one hand, and the nature of sustainable development on the other.

In relation to the development process, this account of Swindon's development reveals important conclusions about the operation of the planning system at national and local levels. A consistent feature of virtually the whole postwar period in Swindon has been the marginal role of the statutory, plan-led planning system in regulating development. The 1947 Act had set up a comprehensive system of development control based firmly on proposals contained in development plans. Subsequent legislation built on this process, introducing the system of structure plans and local plans. Most of the key planning decisions that formed the basis for successive phases of expansion in Swindon, however, have been made outside of this formal, plan-led planning process. They have represented departures from the established planning framework or exceptions to the 'normal' process of development based on planning applications on which decisions are reached in the light of the statutory planning framework.

The earliest phase of eastern expansion was carried out under town development powers, permissions for the western expansion were given following planning appeals in the mid 1970s in the context of delays in bringing out a structure plan, several industrial developments including the Honda development were approved as departures from the agreed planning framework, and the latest northern development area was again allowed on appeal in advance of decisions on the strategic planning framework. Other policy documents, especially the *Silver Book*, have been far more significant in providing a guiding framework for new development, managed on a project-by-project basis via informal master plans and legal agreements. Meanwhile, both the County and the Borough have attempted to use the planning system as a means of delaying decisions, which have subsequently been taken out of their hands by central government. Planning has operated more as an arena in which the different interests of the local authorities and the development industry have been played out, seeking to establish their positions and signify intentions.

Within this, however, important shifts have taken place in the role of the local authority in the development process. The contrast between the western expansion and the northern development area is illustrative of this shift. In the western expansion the ability of the authority to buy up land ahead of development, forming partnerships with private developers, allowed them to exercise far more control than planning powers would have allowed, particularly in the early stages. At the same time, financial benefits came to the authority as land values increased. As the western expansion proceeded and development moved into areas owned by the private sector, so the control and influence of the Borough Council diminishes. This was reflected in the growing level of complaints about the provision of social and community infrastructure. The northern development area, on the other hand, was from the outset more clearly an example of market-led development, with a private sector consortium adopting an overall coordinating role, preparing the master plan and development briefs and funding infrastructure from the proceeds of land sales. The powers of the authority over much of the period were largely confined to conventional planning powers.

As this example graphically illustrates, however, the ability of the private sector to play this role may be compromised by the volatility of land and property markets. As the housing and land market went into free fall in the late 1980s, so the financial basis of the developers' commitments fell apart. Rescuing the scheme required protracted and complex negotiations, and from the local authority's perspective, the ability to reassert a degree of control via imaginative use of land ownership. This has been fundamental to preserving the integrity of the scheme as originally agreed. The sorts of timescales involved in bringing forward large-scale residential developments are also illustrated by the northern sector; the anticipatory phase of this scheme goes back at least to the mid-1970s, with real pressure emerging in the early 1980s. Construction is only just underway in 1996 and completion is likely to take a further 15 years. Swindon's northern development area carries some important messages about the difficulties that might be encountered in the kind of private sector-led 'new settlements' in which the government is currently showing interest.

The history of development in Swindon also illustrates the key role played by a small group of individuals in the local property sector in promoting successive phases of expansion. Local builders

Bradley and associated company Bradley Planning Services were clearly important actors in earlier periods, making some astute land acquisitions and working in close partnership with the local authority. Subsequently, various individuals associated with Bradley moved into key positions within the local policy network. A number of former Bradley's employees went on to establish Chapman Warren Planning Consultants, who successfully promoted the northern sector. One became, for a time, the Borough Council's economic development advisor. Another now works for local planning consultants DPDS, currently promoting southern expansion. Within a broader context where national housebuilders have become more significant players on the Swindon scene, these locally based property professionals continue to occupy an important mediating position.

Looking to the future, the current impasse over the role of Swindon and the strategic policy framework for the County raises questions as to the capability of the planning system to resolve growth conflicts at the local level. While development following the 1991 Planning and Compensation Act is ostensibly 'plan-led', the conflicting positions of the County and Borough Councils seem likely to result in a period of extended uncertainty. This, we would argue, is in turn likely to invite challenges from development interests who are already growing restive about the lack of responsiveness of the new system. It also reveals the weaknesses in the current strategic and regional planning framework, which, as currently delineated, relies substantially on voluntary arrangements among participants whose cooperation cannot be assured or guaranteed, particularly over any extended time period.

Accommodating future growth: planning under pressure

At a broader level, the key planning issue of the late 1990s and beyond is likely to be the projected growth of households in England over the next 25 years or so, carrying with it implications for a massive new housebuilding programme. This is in a context where few things arouse more fierce opposition than the prospect of new development within a local community. In addition, the sustainable development agenda is leading many to ask whether it is possible to meet the implied housing needs without serious damage to the environment. The issue therefore sharpens the debate on sustainability, raising questions of how we trade off apparently incompatible priorities of the conservation, the environment, economic development and social equity.

A new set of household projections, published by the DoE in 1995, forecast that an additional 4.4 million households would be formed in England in the period 1991-2016, a 25% increase on the existing number of households, and almost one million more than the figures that underlay current plans (Table 6.4). The growth pressures are particularly concentrated in the south of the country, especially the arc of counties north and west of London. Underlying this forecast growth in households are a projected increase in the national population, together with trends in terms of household formation. Population is forecast to increase due to lower mortality – people are living longer. There are also new assumptions about international migration – it is expected that England will gain around 58,000 people each year to 2006, due to migration from other countries, primarily the rest of Europe (Table 6.4). At the sub-national level population change is influenced by population movement within the country – counties such as Wiltshire, on the fringes of the South East, are expected to grow due to continued in-migration. In terms of households the average size of households is also falling (from 2.67 in 1991 to an estimated 2.22 by 2011). A complex set of social, demographic and policy influences affect household formation. Divorce, a decline in marriage, and the growing tendency for the young and the old to live separately from their families are among the factors leading to increased household fission and growth in single person households. Added to this, higher incomes lead to higher housing expectations, in terms of aspirations to live separately, space in and around the home and the demand for second homes.

The largest projected absolute growth in households is expected to occur in the South East, particularly the counties surrounding London. The highest percentage changes, on the other hand, are in the regions adjoining the South East, including East Anglia and the South West. High growth is anticipated in a band of counties stretching from Cambridgeshire to the north and west of London through to Wiltshire and into the South West. Growth in this arc reflects both an in-built dynamic – high indigenous growth arising from previous waves of movement into these counties – and continued in-migration. For Wiltshire itself, the projections are for an additional 84,000 households in the 25-

year period (Table 6.5). Around half of this represents growth in the already resident population and half in-migration, a characteristic shared with the adjoining West of England counties of Avon and Gloucestershire.

Table 6.4: Projected household numbers, England (1991-2016)

Region	1991 (000s)	2016 (000s)	Change (000s) 1991-2016	Change (%) 1991-2016
South East	7,081	8,813	1,732	24.5
Greater London	*2,842*	*3,471*	*629*	*22.1*
Rest of South East	*4,239*	*5,343*	*1,104*	*26.0*
East Anglia	832	1,117	285	34.2
South West	1,903	2,448	545	28.6
East Midlands	1,596	2,014	418	26.2
West Midlands	2,043	2,410	367	18.0
Yorks and Humberside	1,993	2,380	387	19.4
North West	2,524	2,971	447	17.7
North	1,245	1,445	200	16.1

Source: DoE projections of households in England to 2016

Table 6.5: Projected change in household numbers, selected counties (1991-2016)

County	1991 (000s)	2016 (000s)	Change (000s) 1991-2016	Change (%) 1991-2016
Berkshire	288	394	+106	37
Oxfordshire	220	296	+76	35
Wiltshire	223	307	+84	38
Avon	388	481	+93	24
Gloucestershire	216	279	+63	29

Source: DoE projections of households in England to 2016

The projected level of growth in this group of counties on the fringes of the South East will pose difficult planning issues. In most cases growth is now expected to be significantly higher than anticipated in current Regional Guidance. Most of these counties, Wiltshire included, were in any case already seeking reductions in Regional Guidance totals for new housing development on the basis of environmental constraints and local opposition. The new figures can only intensify controversy. Wiltshire was arguing for an additional 65,000 dwellings between 1991 and 2011 compared with 69,000 as proposed by the government's Regional Planning Guidance (DoE, 1994). The report on the Examination in Public in fact recommended a figure of 70,000, slightly higher than the RPG proposals and well above that of the County Council (DoE, 1997).

The main basis for challenging the validity of these new projections relates to the issue of migration. The essential question is whether historic trends of movement of people away from London and the South East to locations along the M4 Corridor will continue in the future. Movement to counties such as Wiltshire has, in the past, reflected better relative economic performance, better perceived quality of life in comparison with London, and a ready supply of relatively cheap housing. The future economic prospects in the sub-region remain relatively strong. Employment growth has been high in national terms in the early 1990s in Avon and Wiltshire and they are expected to be among the top performing counties in economic terms in future years (Cambridge Econometrics, 1996). While controversy is now evident over new housing development, there are still significant new developments going ahead (eg, the 10,000 new houses planned in the Swindon northern sector). There are in any case uncertainties over the possibility of deterring migration through restricting housing supply. If the economic or environmental attractions of an area are strong enough, people will come and buy housing in the second-hand market. Higher prices resulting from more housing scarcity would, in turn, increase the incentive for developers to challenge planning constraints and seek further permissions.

Growth pressures in counties such as Wiltshire relate closely to population (and employment) pressures and migration out from London and the rest of the South East (see Table 6.6). This in part reflects planning constraints in Greater London and surrounding home counties. Migration out of the South East, rapid during the 1970s and 1980s, has been lower in the early years of the 1990s as a result of the economic and housing market down-turn (see

Figure 6.6). The heavy reliance of the new household projections on migration trends in the late 1980s and early 1990s period, coinciding with the period when migration out of the South East was lower, means they may seriously in fact *under*-estimate potential movement. Strategic planning policy is now seeking to shift the focus of growth in the South East away from the west and towards the 'Thames Gateway' in the east. This shift is being seized on by counties west of London seeking to restrain growth in their own areas, to argue for lower allocations. The impact of this new development opportunity on the household growth figures for the South East is, however, fairly marginal – Thames Gateway is officially estimated to yield around 30,000 new dwellings, compared with household growth of well over one million in the whole of the South East. Serious capacity constraints in London, coupled with the very difficult politics of development in much of the South East, may well push pressure further out to the adjoining regions. Depending on the line that central government adopts to these projections, and crucially whether concessions are made to NIMBY or 'Not In My Back Yard' tendencies in the South East, places such as Swindon, Peterborough, Northampton and Milton Keynes, which have acted in the past as counter-magnets or 'safety valves' in relation to London and the South East, may well be under even greater pressure.

At a more fundamental level, the trends discussed here represent long-standing and deep-seated features of the changing economic and demographic geography of the UK. A long-standing process of 'counter-urbanisation' has been evident for at least 30 years. Both people and jobs have been tending to move away from large cities and conurbations towards smaller cities and towns and to more rural areas (Breheny, 1995; Atkins et al, 1996). In the period 1981-94 the metropolitan counties and London between them recorded a population loss of over one and a quarter million people, an average of over 90,000 a year. Moreover, recent research by Champion (1996) indicates that the outward flow from the cities has accelerated through the 1990s, after a drastic slow down in 1989/90. For many living in the largest cities there is still a strong preference to move out, motivated by push factors (traffic, pollution, dissatisfaction with urban schools, fear of crime) and pull factors (a preference for suburban or rural living). Growth of population and households in counties such as Wiltshire, and indeed in all counties fringing the South East

Table 6.6: Sources of in-migration into Wiltshire over the period 1984-96

Source area	In-migration (net)[1]
Greater London	9,952
Berkshire	5,382
Hampshire	3,392
Surrey	3,257
Avon	3,054
Hertfordshire	1,866
Kent	1,761
Essex	1,496
Oxfordshire	1,109
Buckinghamshire	1,071
Rest of Great Britain[2]	-1,708
All areas	30,632

Notes: [1] Figures show the difference between in-migration and out-migration between Wiltshire Health Authority Area and the areas listed in the table. Thus, for example, an estimated 15,245 people moved from Berkshire into Wiltshire over this period, an estimated 9,863 moved from Wiltshire to Berkshire, giving a net gain in Wiltshire of 5,382.

[2] Includes some other areas generating net in-migration into Wiltshire but these were outweighed by areas to which there was a net out-flow from Wiltshire.

Source: NOMIS, FHSA Migration data

region, is therefore part of a much broader set of changes associated with an urban to rural shift in jobs and population. The deep-seated nature of this process casts doubt on whether the process of counter-urbanisation can be easily or substantially reversed. In many ways the processes are beyond the scope of policy as it is currently practised. Reflecting on the growth projections, a Swindon planner commented:

> *"If you look at the projections they're talking about major population growth in a ring from East Anglia to Dorset, just beyond the South East fringe. There are no more than half a dozen centres of growth in that band, and they're the same old horse that's being flogged to death.*

> *There is never any attempt to try and see whether*
> *these places should be given a breathing space....*
> *There are no arrangements for looking at the*
> *connections between the regions and so we just*
> *bumble along ... with a lot of internal bickering."*

The 'West of England' sub-region (Avon, Gloucestershire and Wiltshire) could therefore be under pressure to accommodate in excess of a quarter of a million new households over the next 25-30 years. This will be the focus of new Regional Guidance due in 1998, and strategic plans to follow. All of these counties have extensive planning constraints due to green belt or AONB designations and the towns and cities do not possess the large areas of vacant land associated with the industrial legacy of other urban areas. National policy to accommodate the majority of new housing development within existing urban areas is clearly not feasible in this region. Further green field development at the edge of towns and cities, probably requiring amendments to green belt or other protective designations and possible New Towns and settlements, in which there is renewed policy interest, are all on the cards for the future. The potential implications for the Swindon area are clearly considerable, with the possibility of major pressure for additional growth.

The housing market and housing policy

Having discussed the overall framework for planning and housing development, this final section of the chapter looks more specifically at the housing market, housing policy and housing provision locally. In terms of national policy, in the wake of wartime damage, and in the context of severe housing shortage housing policy, the key concern for at least the first 25 years of the postwar period was with the numbers of houses built. Labour and Conservative governments vied with each other in the 'numbers game', in setting targets for annual completions. Throughout this early period two main forms of provision dominated: public sector housing for rent, provided by local authorities and the New Town Development Corporations, and owner-occupied housing provided by the speculative housebuilding industry. Up to 1958, completions of public sector housing for rent exceeded completions by the private sector. After this, private sector housebuilding overtook public sector provision although local authority and New Town output remained significant up to the late 1970s with 100,000 completions a year and around 40% of total completions. Since then, new council housebuilding has rapidly diminished. There was some increase in provision by housing associations, but at levels far below the historic rates of public sector construction.

In the period up to 1959, land purchased compulsorily for public sector housebuilding was priced at 'existing use value' and land prices were therefore considerably less than market values (initially under the 1947 Town and Country Planning Act and subsequently under the 1954 Act). After 1959, however, land costs per dwelling rose sharply, from 2-3% of total capital costs in the early 1950s to 19% by 1975 (Merrett, 1979). Subsidies for council housing were relatively generous, though declining, throughout the period to the mid-1970s, and there were no overall limits to local authority capital spending on housing. This all began to change, initially under the Labour Government in the context of economic crisis and government financial difficulty resulting from the International Monetary Fund imposed cuts in 1976. More rapid and fundamental change followed the election of the Thatcher Government in 1979, which set out to reshape the structure and finance of local government in general and the role of public sector housing in particular. Subsidy was steadily withdrawn exerting upward pressure on rents. Capital expenditure limits were imposed and tightened progressively to a level where little new building could take place. Sales of existing local authority rented housing at substantial discounts to sitting tenants were also encouraged on a significant scale under the 'Right to Buy' legislation. Through the 1980s, national housing policy had been fundamentally reshaped (Malpass, 1990). The formal role of local authorities, which had historically included meeting general housing need, has been redefined as 'enabling' provision of new social housing by housing associations and the private sector, using resources of land, finance and planning powers.

Owner-occupation grew strongly, particularly in the period after 1955, in the context of rising real incomes and secure employment prospects for most households, supported by fiscal measures that effectively subsidised the costs of mortgages. By

1979 54% of households were owner-occupiers. Strong encouragement to owner-occupation was a significant feature of housing policy in the 1980s. The Right to Buy policy implemented in 1980 gave tenants of council housing the right to purchase their houses at significant discounts (of up to 60%) on market values, and also removed housing from local authority control. Nationally around 25% of the council housing stock has been sold. Williams (1992) suggests that about half of the growth in owner-occupation between 1979 and 1990, when it reached 67%, was due to this sales programme. Alongside these changes in the relative roles of the public and private sectors have gone changes in the social and economic characteristics of tenants and owners. For much of the postwar period council housing was built to meet 'general housing needs'; it was certainly a mass tenure housing a high proportion of skilled and unskilled manual workers. Under the impact of council house sales, and in a general context that emphasised the benefits of owner-occupation, the role of council housing has been redefined. Sales have disproportionately been of the best properties (houses) in the more attractive areas and have been bought by the better-off households within the sector. There has therefore been a 'residualisation' of council housing – a growing concentration of the poor, unemployed and those dependant on state benefits in the sector (Forrest and Murie, 1988). At the same time as owner-occupation grew and diversified, relatively more lower income households were depending on the private market for housing. In the context of rising costs throughout the 1980s (see below) the affordability of private housing became an important policy issue. As prices declined in the subsequent housing market collapse, accompanied by rising unemployment generally, however, new problems of negative equity and mortgage arrears and repossessions have emerged.

While owner-occupation grew generally throughout the postwar period, housing production by the speculative housebuilding industry has been extremely vulnerable to fluctuating demand and changing economic conditions with the housing market characterised by significant variation in terms of output and house prices. There have been major periods of boom and slump in recent years. The first, fuelled by the early 1970s 'Barber boom', saw a high level of house price inflation and rising output, followed by spectacular collapse in 1974/75, which saw numerous housebuilders go out of business or taken over by larger companies. Private sector completions fell from almost 200,000 in 1972 to 140,000 in 1974. This period was significant partly because it resulted in a growing concentration and centralisation of the housebuilding industry, as smaller regionally based companies were taken over by larger national housebuilding companies (Ball, 1983). The mid-1980s then saw rapidly rising house prices and output recovering from around 115,000 new houses in 1981 to almost 200,000 in 1988. Pressures were particularly strong in the overheated market of the South East, and this period was marked by growing inter-regional house price differentials. The subsequent collapse of the market from 1989, however, has again seen a slump in output which dropped to 130,000 in 1994. For the first time in the postwar period, there were also large falls in house prices in real terms. There were some signs of recovery by the mid-1990s but at relatively modest rates. The prospects for continued growth in owner-occupation on any major scale may also be less certain than in the past. Throughout the postwar period, the expansion of owner-occupation has been sustained by secure, often lifetime employment, rising real incomes, stable households, a privileged fiscal context. Housing could be treated as a secure asset which would generally increase in value, while relatively high rates of inflation reduced the real cost of borrowing. Many of these assumptions no longer hold. While household growth is set to increase in the early years of the next century, many of these households may be unable or unwilling to meet their housing needs through owner-occupation.

The housing market and housing policy in Swindon

Turning to the local level, in the early postwar period provision of council housing dominated new building in Swindon (see Figure 6.7). By the 1960s, however, owner-occupation was growing rapidly, and from the late 1970s it came to dominate. Little new Council housing for general needs was built during the 1980s. The Borough Council, although Labour controlled for virtually the whole postwar period, had, however, been supportive of owner-occupation from the early 1960s – they themselves built housing for sale. They also pioneered public–private sector partnerships with private sector builders (Salt, 1992). There was a small Council house sales programme in advance of the Right to Buy legislation, and in spite of some ritual opposition to the imposition of sales, many houses were sold to sitting tenants. However, as the parameters of housing policy changed over time, the role of the Borough Council in housing terms has shifted dramatically. In the early period, housing policy locally was strongly driven by the Councils' ambitions in terms of growth and industrial diversification. A ready supply of new Council housing for incoming households and a key worker allocation policy were significant features. In the 1980s, as private sector housing provision came to dominate, the process was increasingly driven by speculative housebuilders. Employment policy and housing policy were thus effectively de-coupled. In the most recent period, housing policy has largely been addressed to the more serious of local needs, with the Borough doing what it can in resource terms to improve an ageing Council stock and to support housing association construction.

Figure 6.7: Housing completions by tenure, Thamesdown (1972/73-1995/96)

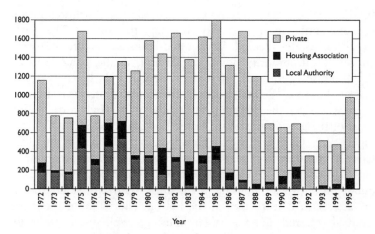

The private housing market in Swindon has been subject to macroeconomic influences as in other areas, although more local factors influencing supply and production have also been important. Thus, while house prices and the housing market went into decline nationally in the early 1980s, the market remained buoyant in Swindon. By this point Swindon was coming more strongly within the sphere of influence of the South East economy and housing market. The western expansion came on stream in this period, with sales fed by high levels of in-migration. Swindon also provides a good example of the increasing dominance of the larger national housebuilders in housing construction. National players became more important particularly in the period after the mid-1970s, as companies expanded into what was seen as a profitable and buoyant market, with an assured long-term pro-gramme of production. Crest's expansion of its activities down the M4 Corridor and its involvement in the northern expansion is typical of this, as is the involvement of a range of other large national builders who have bought into this same development. These private builders have tended, however, to concentrate on only certain market segments, the lower end and the middle of the market. Demand for more expensive up-market housing has been largely met in the second-hand market in towns and villages beyond the Swindon boundary.

Council housing (1953-79)

In the 1950s and 1960s housing provision in Swindon meant predominantly local authority housing for rent. The early expansion estates (Penhill, Walcot and Parks, see Figure 6.2) were entirely local authority housing. Overall, in the years 1953-70 7,300 houses were built for rent by the Borough, but only 1,540 private houses. Private builders concentrated in areas beyond what was then the Swindon boundary, with Highworth seeing most of the growth in private sector housing (Harloe, 1987a) (see Figure 2.1, Chapter Two). However, by the early 1960s, the Council pioneered a local authority 'build-for-sale' programme, partly in response to demands from early migrants to move from public into private housing. Unhappy with the standards of private sector construction at the bottom end of the market, the Council offered good quality housing, with local authority mortgages and only £25 deposits (Harloe, 1987a). This policy was restated in the *Silver Book*, which noted that vacancy rates in the Council sector were increasing, in part due to rising real incomes in the Borough that allowed people to realise ambitions to become owner-occupiers. In the new expansion areas to the west, the planned mix was 40% built by the private sector for owner-occupation, 25% built for sale by the local authority and around 35% local authority rented housing.

By the early 1970s housing need in the Borough began to change. There was substantial growth in demand from second generation migrants, children of the first wave of newcomers to the town. There was also growing demand for housing from older people. Locally generated demand for housing was thus becoming more important. In-migration also continued, and demand was increased by the opening of the M4 which widened the appeal of the Swindon housing market. The property boom nationally, moreover, was leading to price rises in the private sector (see below), and housing shortages was exacerbated by slow progress initially with the western expansion. The Council housing waiting list increased from around 1,500 in the 1960s to 5,000 in 1974. In the early 1970s, however, the Council were building fewer council houses (see Figure 6.7) and a series of reports outlined the need for a building programme of between 500 and 600 local authority housing units for rent each year through the rest of the 1970s. In the context of cuts in public expenditure this proved overambitious, but completions of local authority housing for rent did increase substantially towards the end of the 1970s.

Other developments in the 1970s included a small-scale programme of council house sales in the early part of the decade, although Harloe (1987a) suggests this was not very widely supported by the Labour Group. In 1976, however, the Conservatives took control of the Council and reintroduced the sales policy with discounts of up to 20% on market value. Capital receipts at that time could be recycled back into new Council building. Significantly for the Council, which had initiated a significant build-for-sale programme, a freeze was imposed in 1975 on local authority mortgage lending. By 1974 the Council had increased lending to over £2m a year to support its build-for-sale programme. Other issues were also looming. The local authority had been focusing on the need to expand the supply of housing to meet the needs of population growth. By the late 1970s there was widespread criticism of the Council's repairs service and growing complaints about the condition of some of the oldest council housing and in the eastern expansion area (Penhill and Park). Throughout this period, however, a key worker housing policy had, in effect, allowed all those that required rented accommodation to be allocated a council house, and while needs overall were increasing, waiting times for local authority rented housing were still fairly low at between two and three months.

The private market (1953-79)

As we have seen, private sector housing completions were only a small proportion of the total during the 1950s and the 1960s. However, that changed radically from the early 1970s. The housing boom nationally and strong local demand contributed to large house price rises (around 30% a year in the early 1970s). Swindon, however, remained a relatively cheap housing market compared to other areas in the south. Private sector building rates rose, locally, in the first half of the decade, and represented more than 70% of total housing completions. After falling back somewhat, private sector production revived with the commencement of the first developments in the western expansion at Toothill and in the context of falling interest rates nationally. By the end of the 1970s, the private sector was again contributing more than 70% of total completions, a trend that was to increase into the 1980s. Private sector building rates were reflected in levels of owner-occupation well above the national rate (see Table 6.7).

After 1976 house prices in Swindon started to rise faster than in the South East and South West regions. Annual price rises of up to 50% for some types of houses were being reported in 1979. Increasing demand from those already resident in the town continued to be an important factor, but Harloe suggests that demand from growing numbers of households priced out of the South East market was an increasingly significant component of demand for new housing in Swindon. "Thamesdown is entering a new phase as a reception area for 'overspill' population, but this time not from London but from the overheated housing markets of the South East, especially those lying along the line of the M4 motorway" (Harloe, 1987a, p 18). As we saw earlier in the chapter, the strong housing market in Swindon was beginning to attract the attentions of a number of national housebuilders, notably Crest, who later undertook to promote the northern expansion. Private developers were also acquiring land in the later phases of the western expansion and pressure was being exerted to release land in other parts of the Borough. Development of the town was shifting from the 'employment-led' pattern of the earlier period to the 'housing market-led' pattern that persisted throughout the 1980s.

Local authority housing (1980-96)

As described earlier, the 1980s saw national housing policy substantially reshaped and the role of local authorities as direct housing providers largely eclipsed. A decade of cuts in public expenditure virtually ended local authority building for rent, rents in the public sector increased substantially and the Right to Buy policy introduced in 1980 removed large numbers of houses from local authority control. In Swindon the cash value of the Council's Housing Investment allocation fell from £9.8m in 1977/78 to only £6m in 1984/85, a reduction in real terms, after inflation, of nearly 50%. These trends were reflected in the changing tenure composition of the town's housing stock. In the 1950s and early 1960s local authority housing had accounted for well over half the total housing stock in the town. With new private housebuilding and local authority building-for-sale, this had declined to 30% by 1981 and little more than 20% by the mid-1990s. At the same time, the owner-occupied sector increased from 54% in 1961 to 63% in 1981 and 75% in 1995, above average for the country as a whole.

The financial squeeze on local authority housing provision is evident from completion rates during the 1980s (see Figure 6.7). In the early part of the 1980s completions fluctuated somewhat, but struggled to get above 200 to 300 a year. In 1988, for the first time in 40 years, there were no council houses built in Swindon. Soon after that, local authority provision ceased altogether, leaving only a small housing association building programme alongside private sector speculative housebuilding. Housing associations became active in the town from the early 1970s and have maintained a small though fluctuating output throughout the period. By 1995 there were just over 12,000 council houses in Thamesdown, down from a peak of 18,000, and just over 2,000 housing association properties. By the mid-1980s the waiting list for council housing was up to 3,500, and the council withdrew their key worker housing policy and moved from a date ordered allocation system to a points system. A high proportion of new council construction in this later period was smaller units for older people. This was in response to the increasing demand for this sort of accommodation from the mid-1970s on, but significantly as well, older persons accommodation was exempt from the Right to Buy and the Borough Council could therefore retain ownership.

Thamesdown was initially reluctant to go along with the Right to Buy legislation introduced in 1980 – employing, for example, delaying tactics such as refusing to supply tenants with application forms.   Following a short period of struggle with the DoE, however, the Council had to give way and began to process applications normally.   Applications to buy built up rapidly, encouraged by statutory discounts on market values.   However, Council house rents were also being driven up sharply by central government policy, including restrictions on the extent to which they could be subsidised by local authorities.   Rents were increased by between 20% and 40% in three successive years to 1981.   Sales therefore accelerated in the early years of the 1980s.   By the beginning of 1986 Thamesdown had sold almost 3,000 council houses (18% of the stock) and applications for a further 1,000 were being processed.   Sales rates varied in different parts of the town – Eldene and Liden, both higher quality mixed-tenure estates built in the 1970s, had sales rates of up to 45% of the stock. Subsequently, the pace of sales declined somewhat, but by the middle of 1996 5,800 council houses had been sold under the Right to Buy (32% of the total stock).   Again, the newer, mixed tenure estates such as Eldene, Liden and Toothill, had proved particularly popular, as had the rural areas.   A high proportion of older, generally lower quality council housing remains in local authority control; sales in areas such as Pinehurst and Penhill, built in the early phases of town expansion, have been relatively low.

With the decline in the council building programme and the loss of stock through the Right to Buy, various indicators of housing stress began to get worse.   The waiting list went up to 5,000 in the early 1980s, though declined thereafter, presumably as the prospects for many of actually securing council housing declined.   In 1996 the waiting list stood at 3,500, of which 900 were single people, the vast majority aged under 30.   Homelessness also increased throughout the 1980s.   In 1981 190 families were rehoused as homeless, representing around 10% of all lettings.   Homelessness then increased steadily for the mid-1980s (see Figure 6.8).   In each of the six years since 1989, around 500 families have been accepted as homeless and offered some kind of accommodation.   This typically represents less than one fifth of total applicants for official recognition as homeless – many of the remainder are classified as non-priority cases (young single people or childless couples) or as 'intentionally homeless'.   By

Table 6.7: Housing tenure, Swindon and Great Britain (1971-91) (%)

Year	Owner-occupied		Local authority rented		Private and housing association rented	
	Swindon	Great Britain	Swindon	Great Britain	Swindon	Great Britain
1971	60	51	30	31	10	19
1981	63	56	30	31	7	13
1991	73	66	18	21	9	13

1995 around a third of all lettings were to homeless families, while a further 400 families were living in temporary accommodation such as hostels. This in itself clearly demonstrates the shift in the role of the Council as a housing authority, even in what is on other indicators, a relatively prosperous town. As an indication of the growing volume of homelessness problems the homelessness section in the local authority has increased in staff numbers from 2 to 13 in the last 10 years. A further feature of the last few years has been the increasing numbers who are homeless as a result of mortgage arrears and repossessions, though the depressed housing market has also expanded the supply of private rented accommodation offered to the council on a short-term basis by owners unable to sell.

Figure 6.8: Homeless households, Thamesdown (1982-92)

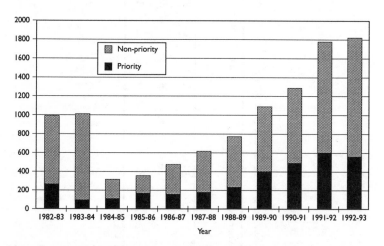

Note: Figures relate to numbers of households which approached Thamesdown Borough Council and those accepted and registered as homeless over the financial year.
Source: Thamesdown Borough Council

Complaints about the condition of much council housing in the Borough, with tenant organisations lobbying for increased spending on improvement and repairs, was a recurrent feature of the early 1980s. At this time spending on improvements to the existing stock was in competition with efforts to increase the supply of older persons' accommodation, where needs were also severe, in the context of declining resources. In 1986/87 spending on the existing council stock was £2.5m (compared with just over £1m on new building) out of a total capital programme of £9.5m. By 1994/95 spending on council house improvement was £3.5m, out of a total capital programme of £8.5m. It is evident that resources had not been sufficient to deal with the growing problems in the council stock. In 1995 almost 6,000 of the 12,200 council houses were identified as needing renovation, and 2,600 dwellings were designated as defective under the Housing Defects legislation and not yet reinstated (Housing Investment Programme, Needs Appraisal). Many of the latter were industrially built units, and required major works. The total cost of improving the whole stock was estimated as £16.5m (Thamesdown Borough Council, 1996).

Part of Swindon's problem had been its treatment under the government's housing finance allocation system. Because of its development activities, involving land sales for employment and housing development, plus a relatively high level of Right to Buy sales, capital receipts had been a major source of finance in the authority. As receipts are netted-off, the resources an authority is deemed to need under the Housing Investment Programme system, the authority's basic credit approval for new housing investment, has typically been low or non-existent. From Thamesdown's point of view they were unfairly penalised, as a high proportion of the capital receipts actually received from land sales had been recycled into supporting infrastructure provision, and were not in practice available for housing expenditure.

The private market (1980-96)

While the housing market nationally was fairly stagnant at the beginning of the 1980s, private sector housebuilding in Swindon continued to expand. Completions during the early 1980s were sustained at over 1,000 a year, dominated by building in the western expansion. As development in West Swindon proceeded, the tenure mix, however, shifted considerably from the Council's initial plans. While the first Toothill urban village contained around 35% council housing for rent, subsequent phases were primarily owner-occupied housing. Freshbrook was 90% and Westlea and Shaw were 100% owner-occupied. This was a function of the increasing role of private sector builders in the later stages where much of the land was owned by local builders Bradley or by Wimpey, and of the worsening financial position of the local housing authority. Generally, builders at this time were catering for middle of the market, where Ball (1980) suggests profit margins were extremely good. There was one small scheme for up-market housing. In 1984 King Homes completed a small scheme of luxury houses at Shaw, complete with recreational facilities for the occupants, ranging in price from £94,000 to £160,000 (a standard three-bedroom estate house at the time cost around £45,000 locally). Harloe (1987a) reports that by 1984 many of the prestigious London estate agents had opened offices in the area and that firms of executive relocation agents were also active. However, the attractions of Swindon for the expensive end of the housing market were clearly very limited. Most of the demand for executive upper income housing was being felt in the surrounding rural area, in towns such as Marlborough, Malmesbury, Devizes and Melksham. Throughout the early 1980s, builders locally were complaining that land supply problems were a major constraint. As much as anything this reflected the concentration of ownership of land allocated for development in the western expansion and other areas (a Borough Council report in 1984 estimated that 80% of private sector output was provided by just five developers). Smaller local builders were commonly seeking to build in the smaller towns and villages in the rural parts of the Borough where, however, strong restraint polices applied.

Total housing completions picked up rapidly with the booming market of the mid-1980s, to a peak of around 1,800 – 1980-88 was the peak period for output in west Swindon (see Figure 6.3). Thereafter, the slump in the housing market hit Swindon with a vengeance. Completions fell from just over 1,800 in 1986 to around 1,000 in 1989 and virtually stalling at a low point of around 350 by 1993. While Swindon had been largely insulated from the national housing market slump of the early 1980s, in the late 1980s and early 1990s it suffered dis-proportionately. In part this reflected the problems of land supply created by the hiatus in the northern development area. By 1990 the western expansion was nearing completion and housing completions there were down to a trickle, while protracted negotiations continued in the northern sector. It also, perhaps, reflects the high proportion of housing supplied by a small number of major housebuilders, whose individual decisions consequently have a big impact on total output. With prices falling in real terms and demand in a trough, there was little incentive for builders to bring houses onto the market.

At the beginning of the 1980s average house prices in Swindon were still low compared to both the South East and South West averages. As prices rose during the decade the gap narrowed. Between 1985 and 1988 average house prices almost doubled, although Swindon still remained cheaper than most of the rest of Wiltshire and the outer South East. Since then prices have declined sharply – by around 25% since the 1987/88 boom – and the latest Housing Market Report for the County detects few signs of recovery. Regional house price differentials are now much narrower, however, and Swindon is likely to be less attractive simply in terms of house prices to those working in the South East. But migration into the County has not declined much in recent years, despite recession and the reduced house price advantage. Houses in the northern development area started to became available in 1995 (Figure 6.3), and completions are expected to build up to around 400-500 houses a year in the latter part of the 1990s. The houses here are mainly for the mid-level, trade-up sector of the housing market. As families have moved into the northern sector, it has been reported that many 'for sale' signs have appeared in the western expansion; the feeling is that part of the early demand for houses in the north has been from those trading up within the Borough.

The enabling local authority?

In the context of public expenditure cuts and shifting central government policy Thamesdown was forced to consider ways of meeting housing needs other than building council housing for rent. Current efforts are focused on partnership with housing associations and private sector builders. As noted earlier, the Council has, for many years, had a policy of building-for-sale and working in partnership with the private sector, though generally in a situation where land ownership offered them a high degree of control. Since 1971 over 2,000 houses have been produced through the 'nominated purchaser' and build-for-sale schemes, typically offering a small discount on market price together with a 100% local authority mortgage. The successful partnership scheme with housing developers, Rendells, in the late 1970s produced 400 homes at Eldene, Liden and Toothill on land made available by the local authority. A further scheme in 1986 involved a partnership with development group PROBE (involving Lovells, the Nationwide and Halifax Building Societies), producing 300 homes for single people and first-time buyers built on redundant school land bought from the County Council. More recently, projects with Lovells and Crest have involved low cost ownership schemes, where Thamesdown provides the land and maintains a 30% equity share in the finished houses. Diminishing local authority land stocks have been a constraint on further activity. A partnership with five or six housing associations locally is supported by Local Authority Housing Association Grant, although this is declining in value, partly as capital receipts from land and house sales dry up. The main current project is a housing association consortium development on part of the old railway works (Tarmac) site, expected to produce 80 units. There is also a Foyer project planned, offering homes and training for 60 16-24-year-olds. These represent innovative projects. They are, however, even in total, clearly very small in scale compared both to the kinds of council house building programme undertaken in the past, and to the scale of housing needs being expressed in the Borough.

A housing needs survey carried out by consultants for the Borough in 1994 revealed around 6,000 households in serious housing need, but unable to afford a mortgage, of which 2,400 were concealed households (typically families and couples sharing with others) unable to afford a mortgage. This information was being used to underpin the use of planning powers to require a contribution of affordable housing from all new residential development. An overall target of 2,000 for the remainder of the local plan period (to 2001) was set. The major difficulty with this was that the northern development area, which represented the main new source of houses in the Borough, gained permission before the change in government advice in PPG3 allowed planning authorities to negotiate affordable housing on private sector housing sites. While some land here may be made available to housing associations (presumably at market value) its contribution overall will not be great.

The late 1990s thus saw the housing market in Swindon almost totally dominated by national housebuilding companies. Land supply was even more concentrated in relatively few hands.

This represented the culmination of a trend that goes back to the early 1980s, when the housing market in Swindon was being described as providing a 'safety valve' for housing pressures generated in the South East (Harloe and Boddy, 1988). Speculative developers had been positioning themselves for a new round of expansion. The local authority role, on the other hand, was very much that of fire fighting, using planning powers and engaging in strategic planning debates at county and regional level to try and hold the line against development pressures.

Since the 1950s and 1960s, as argued earlier, the development of Swindon has moved from an 'employment-driven' model to a model which is increasingly dependent on housing-led growth. As a senior planning officer in the Borough Council observed in 1996:

> "The history of the last 15 to 20 years of housing development has been entirely speculatively driven.... From a planning point of view we try to keep things in balance ... there needs to be a balance between employment land and housing, but the reality on the ground is if the developers think they can get permission anywhere, they'll go for it, and that's really the history of it."

Alongside this, there has been a major decline in the resources available to the local authority to control or participate in development. Unusually, perhaps, for a Labour-controlled local authority, the Council in Swindon had, for many years, followed a housing policy which aimed to secure a high level of owner-occupation, including build-for-sale schemes and land disposals to private developers. By the 1990s, however, the proportion of owner-occupation in the Borough actually exceeded the national average. The stock of local authority-owned housing remains significant, much of it, however, as noted, in need of improvement and modernisation. Capital expenditure controls, and from 1997 new 'rent-capping' controls in the public sector severely restrict the ability of the local authority to spend on the existing housing stock. In this context a policy of disposing of the council stock (to a housing association or Local Housing Company under the terms of the 1996 Housing Act), while politically unpalatable, may become unavoidable.

The shift, overall, in terms of the local authority role as housing developer and housing authority is clear.   Where previously it was expansionist, development-oriented and outward looking, it is now, essentially, inward-looking and preoccupied essentially with housing problems, with unmet needs within the Borough and with a deteriorating council-owned housing stock. Housing policy issues, so far as the Borough Council is concerned, are now increasingly issues of housing need and increasingly bound up with social issues more generally.   Chapter Seven goes on to address such issues in the context of the models of social policy and social development built in to the town's postwar expansion and the impacts, more generally of social change over this period.

seven

Social policy and social change

Economic transformation in the postwar period has been mirrored by equally far reaching change in terms of social structure across the country as a whole. Within Swindon, economic change, physical expansion and population growth on a massive scale (described in earlier chapters) have been reflected in major shifts, locally, in social structure, patterns of social change and ways of life. This in turn has provided the context for social policy and for the provision of social and community infrastructure and support in Swindon which has been framed in response to the massive scale of physical expansion and population growth over the last 25 years. Swindon is notable for the fact that very active and explicit commitment to social and community development represented an integral component of policy at the local level throughout the postwar period. As with strategy in relation to economic development and physical expansion, however, there have been significant shifts in direction over time.

Strategies for social and community development were initially framed in the early postwar years in relation to the new expansion areas and the integration of the in-migrant population. They were further developed and formalised in plans for further expansion set out in the *Silver Book* in 1968 which represents something of a baseline against which to judge what has been achieved in subsequent decades. By the early 1980s and with the policy rethink around *A new vision for Thamesdown*, there was increasing concern over levels of provision and support in relation to the existing population and older communities. Most recently, with Swindon gaining unitary status in 1997, the Borough Council took over responsibility for education and social services, representing major, high-budget areas of social and community-based service provision in their own right. Established forms of social and community provision and support were redefined and restructured, dwarfed by these new statutory services. Having looked in some detail in previous chapters at the economic and physical expansion of the town and the planned development of industry and housing, this chapter focuses in more detail on issues of social development and patterns of social change. As with issues around economic and physical growth, the scale and pro-active support of town expansion and development raises key issues in terms of social and community development and patterns and processes of social change, which are of considerable relevance to broader debates.

Postwar expansion and social development

Commitment to town expansion in the early postwar years was based on a firm belief in the benefits of economic growth and diversification linked to national policies of overspill and population dispersal. These were seen as essential to Swindon's survival and ultimate prosperity. The benefits of growth both to existing and new residents in terms of jobs, amenities and housing were clear. However, growth and physical expansion, with widespread upheaval and transitional problems, also brought with it a variety of social pressures and concerns. Harloe (1975) describes how, in this context, social and community policy was primarily focused on the newcomers who came to Swindon from London:

> ... All these benefits might have counted for very little if the influx of newcomers had so disrupted town society that the attitudes of hostility and bitterness resulted. So it was inevitable that most of the social development programme was directed towards the newcomers, rather than towards the existing inhabitants who presumably had already achieved a stable pattern of social life in the town. In other words, the main problem thought to exist was one of integrating the

> immigrants into the existing way of life in the
> town. (Harloe, 1975, p 100)

The new in-migrants faced a range of difficult social issues on their relocation to Swindon. Many were very satisfied with the improvement in terms of housing compared with their former circumstances. A survey carried out in the early 1960s (Cullingworth, 1961), however, suggested widespread feelings of insecurity associated with a fairly limited local labour market and some dissatisfaction with the terms and conditions of employment in Swindon as compared to London. The newcomers also felt that the town lacked amenities and reported a sense of isolation. This was noted as a particular problem for women who tended to be 'home alone' during the day with limited social contact.

With levels of wages in Swindon less than in London and increased expenditure associated with furnishing a new home, financial pressures were reported to have increased. This often meant that many women had to seek work in order to help pay the bills and Harloe (1975, p 104) noted that, "the remarkable increase in the number of working women in the town was one of the most striking results of expansion". While he described how this new trend might have helped to relieve the boredom and isolation faced by women at home all day, this might have caused further stresses in some households where the employment of both partners may have brought with it new pressures and strains on childcare and family relationships.

In policy terms, the provision was oriented to the needs of these new arrivals and integrating them as fully as possible into the existing community. The Borough sought to encourage a cohesive and integrated community through the active involvement of neighbourhood workers whose remit was to bring people together by encouraging local group activities. They were also an initial point of contact, welcomed new arrivals, provided information about the town and answered queries from newcomers. While similar approaches were developed in fully fledged New Towns, this represented an innovative and distinctive part of Swindon's approach to community development at the time. Multi-purpose 'common rooms' were provided on each estate, owned by the Council, and made available to local groups as a place to meet and develop local contacts. They were also used for clinics and public meetings and were intended to form a central community resource and focal point within each local area. These forms of provision reflected the particular philosophy under-pinning social development policy at the time summarised by the social development officer (quoted in Harloe, 1975, p 119):

1. *Freedom* – that a 'free' or 'plural' society was the desirable end or aim ...

2. *Control* – that nevertheless some degree of control by the local authority was necessary if a stable community was to result. The control proposed in this respect was to retain ownership of accom-modation and some degree of selectivity as to user.

3. *Stimulus* – that some stimulus would be required to encourage the most rapid community development of the new neighbourhood units by providing during the formative periods: (a) somewhere to go; (b) some-where to turn to for help ... 'the someone to turn to' was to be met by providing neighbourhood workers who were qualified social workers resident on estates during the formative years but essentially temporary in nature, working to produce a stable community from which they could ultimately be withdrawn.

4. *Integration* – that hostility should be avoided between new communities on the new neighbourhood units on the one had and the existing social pattern of the railway town on the other.

The Borough Council attempted to ensure integration of newcomers and to create social balance between older and newer residents by avoiding concentrating newcomers in particular parts of the town. It aimed to disperse housing applicants across the town so that the full public housing stock was used for accom-modating newcomers and applications from existing residents alike. Both established residents and newcomers were therefore given access to older and newer housing.

The underlying assumptions of this model were that the local authority could and should intervene to reduce potential social conflict and should retain control of community assets on behalf of the community as a whole. As Harloe (1975) notes, there have been numerous criticisms made of this model on the grounds that it is paternalistic, elitist and disempowering for local residents. According to some critics, this type of model is essentially a recipe for social control by the local Council. In some ways, it is perhaps unsurprising that this was the model originally adopted with the first expansion of the town. It may be seen as paralleling the paternalistic policies of the former GWR which had so permeated the culture and ethos of the town and its leaders up to this point. Just as the GWR had largely sought to provide for both the economic and social livelihood of the residents of Swindon, so the local Council consciously sought to save the town from anticipated economic and social degradation associated with its decline. Indeed, a significant number of elected Councillors at the time were drawn from the ranks of the former GWR or had close links with it and may well have absorbed from their GWR experience this more extensive type of provision and intervention as necessary components of stability in the town.

Commitment to integrating newcomers and existing residents by means of housing allocation policies was judged to have achieved a degree of success at least in the earlier years of planned expansion. Neighbourhood workers and locally based community provision were also widely thought of as a valuable contributions to meeting the needs of individuals. Other aspects were more open to question (Harloe, 1975). The basic premise that the Council should itself be a controlling authority which provided for local social needs according to its own perceptions of what those needs were was one issue. Policy also focused on areas where the Council could clearly have a powerful influence such as domestic, leisure and planning issues. Actively trying to attract and retain employers, the Council refrained from involvement in potentially contentious issues, such as working conditions and terms of employment which concerned some newcomers in particular. There was also a degree of inflexibility in implementing the policy. Where ideal solutions were not forthcoming because of financial or political constraints (eg, in the provision of community rooms and play areas for some areas such as Penhill), there was some unwillingness to consider other solutions which might have met needs on a temporary basis.

There were also problems arising from the split in service provision between the Borough and County Councils. The Borough had responsibility and a degree of control over housing and community provision, while the County dealt with other key areas such as education, health and welfare. While coordinated effort across these service areas would have potentially been most effective, consultation and effective joint working between the two local authorities was limited. Indeed, both political and budgetary barriers hindered the adequate provision of services to support the social infrastructure of the growing population. Politically, moreover, the County was unwilling to support levels of provision which it perceived would disproportionately benefit Swindon at the expense of other areas of Wiltshire. This meant that key aspects of the social needs of the expanding town were less adequately met. Harloe (1975) described how particular conflicts arose between the Borough and County Councils over provision of services such as hospitals and education and indeed these continue to be important issues in the current context of Swindon which have yet to be resolved satisfactorily.

Tension between the local authorities was further exacerbated by central government policies. Educational provision was an important example of this. The Ministry of Education, faced with public expenditure cutbacks, would not sanction the construction of new schools in the expanding areas of Swindon. The argument was that more schools should not be built until the students were actually in place and requiring more space. The underlying logic of this was that service provision should rise to meet demand rather than anticipate it. Problems arose, however, in that school provision then tended to lag behind demand. The construction of new schools required a period of approximately three years during which time local capacity in the expanding areas fell short of the necessary places. This led to a situation in which students had to be bussed around Swindon to attend schools with spare capacity outside their local area:

> The first school, far from being available at or near the start of development was opened just about the same time as the last houses were completed. The other schools took even longer to arrive. Meanwhile the children had to be taken by bus to other parts of the town where there were places available. To some extent this was reasonable, but the early educational planning was so ineffective that these schools soon became overcrowded, and it is likely that the standards of education in the town were adversely affected. (Harloe, 1975, p 113)

The County Council was itself unwilling to recognise that Swindon should receive an additional allocation from the education budget for more teaching staff or schools. This was again related to the perception that Swindon should not receive more provision at the expense of the rest of the County. Both national government and the County Council were thus unwilling to accept that the expanding town faced quite exceptional circumstances and needed special provision to cater for the needs of a rapidly growing population. Short-term thinking, economic constraints and political sensitivities appear, therefore, to have precluded meeting the longer term interests of Swindon as perceived by the town's leaders at the time.

The new city and the western expansion

The *Silver Book* proposals which framed the second phase of expansion from the early 1970s set out a blueprint for 'success' in terms of social development and identified criteria against which this could be measured. The *Silver Book* also sought explicitly to incorporate the lessons learned from the previous experience of town expansion. The overall approach was encapsulated in the notion of a 'hierarchy' of interlocking systems of social provision which would address different types of individual and social needs. These ideas were reflected in the physical and community planning of the later stages of development in East Swindon but also particularly in the western expansion. Greater emphasis on integrated systems of social provision and on involving a variety of different agencies to deliver social welfare services marked a break from the previous 'go it alone' strategy of the Council.

A three-level hierarchy of social provision included urban villages, district centres and the town centre itself. At the lowest level, the urban village was envisaged as a means of satisfying the most immediate needs of individuals within their own local area. At the heart of the urban village was a neighbourhood centre which would serve a specified number of households and provide primary and middle schools, basic medical facilities, play areas, local shops and a pub. Also to be located there was the multi-purpose meeting space for community activities, an element carried through from the first phase of expansion. The idea was to provide a sense of identity, distinctiveness and cohesion to new housing estates in order to facilitate community development. Each 'village' was to be individually named and "different in character to the others so far as this is practicable" (Swindon Borough Council et al, 1968, p 97). The architects of this approach were keen, however, to point out that while each village was to provide for the needs of local residents, they were not intended, "to convey the impression that an attempt is being made to create within a town a number of self-contained and introvert communities with a social life based upon a community centre..." (Swindon Borough Council et al, 1968, p 97). This was viewed as a model which had previously been attempted elsewhere and discredited. The role of neighbourhood workers developed in East Swindon and described by the *Silver Book* as "of great value" in integrating new arrivals into the town was also incorporated into developments in West Swindon.

The urban village, with its mix of housing types and tenure, was an attempt to rectify problems identified with earlier housing and social provision in the eastern expansion. As explained by a local authority officer in 1996:

> *"They physically planned West Swindon dif-*
> *ferently, deliberately, this urban village concept,*
> *than they had in the east. That was one reaction*
> *to the inadequacies and the other one was the ...*
> *planning to put in the social infrastructure as well,*
> *you know, recognising that that need, that*
> *something needed to be done to make it move on*
> *faster. And I think the provision here was an*
> *effort to make it happen faster you know, to speed*
> *a process up."*

The emphasis on creating 'balanced communities' through integration of newcomers and established residents was also carried through into the western expansion. Additional attempts were made to disperse those from the same areas of London or working for the same employers and to achieve a mix in terms of age and 'social class' within each community. According to the *Silver Book*:

> Various studies indicate that one of the main
> disadvantages of previous developments has been
> the failure to achieve a balanced community, both
> with respect to age composition and social class.

The former problem requires action to attract a wider age range although it is recognised that the possibilities for doing this are limited. It is proposed to minimise the latter by creating within each village separate estates of houses for letting, local authority houses built for sale, and private enterprise houses.... (Swindon Borough Council et al, 1968, p 98)

Key features of the second phase of expansion in West Swindon, therefore, were the attempt to design balanced communities by bringing together people from diverse social backgrounds and ensuring that social balance was achieved by planning housing of mixed tenures in each area. While it was acknowledged that this alone would not necessarily break down social barriers, it was felt that positive interaction and integration of people from different social backgrounds would most likely be achieved by bringing them together in the same urban villages.

District centres, the second level of the hierarchy, were to provide social amenities on a larger scale to meet the needs of groups of urban villages. Facilities such as comprehensive schools, swimming pools and libraries which would require a larger population than an urban village to sustain them would be located at this level, alongside retail provision. Overall, the district centre was envisaged as the focus where most of the routine needs of residents of the district would be met. In the early years of the western expansion, the need to attract a more diverse range of employers to the area was increasingly apparent. The Council identified the need for showpiece amenities as a means to 'sell' Swindon to potential inward investors. Recreation and leisure facilities provided at district level played an important role in the Council's strategy both of creating a desirable environment in which to live and work and of persuading employers that Swindon was the sort of place to which key workers could be persuaded to move and where they could successfully recruit in order to meet future needs. As one former Councillor commented in 1996:

> "*I mean the policy of Swindon when it comes to the expansion as a whole was really, to get the commerce and industry to come here, you've got to sell it to them, haven't you? I mean with all the advertising.... But we had to encourage people*

> *to come here and want to set up industry and
> commerce.... So we used, I mean we used to take
> them round in a coach. Take them over the golf
> course, down the Oasis, and museums, you know,
> whatever. Put a day on, a show.... [They would
> say] our employees want to be able to do things in
> their own time. What can you offer? And like
> down to the swimming facilities, golfing, cricket,
> you name it, football pitches, everything. We
> showed them round and they liked it, and they
> came."*

This view was shared by a senior officer of the authority:

> *"When Swindon decided to rescue itself from what
> would have been the demise of the railway, and
> the demise of car manufacturing, as it was thought
> it was going to be,... in attracting new industry
> and new service sector people, it was based on
> relocation, or people ... investing here. It was
> obviously key that the facilities there were here ...
> there had to be things to show them, places like
> Oasis and Link, all the landscaping, it had to give
> the impression of somewhere that was a good
> environment. I have to say, it's a bit cosmetic in
> places because not all of the infrastructure has
> survived or kept up with the pace of development,
> but outwardly it looks like a fairly good place for
> young families, which is obviously what the key
> is."*

The town centre, the third and final level of the hierarchy, was
envisaged in the *Silver Book* as the major focus for shopping and
commercial activities serving both the wider town and subregion
planned in anticipation of a projected population of around
240,000 by 1986 and 300,000 by the year 2001. A major health
centre with offices for associated social services was part of this
original vision for the town centre. The town centre was also
planned to include a new civic centre which would contain, "a
new library, arts centre, museum, art gallery and civic hall"
(Swindon Borough Council et al, 1968, p 99).

   In terms of overall approach, the *Silver Book* anticipated
increased joint working between agencies providing social and

community welfare services. The proposed link between medical facilities and social services offices was one obvious attempt to improve communications between agencies and to encourage a more holistic approach to meeting the needs of local people. It also specifically set out a model of service provision which would entail closer working relationships between local voluntary agencies and the statutory authorities in delivering social welfare services:

> Liaison with the other bodies concerned with meeting the social and spiritual needs of a very rapidly rising population is however seen to be of equal importance [to the services provided by local authorities] and machinery for this purpose should be established as soon as possible. In this connection great benefit would be derived from the establishment of a Council of Social Service or a Community Council representing and co-ordinating the many voluntary social organisations which will be involved. (Swindon Borough Council et al, 1968, p 100)

The voluntary sector was seen as particularly important in ensuring that new areas of social need were identified and addressed. Its role was perceived of as catalytic in meeting the demand for new services ahead of the local authorities and demonstrating needs which might subsequently be met by mainstream statutory provision. It was recognised that to make this joint model of social welfare provision work, a significant amount of coordination would be required to avoid overlap and duplication of activities between the public and voluntary sectors as well as between services provided by different voluntary bodies. The active involvement of a body such as a community council or council of social service was seen as essential as it would be in an 'ideal position to oversee the whole field' and therefore to adopt this coordinating role. Other parts of the document suggested the possibility of integrating a number of different social, health and welfare organisations and the viability of this type of model was also explored:

> The Communicare experiment which has been initiated at Killingworth New Town attempts to meet within a single framework those needs of

> the community which are elsewhere met by
> uncoordinated health and welfare organisations.
> This is perhaps an ideal solution and one which
> may not be wholly attainable in practice, but in
> Killingworth at least the work of organisations
> providing material and spiritual welfare has been
> more closely integrated with the aim of producing
> a more efficient and more effective service. In
> view of the radical nature of this experiment,
> representing as it does a marked advance in social
> thinking, it is suggested that serious consideration
> should be given to a similar arrangement in
> Swindon. (Swindon Borough Council et al, 1968,
> p 113)

These recommendations all suggest a policy shift towards a model
of local authority working which valued the combined but
distinctive efforts of a range of different players in service
provision. This was something of a departure from the earlier
postwar model of development in which the Borough was less
concerned with working closely with other actors in planning and
implementing social welfare provision. This, then, was the policy
framework which was intended to serve as the strategy for social
development into at least the early 1980s. It provided a statement
of principle and approach by the Council which has not been
repeated since.   The extent to which this vision has been
successfully achieved is explored in greater detail later in the
chapter. By the early 1980s, however, the local authority's own
circumstances had changed.   Its resources were starting to be
squeezed, including its capacity for capital expenditure. The local
authority was also aware from its experience in West Swindon that
its ability to provide the full compliment of social provision
necessary for effective town expansion in isolation was limited.
Here, therefore, we can look briefly at developments in North
Swindon representing the latest phase of expansion.

The northern expansion

As described in previous chapters, the Borough Council was much
less proactively involved in the northern expansion and had indeed

opposed it initially, albeit partly on tactical grounds, along with the County Council. In the context of the early 1980s the Borough's capacity to steer the development process was much diminished. As noted in previous chapters, moreover, belief in the obvious benefits, both economic and social, of continued expansion, was also starting to be questioned. There was growing concern that levels of social and community-based provision had fallen behind the economic and physical expansion of the town. There was also concern that provision and support for older areas of the town and longer established communities had suffered through the concentration of resources and effort on the needs of the expanding areas and new communities. The perceived need for a period of consolidation or catching-up developed as much from a concern over social and community provision in the town as from anxieties over the impacts of continued economic development and physical expansion.

The framework was being established, meanwhile, for a third phase of major expansion, led and steered largely by the private sector. The powers and influence of the Borough Council were much reduced compared with earlier phases of expansion. In terms of social and community provision, moreover, it had fewer resources, less enthusiasm and a somewhat ambiguous sense of where this growth fitted into any overall plan for Swindon's future. In terms of physical planning as such, the Borough Council had established a master plan for the northern expansion. This set out an overall model for development similar to that of West Swindon, with 'urban villages', neighbourhood centres and a district centre. It represented at one level, then, the final stage of the *Silver Book* proposals. There were major question marks, however, over the capacity of the Borough Council to deliver the forms of social and community provision and to carry through into this final phase of development the philosophy underpinning the original *Silver Book* proposals. *A new vision*, in effect, stated just this – with the northern expansion, the Council had lost the capacity to implement social and community development in line with its long-standing aspirations. A local authority officer described in 1996 how the new development had been taking place without a sense of corporate mission and purpose underlying the workings of different Council departments.

> "... *I mean if you said to me, give me a copy of your corporate strategy, I'd give you one, but the*

> *health warning that I would personally put on*
> *that is that it's in a sense, it's something that is*
> *basically a staple through a lot of departmental*
> *statements. There's nothing ... so it's interesting*
> *really ... how come it's been a successful local*
> *authority.... It's been riding on the back of a*
> *vision that was created as much as forty years*
> *ago."*

Coinciding with the latest expansion and offering a new power
base from which to create and implement policy is the move to
unitary authority status and the creation of Swindon Council in
April 1997. While this means that more control over service
provision will ultimately rest with the Borough, the transitional
phase was described as both time consuming and destabilising for
members and officers of the local authority. At the same time, a
major restructuring of the Council was also undertaken which
itself made it difficult to take forward plans at the strategic level.
In relation to social development specifically, this period of change
and upheaval has meant that the level of resources available for the
types of social and community development work which the
Borough has traditionally undertaken remains uncertain. Despite
these potential concerns, Council officers and elected members
have expressed their enthusiasm for the opportunities presented by
unitary status to embark on more integrated planning and service
delivery for social welfare and to work in close collaboration with
other service providers.

> *"... On the positive side ... the opportunities to*
> *work very closely with social services and*
> *education are tremendous. We've tried to build*
> *those relationships in the past and there always*
> *has been this sort of Chinese wall of we work for*
> *the County and we work for the Borough. At the*
> *management level, there's been very good*
> *relationships but that's been soured by the*
> *political dimension.... So I think that the break*
> *from the County is excellent.... The opportunity*
> *for us to work with social services and education*
> *in that enabling role, the partnership role ... is*
> *very good."*

As part of the restructuring process, the community development department of the Council which has, in various guises, over the years, been responsible for the management of the neighbourhood workers, supporting the voluntary sector, the provision and maintenance of community buildings, the development of a play service and the overseeing of equal opportunities initiatives in Swindon, has been merged with the leisure services department. The new community and leisure services department will be accountable to a Council committee of the same name and will merge the activities of the two former departments as well as acquiring a new remit for youth and community services and library services which have previously been under the auspices of the County.

The community development department and leisure services had both played a key role in the Borough's strategy for social development in West Swindon from the late 1960s and early 1970s. The precursor of the community development department, the social development section, was also closely involved with the planning and implementation of social facilities and the fostering of community networks as far back as the first expansion in the 1950s. The priority attached to each of these functions by the Council is clearly demonstrated by their continued commitment to maintaining the substantial budget allocations made to them, even during periods of financial stress. For example, while both departments suffered cutbacks in the Council-wide budget reductions of 1992, neither was disproportionately affected in relation to other departments despite the fact that both are defined as areas of 'discretionary spending'. This means that while the Council was not obliged to provide services in these areas statutorily, it has chosen to do so as part of an ongoing commitment to leisure and community development activities in Swindon. A question remains, however, as to future priority to be attached to the new department specifically because of its largely discretionary nature. In the light of the incorporation of the major mainstream statutory services represented by education and social services into the new Council, both of which are priority areas for social spending and are service areas which the Council is obliged to resource, the funding available for traditional leisure and community development facilities may be more vulnerable to budget restrictions in future. It may therefore be that while leisure services and community development have been prioritised as important players in the past, they may fare less well in the future when they are forced to compete for resources with education and social services.

The wider regional context of social welfare provision has also been one of upheaval and transition with restructuring occurring in the district health authorities as well as Wiltshire's social services department. This period of flux and uncertainty among three of the key actors providing and funding social welfare provision in the area has reportedly impeded progress towards strategic and coordinated planning. As one voluntary sector representative observed, this has had important implications for voluntary sector providers which need to liaise closely with these organisations and rely upon them to a large extent for their funding.

> "... An amazing thing that has happened in recent history is the enormous changes in the local statutories and we are just going through the third one now. The health authorities have organised and reorganised, social services has reorganised, and now the Borough is. And if you look for consistent personnel in those departments, those key departments ... you will find them thin on the ground. And if you look for consistent policies as well.... [We've] rung up to find desks not staffed, policies changed, nobody can give answers, 'because we are in the middle of changing'. It's been horrendous really. We've been trying to relate to such a moving target that it's, there's been no opportunities for development...."

In addition to these changes, the broader national policy framework within which local authorities are (to a greater or lesser extent) striving to operate involves an attempt to move towards 'enabling' others to provide services rather then providing services directly themselves. Coinciding with this has been a new emphasis on the marketisation of services and the imposition of new ways of working, such as compulsory competitive tendering, the purchaser–provider split and greater emphasis on input from service users in the planning, purchasing and evaluation of the services they receive.

Comparing this new context for local authorities to the ways in which the Borough has traditionally tended to operate, these ideas do not fit easily within the conceptual framework which has guided much of the Council's actions throughout the past 50 years. There are therefore a number of challenges and tensions which the new Council must confront in its move to unitary authority status. Not least of these will be the conflict of moving towards a stronger and more coherent power base while simultaneously being constrained to operate within this new environment in which enabling rather than providing is the goal. A local authority officer described these challenges in the following way:

> *"... It's going to be a changing environment for us. I don't think we'll any longer be seen as the bricks and mortar provider. We might move much more into an enabling role. Helping get the best out of the community, or helping them get the best out of the community because if we're not careful, if we carried on the way we are, you could almost be back to the nanny state again where the Council will provide and we'll do everything.... We'll have to be much more willing to be a willing partner with other people, whereas I think in the past the Council's taken the lead, and 'We are the Council, we're in charge, we will do it!' Now we're going to have much closer partnerships with other agencies and other groups."*

The question then remains as to how these policy shifts might affect the planning and implementation of social development policies in Swindon and how this will particularly impact on the latest phase of expansion in the northern sector. In theory, the northern sector should benefit greatly from lessons learned in the two previous phases of expansion in Swindon. However, as the national policy framework has imposed increasing constraints on the autonomy of local authorities and the Borough's own access and ability to use resources has decreased, it is potentially no longer in a position to act upon all of the lessons it has learned.

Several aspects of social provision in this phase of expansion are therefore different to earlier approaches, by necessity more than design. For example, a basic tenet of both of the previous expansions was the policy of 'dispersal' whereby people of different ages and socio-economic status should be integrated together in each area by providing housing of mixed tenures. This was seen as a means of minimising social conflict as well as avoiding potential structural problems which might arise if a demographic balance was not achieved in each new area. While this did not necessarily work out perfectly in practice, it was nevertheless established as a key goal for successful social development. In the current expansion, however, the estate is to be almost entirely private, owner-occupied housing with the 'social mix' determined essentially by market forces combined with the strategy of the developers in terms of the types of housing they build.

Similarly, while previous experience has highlighted the importance of providing the social infrastructure and community facilities at the earliest possible stage in the new area's development, the Borough cannot dictate precisely when these facilities are to be provided in the northern sector. As development is expected to occur at a fairly slow pace in the area, the social implications in terms of isolation and the lack of a comprehensive social infrastructure has been identified by some local policy makers as a source of concern:

> "Northern sector is almost entirely privately owned, and so the developers come with their massive structure plan and planning application, and we're working hard ... to say, 'But where's the leisure provision, where's the social provision?' And it's very difficult because the developer is obviously trying to do the least he can to satisfy us, whereas we were trying to do the best we could in the early days.... It's based on the chimney pot thing. As you get 200 chimney pots you get another acre of land, and when you get 1,000 chimney pots, you get a library or something. Now because of the recession, the northern sector is happening very slowly. It's not a great mushroom development anymore, it's a very slow, controlled one. It'll be years before some of those facilities actually arrive.... If you don't put good facilities early in the stream, you finish up with a

very difficult housing situation, with very lonely,
very detached people...."

The issue here is similar to that discussed in relation to educational provision in the previous expansions. That is, while it is recognised that services need to be planned for and in some senses provided at the outset of a new community area, until some milestone is reached in the area's growth, provision is deemed unfeasible or unacceptable. While in the eastern expansion the Borough was having to negotiate with the County and national officials over provision of more resources for expanding areas, in the case of the northern expansion, the Borough is having to negotiate with private developers. In both cases, local leaders could clearly see what was required and had the will to provide it. They could not, however, do so in isolation and had to rely on the resource input of others whose focus and motivations were less exclusively linked to the well being of the Borough's residents. In the current context, a policy officer described the challenges and tensions of making private sector developers responsible for providing community facilities in the new areas.

> *"You can't pursue the developers to do as much as*
> *we would have done if we'd been controlling it,*
> *because it was eating into their profits. So they*
> *know they have a social responsibility and they*
> *have to do something, but they'll do the least they*
> *can."*

The role of the neighbourhood workers in facilitating community development will also change, having been largely cut back to that of information provider. Indeed, by 1997 there was only one part-time neighbourhood worker in the area and their remit was largely to provide information and 'welcome packs' rather than as was previously the case, to combine the role of social worker, community network facilitator and information provider in one. The paring down of provision is largely a response to the limited resources available for this work and alternative methods of encouraging community development and financing community facilities were being considered.

> *"The developers will be providing the physical kit*
> *as it were, what we then have to resource are the*
> *revenue and running costs and the support to*

> *enable that to happen and I think we have to*
> *acknowledge that it is increasingly difficult.... So*
> *we are looking at what else we can do, what other*
> *sort of models are there for enabling local people*
> *to have proper meeting places and come together*
> *and own and control that with increased*
> *support.... I think of necessity we will have to*
> *look at how those [community buildings] are*
> *resourced and managed. It may mean shifting*
> *resources around; we haven't to date looked at*
> *how else will we provide support if we don't get*
> *extra staff resources up there. The expectation*
> *and the hope and the anticipation is that*
> *eventually we will."*

These issues clearly demonstrate the current constraints on the Council to implement fully the lessons of the past. While policy officers are therefore clear about the potential implications of delayed or inadequate social facilities in the newly developing areas, they cannot access sufficient resources to rectify the situation.

To sum up, the model of social provision sustained by the Council from the early postwar years was, to some extent, inherited from the GWR and refined over the years into the vision which was articulated most clearly in the *Silver Book*. This approach had not, however, been explicitly or comprehensively redefined in the light of changing circumstances. The extent to which the Council's approach remains appropriate has been questioned both by officers and elected members of the former Thamesdown Borough Council:

> *"It's always had a paternalistic attitude, and this*
> *goes back to the Great Western Railway days.*
> *They were paternalistic, they provided houses,*
> *hospitals, schools, whatever. Their workers, and*
> *of course the people when this authority was first*
> *created back at the beginning of this century, the*
> *people that became Councillors, that's where they*
> *came from, because that was the biggest employer*
> *in town. And so they came with those sort of*
> *attitudes, and this Council has always been to*
> *some extent a paternalistic organisation. And it is*

> *finding it difficult to adjust to economic realities, I suppose, of the late 20th Century, when the provision of social facilities is not seen as a very high priority."*

There are clear signs that this earlier model of community development and the provision of extensive social support and active intervention by the Council is no longer sustainable. This is both because of economic constraints which preclude the effective implementation of this sort of model and because it is seen as an attempt to cling on to historic models of extensive municipal and state provision which, in the current context, are losing their appeal and support. However, there is evidence of a degree of underlying conflict between those who would still like to see Swindon carry on in this role as extensive social provider and others who would seek to find new solutions and create a new model of social provision, potentially with increased involvement from other types of providers.

> *"Community development, to some extent, has not lost its way, but has become a bit less fashionable than it was.... Its ... resources have been cut back over recent years in real terms and it seeks the kind of focus on maintenance of what exists.... It used to be much more of a catalytic role and the reason why it can't be so much of a catalyst, there's nothing to actually kind of come onto the catalyst. There are no government funds.... So again, it's almost like we're forced into the stresses of consolidation. It has been growing, it has been kind of maintaining community groups, the ethos of people's self-development, group development.... I think it has big ideas, but it's got less kind of opportunity to actually take them forward at the moment.... And if it sees a new idea that it wants to take forward and support, it very often has to come back on an old idea. And that old idea may still be valid, but it has to, it may not be so much kind of appeal, so it is much harder to achieve things...."*

The Borough Council has thus been actively involved in social and community development as an integral component of economic development and town expansion since the early postwar years. Much has been achieved in terms of patterns of social and community infrastructure and leisure facilities. At the same time, provision has tended towards paternalism, implementing a particular model of social and community development in line with the Borough's perception of appropriate forms of action and intervention. More recently, both the vision and the means of achieving it have been challenged by economic constraints and indeed by social change and different ideologies of social and community development. These have caused the Council to re-evaluate its own power base, to reconsider its own goals and to seek new methods of meeting its aims. The transition to unitary authority status provided the opportunity for restructuring and redefinition of priorities. It is too early, as yet, to discern what this will mean in practical terms. While this is evident across the Council as a whole, it is perhaps particularly so in the area of social policy and welfare provision, where major new services will come under the Council's remit and existing providers in the form of the new community and leisure services department will face new challenges to its traditional place and role within the Council.

Social change

Having looked in some detail at the development of social policy and social provision in Swindon, the rest of this chapter focuses on patterns of social change and key social issues on the ground. In doing so, it considers in particular patterns of social integration and social exclusion in the context of Swindon as an economically buoyant and relatively prosperous locality. It adds, therefore, to national debates around social integration and exclusion. Swindon, as described in earlier chapters, is clearly, at one level, a very successful locality in economic and labour market terms. The town's economic base has been fundamentally transformed in the last 25 years or so. While it is by no means immune from external economic forces it has experienced below-average levels of unemployment since the mid-1970s, it has suffered less in recession and it has tended to recover earlier than the rest of the country. Active social and community strategies in the postwar period aiming to secure what the *Silver Book* termed "integrated and balanced communities" described earlier in the chapter, have thus been juxtaposed with a particularly strong performance in economic terms.

Social class and social integration

Social integration has been a fundamental principle of the Borough's strategy since its early attempts during the 1950s to integrate new arrivals to the town with more established residents. The underlying aims of the policy were primarily to avoid social conflict and structural problems linked to demographically un-balanced communities. Social integration and social exclusion have also been major policy concerns for urban areas at national and European scales in recent years, taking forward debates around the 'rediscovery' of poverty in the 1960s and early 1970s. This section therefore explores the extent to which Swindon could be described as a socially integrated community and the evidence for social deprivation and social exclusion in what is, on the face of it, something of a boom town in economic terms.

Social structure and social class: the sort of massive shifts in industrial and occupational structure described earlier in Chapter Three, have been reflected in turn in major change in terms of class structure (Table 7.1). In broad terms, in the decade up to 1991, there was rapid growth in non-manual groups locally. Managerial, technical and professional groups expanded particularly rapidly and there was also significant growth in the skilled non-manual group. There was significant decline, on the other hand, across both skilled and less skilled manual groups. The overall pattern of change locally mirrored shifts in terms of class structure at the national level. The scale of growth and decline was, moreover, considerably more rapid locally than nationally, resulting in a particularly sharp shift in the overall balance of the town's social structure towards white collar, clerical, managerial and professional groups (Table 7.1). To some extent, rapid change locally in the 1980s brought the town more in line with the overall class structure at national level, having previously been dominated to a large extent by more manual, working class groups.

Table 7.1: Social class, Swindon, and England and Wales (1981-91)

Social class	Swindon			England and Wales		
	1981 (%)	1991 (%)	Change in share (1981-91)	1981 (%)	1991 (%)	Change in share (1981-91)
Professional (etc) occupations	4.3	5.9	37	5.8	6.8	18
Managerial and technical	20.8	30.2	45	25.0	31.4	26
Skilled non-manual	13.4	15.7	17	13.6	13.8	2
Skilled manual	32.9	25.3	-23	31.6	26.9	-15
Partly skilled	19.1	15.8	-17	15.8	13.7	-13
Unskilled	5.5	4.4	-19	5.2	4.6	-10
Other	4.1	2.7	-35	2.9	2.6	-13
Total	100.0	100.0	0	100.0	100.0	0

Source: Census of Population, OPCS

More detailed analysis, however, shows quite marked variation in class and social structure across the town as a whole (Table 7.2). Less than 16% of the population in Gorse Hill, Park and Whitworth (see Figure 7.1) can be categorised as 'middle class', all areas with a high concentration of older local authority housing. This compares with over 40% in Eastcott and Lawns in the older urban core, the more rural Blunsdon and Ridgeway, and Toothill in West Swindon. Freshbrook, also in West Swindon and the remaining rural wards also had well above average concentrations of middle class residents.

These sorts of patterns are, in part, a function of housing tenure and the impacts of housing policy. The ideal of integrated communities within the town has, however, proved difficult to realise in practice. Despite the scale of population growth and new housing provision the capacity of the Borough Council to achieve integration has clearly been limited. Even in areas where it was developing mixed tenure housing and where integration might perhaps have more easily been achieved, barriers remained.

> It is interesting to note that although the Council adopted the policy of integrating Londoners and local applicants on the newer estates (unlike some towns, where segregation resulted in ill-feeling between the new and established communities) it made no effort to mix the classes within the new housing areas. The local authority rented estates were separated from the owner-occupied areas of Walcot and Lawns by a broad dual-carriageway, which has remained an effective physical and social barrier ever since. (Thamesdown Borough Council, 1983)

However, the changing context of national housing policy (described in Chapter Six) eroded the Council's ability to develop areas of mixed tenure housing in more recent years. As noted earlier, the tenure mix in the western expansion shifted towards largely private, owner-occupied housing in the later stages as the Borough Council's direct role in development based on ownership of land diminished. Housing development in the northern expansion is virtually all owner-occupied. This shift was further reinforced by the government's 'Right to Buy' council house sales policy from the early 1980s. This resulted in a sizeable proportion

Figure 7.1: Ward boundaries, Thamesdown/Swindon

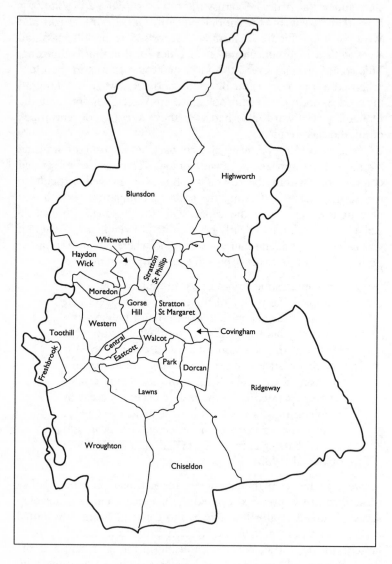

of local authority owned housing being transferred into private ownership. It also had a selective impact in that, as nationally, it was the better housing in more desirable areas which tended to be sold. Less well-off tenants tended increasingly to be concentrated in the residual, poorer quality stock on the less popular estates, reinforcing social fragmentation. The pattern of housing tenure at ward level (Table 7.3) indicates the strong pattern of differentiation in terms of housing tenure within the town.

Over 80% of households in Covingham, Haydon Wick, Eastcott, Lawns, Stratton St Margaret, Toothill and Western wards are owner-occupiers. On the other hand, around 60% of all households in Park and Whitworth are still local authority tenants. While social integration was clearly set out as a key goal in the *Silver Book*, on this sort of evidence there is little to suggest that this has been achieved to any great extent.

Similar contrasts are evident in the distribution of workers in different types of industry. Manufacturing workers are par-ticularly concentrated, as would be expected, in the more working class areas of the town (Table 7.2). Swindon as a whole still has a slightly above average concentration of jobs in manufacturing, although this partly reflects growth in newer manufacturing sectors and the growth of Honda. It also has an above average concentration of workers in the newer, white-collar, 'information industries'. The latter tend to live particularly in the western expansion and other more middle class wards (Table 7.4).

As noted earlier (see Chapter Three), Swindon has experi-enced below average rates of unemployment since the mid-1970s. It has, however, been far from immune to the impacts of economic recession, with unemployment rising locally to nearly 10% of the workforce in early 1986 (over 10,000 people in total). Allowing for the impact of changes both in government policy and statistical definition, it rose close to this level again in 1993. There has also been a persistent level of long-term unemployment in the town. Around half of the unemployed in recent years had been unemployed for more than a year. It was only when unemployment as a whole dipped below about 4% in the period 1989-90 that demand from employers started to eat into the underlying level of the long-term unemployed – there were signs of the same thing by 1997 as unemployment again dipped well below national levels. Despite the overall context of prosperity, therefore, Swindon has experienced significant levels of

Table 7.2: Social class and labour market position by ward, Swindon (1991)

Ward	Population	Working class	Middle class	Manufacturing workers	Information workers	Unemployed	Men on the scrap heap	Young unemployed	Young people on YTS
Blunsdon	2,764	57.8	41.5	19.0	50.3	5.7	11.2	7.9	10.3
Central	7,066	70.3	28.1	24.2	45.3	11.8	22.1	10.5	18.5
Chiseldon	2,583	62.8	36.6	15.2	45.5	5.1	8.2	7.2	9.1
Covingham	4,128	71.6	27.6	28.4	47.1	3.7	5.4	5.3	8.3
Dorcan	9,876	74.0	26.0	23.1	47.2	6.0	11.4	8.2	19.2
Eastcott	8,364	58.1	41.3	20.1	54.7	8.3	11.1	10.3	13.8
Freshbook	9,630	61.9	37.9	21.6	57.0	5.0	11.0	7.1	8.3
Gorse Hill	9,075	84.8	15.2	28.5	29.0	11.2	19.6	12.1	17.9
Haydon Wick	7,355	67.8	32.0	27.7	51.7	3.8	9.5	4.2	11.1
Highworth	8,749	62.1	37.2	23.5	49.9	4.6	6.2	5.0	10.2
Lawns	9,078	49.9	49.4	15.9	66.5	5.0	9.1	5.4	14.5
Moredon	8,945	73.6	25.9	29.6	37.9	9.1	14.9	13.3	17.3
Park	10,264	85.9	12.9	23.1	28.2	14.9	13.6	17.8	20.2
Ridgeway	3,120	47.0	53.0	13.4	61.1	4.1	3.8	5.9	13.0
Stratton St Margaret	13,224	67.5	32.3	25.5	51.4	3.9	9.5	5.7	11.9
Stratton St Philip	7,720	75.9	23.8	25.4	39.9	6.5	10.5	8.7	21.6
Toothill	15,924	58.9	40.1	21.5	55.2	5.1	8.6	6.8	9.6
Walcot	7,774	79.5	19.9	28.0	38.2	12.3	14.3	13.3	25.4
Western	9,162	75.1	24.5	27.5	39.6	6.7	10.2	8.7	20.5
Whitworth	7,525	85.8	14.2	29.8	22.5	15.5	16.3	19.9	14.9
Wroughton	6,880	65.5	34.5	16.4	43.2	5.4	12.2	8.3	10.9
Swindon		*68.6*	*30.9*	*23.7*	*46.4*	*7.3*	*11.7*	*9.4*	*14.9*
England		*65.2*	*33.9*	*20.6*	*45.0*	*9.1*	*28.2*	*10.8*	*26.3*

Source: Derived from Census of Population (1991). Indicators defined as in Forrest and Gordon (1993); Gordon and Forrest (1995). Ward-level analysis conducted for this study by Dr D. Gordon.

unemployment in absolute terms, rising sharply in periods of recession and persistent levels of long-term unemployment.

Differences in term of levels of unemployment in different parts of the town are also particularly marked. The 1991 Census allowed unemployment rates to be measured at a detailed ward level. According to the Census, just over 7% of residents in Swindon as a whole were unemployed at that time compared with 9% in England as a whole. However, 15% of all those living in Park and Whitworth were without work (Table 7.2) and unemployment was well above 10% in three other wards: Central, Gorse Hill, and Walcot. In Covingham, Haydon Wick, Ridgeway and Stratton St Margaret, on the other hand, unemployment was 4% or less. Similar patterns are evident in terms of older unemployed men and the young unemployed (Table 7.2): in Central and Gorse Hill wards 20% or more, over one in five of older men between 55 and retirement age were not working. In Whitworth and Park nearly one in five of the younger potential workforce aged 16-24 were unemployed. As one local authority officer described the situation:

> "We were of course hit by unemployment and it then became very clear that we had a whole generation of young people coming up through Parks and Walcot who had never had jobs and didn't look as if they were going to get jobs. At the same time, we had the older members of the workforce in that area also disproportionally affected by unemployment ... one would have to

---

Notes to Table 7.2: *Working class*: occupations with either relatively low pay and/or strong trade union activity, Standard Occupational Classification groups 4 to 9. *Middle class*: professional occupations with either relatively high pay or little trade union activity. *Manufacturing workers*: Standard Industrial Classification 1980 divisions 2-4. *Information workers*: occupational groups working with information, defined in terms of the Standard Occupational Grouping (see Hepworth et al, 1987). *Unemployed*: % of economically active population who were unemployed. *Men on the scrap heap*: men aged 55-65 who were either unemployed, on a government scheme or otherwise inactive as % of economically active men aged 55-65. *Young unemployed*: % economically active 16-24-year-olds who were unemployed. *Young people 16-17 on YTS*: 16- and 17-year-olds on YTS as % of all 16- and 17-year olds in employment.

> *say that if the policy of expansion was about
> bringing a large and flexible pool of labour to the
> town to attract industry, which it undoubtedly
> and explicitly was, that pool of labour in Walcot
> and Parks ... they were the first to feel the effects
> of economic disadvantage in the down-turn and
> probably the last to feel the benefits.... Even when
> the economy was taking more people ... in the
> Parks and Walcot area, there weren't the
> opportunities for the young people to get into the
> labour market, the older people had been cast out
> of it and there was nothing on offer for that
> community."*

Table 7.3: Housing tenure by ward, Swindon (1991)

Ward	Owner-occupied	Local authority[1]	Privately rented
Blunsdon	78.7	11.8	9.5
Central	67.2	16.9	16.0
Chiseldon	72.4	16.9	10.7
Covingham	94.9	1.2	3.9
Dorcan	73.4	11.8	14.8
Eastcott	81.2	1.1	17.7
Freshbrook	78.4	12.7	8.9
Gorse Hill	66.4	26.1	7.5
Haydon Wick	88.9	3.6	7.5
Highworth	74.0	14.0	12.0
Lawns	87.1	0.7	12.2
Moredon	62.2	31.3	6.5
Park	39.2	57.5	3.3
Ridgeway	74.8	11.5	13.7
Stratton St Margaret	90.2	3.4	6.4
Stratton St Philip	73.9	21.6	4.5
Toothill	80.5	11.4	8.2
Walcot	59.5	35.6	4.9
Western	82.6	8.5	8.8
Whitworth	34.5	62.6	2.9
Wroughton	73.3	13.2	13.5
Thamesdown	73.0	17.9	9.1
Great Britain	66.3	21.2	12.5

[1] Includes households renting through a job or business or renting from a housing association.

Source: Census of Population, OPCS

Long-term unemployment again follows the same sort of patterns. Over 40% of those unemployed in Park, Walcot and Whitworth in 1993 had been out of work for at least a year compared with 35% for the Borough as a whole and only around 25% in the better off wards (Thamesdown Borough Council, 1994b).

Poverty and deprivation: patterns in terms of social class, employment and unemployment and housing tenure indicate the very significant scale of variation in the circumstances of residents in different parts of the town. They suggest a quite significant level of fragmentation and difference in contrast to the goals of social integration and balanced communities. A number of indicators also point more specifically to major variation between different parts of the town in terms of poverty and deprivation. This is not to suggest that Swindon has levels of poverty and deprivation which are particularly marked by national standards. These figures show, however, that residents in parts of the town do experience levels of poverty and deprivation which are significantly above average by national standards.

Simple indicators, such as households without a car or without central heating, show very clear contrasts between different parts of the town (Table 7.4). Lack of a car is not only associated with income level but is also a more specific indicator of mobility and access. Around half of households in Park and Whitworth do not have a car and over 40% in Central, Gorse Hill and Walcot. The proportion of children in each area 'living in households with no wage earner' is also a sensitive indicator of deprivation and social need. A similar pattern emerges, but the contrast between areas is particularly marked, with over a third of all children in Park and Whitworth living in poor families. This compares with only 13% for Swindon as a whole (itself less than the national average of just over 14%) and around 5% in the best off areas. While lack of a family wage-earner may in some cases be temporary, a significant proportion of children in the worst off areas are likely to be growing up in a culture of unemployment, excluded from the benefits of economic independence and full social participation. Long-term illness (discussed in more detail below) is also commonly associated with a higher incidence of poverty and social need, and the same pattern is evident from Table 7.4. The same is true of homelessness and housing need, a more direct indicator of deprivation, discussed in more detail later.

Table 7.4: Poverty and social exclusion by ward, Swindon (1991)

Ward	Population	Households in poverty	Lone parents	Large families	Housing need	Long-term ill	Children in poor households	No car	No central heating
Blunsdon	2,764	12.4	0.9	5.1	3.0	5.1	6.4	14.1	9.8
Central	7,066	23.7	2.3	4.9	4.9	9.6	15.4	46.1	23.4
Chiseldon	2,583	13.5	1.2	5.1	2.0	6.0	6.3	14.5	10.2
Covingham	4,128	8.0	2.3	1.8	2.6	5.6	4.6	10.8	4.5
Dorcan	9,876	16.1	4.1	4.2	0.3	5.3	9.8	20.7	2.5
Eastcott	8,364	17.5	2.0	3.7	1.6	6.2	9.1	35.8	20.8
Freshbook	9,630	12.1	4.2	4.7	0.0	4.3	10.3	15.4	7.1
Gorse Hill	9,075	24.6	4.6	4.9	1.9	8.9	23.6	41.2	27.1
Haydon Wick	7,355	10.5	1.6	2.1	0.3	5.6	4.6	14.0	6.3
Highworth	8,749	14.7	2.3	3.1	1.7	4.7	7.2	19.7	8.1
Lawns	9,078	11.2	1.0	3.1	1.7	6.7	4.5	20.9	4.6
Moredon	8,945	22.5	3.2	7.4	1.5	8.6	16.5	32.4	23.4
Park	10,264	32.8	7.6	6.9	3.8	12.3	32.3	48.1	52.6
Ridgeway	3,120	11.8	1.3	4.2	1.7	5.6	5.5	10.3	10.2
Stratton St Margaret	13,224	11.0	1.5	2.5	0.8	5.4	4.8	15.9	6.2
Stratton St Philip	7,720	17.2	2.4	3.0	1.7	6.6	10.7	24.0	12.0
Toothill	15,924	12.2	4.0	3.5	0.6	4.4	10.7	15.9	10.7
Walcot	7,774	26.2	5.2	7.2	2.9	10.4	24.8	42.5	35.2
Western	9,162	17.4	2.2	4.5	1.9	6.7	11.2	32.6	14.8
Whitworth	7,525	34.9	8.2	4.8	2.3	11.2	33.7	50.5	53.4
Wroughton	6,880	15.3	1.8	3.7	0.8	6.4	6.1	22.5	7.7
Thamesdown		17.9	3.3	4.3	1.7	6.9	13.3	27.3	17.3
England		18.7	3.7	4.5	1.5	8.3	14.3	27.0	17.0

Source: Derived from Census of Population (1991). Indicators defined as in Forrest and Gordon (1993); Gordon and Forrest (1995). Ward-level analysis conducted for this study by Dr D. Gordon.

More sophisticated indicators combine different types of information from the Census in order to derive a composite measure of poverty and deprivation. The poverty index derived by Gordon combines Census data with survey data from the national Breadline Britain Surveys to provide an estimate of the proportion of households in a particular area living in poverty (Gordon and Forrest, 1995). Poverty is defined as circumstances "where resources were so seriously below those commanded by the average individual or family that the poor are, in effect, excluded from ordinary living patterns, customs and activities". While relatively complex to calculate, this is probably the best of the various indicators available and the resulting index is simple to understand providing a straightforward estimate of the proportion of all families in a particular area who are, on this basis, 'poor'.

Figures calculated by Gordon specially for this study indicate that just under 18% of households in Swindon could be defined as living in poverty, slightly below the average for England as a whole of around 19%. The index shows, however, wide variation between different parts of the town (Table 7.4). Around a third of households in Park and over a third in Whitworth were living in poverty in 1991, and around a quarter of households in Central, Gorse Hill and Walcot. This very much confirms the picture built up from simpler indicators. It also gives a very clear picture of levels of poverty in these wards compared with the national picture. On the other hand, the proportion of poor households was well below the national average in a wide range of wards. These included, as might be expected, the more rural areas such as Blunsdon and Ridgeway, and also Toothill and Freshbrook in West Swindon, and middle class Lawns. Areas with the lowest

---

Notes to Table 7.4: *Households in poverty:* a weighted index of poverty based on six Census variables: unemployment, limiting long-term illness, non-home ownership, no access to car, lone parent households, social class IV and V, using the *Breadline Britain* survey to weight the variables (see Gordon and Forrest, 1995). *Lone parents:* lone parent households as % of all households. *Large families:* % of households with three or more dependent children. *Housing need:* homeless persons in hostels, B&B. sleeping rough plus the number of concealed families, as a % of permanent households. *Long-term ill:* % of resident population of working age with limiting long-term illness. *Children in poor households:* children in households with no earners as % of all children. *No car:* % of households with no car. *No central heating:* % of households without central heating.

concentration of poor households also included the more working class areas of Covingham and Stratton St Margaret.

Figures for Swindon provided in Table 7.4 provide a snapshot for 1991. There is clear evidence nationally, however, that the gap between the rich and the poor has been widening. Real incomes of the poorest 10% of households fell by 13% between 1979 and 1993. Those of the next 10% up the scale rose by only 4%. The higher up the scale, however, the bigger the increase, with incomes of the top 10% rising by some 65% (HBAI, quoted in the *Guardian,* 28 April 1997). Locally, some indication of trends between 1981 and 1991 is given by the alternative 'Jarman' index of deprivation. Again, based on a range of Census indicators, this was originally developed as a basis for planning health-related services but usefully provides a more general indicator of relative levels of deprivation. It shows a similar overall pattern to that for poor households outlined above, with Whitworth, Central, Park, Gorse Hill and Walcot the most deprived areas (Table 7.5). Significantly it shows worsening deprivation in all of these, with the exception of Gorse Hill, where the situation changed little. This was particularly marked in the case of Whitworth, Park and Walcot. In several of the less deprived wards, on the other hand, the situation improved over the decade to 1991.

Overall, then, these figures suggest that there has been a widening gap between the most deprived parts of the town and the least deprived. A relatively prosperous economy at the heart of the M4 Corridor thus shows marked patterns of inequality and an increasing gap between the most and the least deprived areas which mirrors the national picture. This lends some support to the view that patterns of economic and labour market change in economically more buoyant localities actually serve to generate increasing levels of inequality. This is contrary to the argument that the benefits of growth and prosperity automatically 'trickle down' to the benefit of all.

Homelessness: the previous section has looked in some detail at poverty and deprivation in the population as a whole. This section now goes on to look at social integration and social exclusion in relation to three more specific groups, the homeless, disabled people and, finally, the black and ethnic minority population.

Table 7.5: Deprivation by ward, Swindon (1981-91)

Ward	Jarman deprivation index[1]		Trend 1981-91[2]
	1981	1991	
Covingham	-22.1	-21.2	No significant change
Ridgeway	-13.3	-21.0	Improvement
Haydon Wick[3]	n/a	-16.8	New ward
Stratton St Margaret	-17.7	-13.9	Deterioration
Chiseldon	-1.9	-13.2	Improvement
Lawns	-14.8	-9.8	Deterioration
Highworth	+1.7	-6.6	Improvement
Wroughton	-3.1	-5.7	Improvement
Blunsdon	-15.0	-5.4	Deterioration
Stratton St Philip	-5.4	-4.9	No significant change
Freshbrook[3]	n/a	-3.2	New ward
Dorcan	1.9	-2.1	Improvement
Toothill[3]	n/a	+1.2	New ward
Western	+2.2	+4.1	Deterioration
Eastcott	+12.4	+9.0	Improvement
Moredon[3]	n/a	+10.5	New ward
Walcot	+9.8	+18.0	Deterioration
Gorse Hill	+23.1	+22.5	No significant change
Park	+16.7	+22.9	Deterioration
Central	+22.2	+24.6	Deterioration
Whitworth	+18.9	+27.8	Deterioration

Notes: The Jarman deprivation index is derived from eight census variables including: people of pensionable age and living alone; children aged under 5; households in social class V; unemployed people; one-parent families; people in households which are overcrowded; people in households which have changed address in the past year; people of ethnic minority background.

[1] A positive score indicates an area experiencing more deprivation as indicated by the Jarman than the national average; a negative score indicates an area experiencing a lower level of deprivation.

[2] This column reflects the difference between the figures for 1981 and 1991. Where the level of deprivation is greater in 1991 than in 1981 then a deterioration in the situation is recorded and so on.

[3] Areas affected by significant boundary changes since 1981.

Source: *Thamesdown Trends*, Thamesdown Borough Council (1996, p 56); originally Swindon Health Authority

Again, while it is not implied that there are particular problems and issues relating to these groups locally, compared with the rest of the country, examining their situation in what is a generally an economically buoyant locality is particularly relevant. The issue of homelessness represents a particularly sharp counterpoint to the overall image of Swindon and the M4 Corridor. The point is not that homelessness is particularly marked in Swindon relative to other places but that it exists to any significant extent at all, as an issue and as a problem. The prevalence of homelessness in Swindon would perhaps surprise many who live in the town as it tends to be a relatively invisible problem. As someone working locally with a homelessness organisation put it:

> *"I think the public, the mainstream public are generally shocked that there is even a homelessness problem in Swindon and that's borne out by the fact that when we have these appeals, we are just inundated with good quality clothing.... I mean, I still think that the Swindon public are surprised, find it hard to believe that there is that level of problem here, they may see the occasional street drinker...."*

This lack of visibility or recognition of the problem may have hindered the success in Swindon of *The Big Issue*, the national magazine sold by homeless people to help them earn money and be reintegrated back into mainstream society. Launched locally in March 1996, after five months the magazine was forced to shut down its operations in the town due to very low sales. Representatives of *The Big Issue* suggested specifically that homelessness was not perceived as a problem in Swindon and this had hindered sales.

Official local authority figures show a sharp increase in homeless households since the mid-1980s (see Figure 6.8, Chapter Six). Homelessness may, however, take a number of forms including those sleeping rough, those living in hostels, and families placed in B&B accommodation. A broader definition of 'housing need' would include 'concealed households' sharing with relatives or friends. Homelessness is therefore difficult to define and measure very exactly, particularly given the mobility of homeless people and the fact that they may not be registered or accepted by a local authority as 'officially' homeless under government provisions, and therefore do not appear in official figures. Thamesdown Council undertook its own survey of homelessness in 1991 and found that:

> 1,099 persons were homeless in Thamesdown during July, a total of 681 households.... Nearly

one half of the homeless during July were staying
in hostel accommodation. A wide range of other
accommodation was also used, particularly by
homeless single person households. Figures
relating to the number of people sleeping rough,
although not conclusive, indicated the numbers in
this category were low. (Thamesdown Borough
Council, 1991b)

By 1993, when the Council repeated this exercise, they found that:

During May 1993 there were around 1,800
people homeless or threatened with homelessness
in Thamesdown. This represents an increase of
around ... 35% since 1991. There has been a
marked shift in the pattern of homelessness
within the Borough since 1991, with the number
of homeless children and women having increased sharply; the former by 91% and the latter
by 36%. (Thamesdown Borough Council, 1993a)

Overall, the 1993 report described the situation as "remaining
bleak" and while the rate of growth of homelessness appeared to
be slowing down, the proportion of the population who had been
homeless for longer periods of six months to two years had
increased. It noted as well a "worrying trend towards an
increasing incidence of homelessness amongst the most vulnerable
groups". Lone-parent households represented 4% of the
Borough's households according to the 1991 Census but
comprised 19% of homeless households, locally, in 1993. The
largest number of homeless people were aged between 18 to 34
years. The largest increase, however, was among children in the
10 to 14 age range, up by 154% between 1991 and 1993,
representing increasing homelessness among households with
children. People from black and minority ethnic communities
were also disproportionately likely to become homeless,
representing about 3% of Swindon's population but 9% of the
homeless population in the Borough. These findings in the early
1990s formed the justification for Council funding of a 'breakfast
club' for homeless people in the town. More recently the Council
opened a 'foyer' providing housing and training for young homeless people in 1996.

In the voluntary sector an umbrella group for organisations working with homeless people in the town was also established in 1993 – Homelessness Organisations Stick Together in Swindon (HOSTS). According to a representative:

> *"We saw a need for people working on the projects to have an umbrella group to enable information [and] experience to be shared [and] for support.... We thought there was a real need for that because it came out of Broadgreen Breakfast Club starting and that's not knowing, having any contact names or having any identity with people in other projects or the health service or social services, so that's how it was born."*

HOSTS were actively involved in seeking the provision of a night shelter and a day centre for homeless people in Swindon. While there was already some hostel provision in the town and the new foyer had opened for young people, a gap in services had been identified for those with multiple difficulties, such as drug or alcohol abuse as well as homelessness.

Race and ethnicity: around 3% of the population of Swindon are from black and other minority ethnic groups, less than the average for the country as a whole of 5.5% (Table 7.6). This, nevertheless, represents the largest concentration of people from black and ethnic minority groups in Wiltshire as a whole and a significant proportion of the population in its own right.

The specific history of the town's development and expansion raises particular issues. The *Silver Book,* for example, highlighted the needs and special provisions made for a number of different subgroups within the population (including children, young people, older people and disabled people). Despite the fact that there was already a small non-white population locally, reflecting earlier waves of in-migration and manufacturing growth, nowhere in the document were the needs of black and ethnic minority groups specifically addressed. This is perhaps symptomatic of the era in which the *Silver Book* was written. It may also reflect the fact that the key social and demographic issues raised by town expansion were perceived as focused around achieving balanced and integrated communities in a context of major growth and in-migration. This was seen largely in terms of the mixing of the overwhelmingly white existing population and newcomers to the town.

Table 7.6: Profile of ethnic groups, Swindon, Wiltshire and Great Britain (1991) (%)

Ethnic group	Thamesdown	Wiltshire	Great Britain
White	96.9	98.3	94.5
Black Caribbean	0.4	0.3	0.9
Black African	0.1	0.1	0.4
Black other	0.2	0.2	0.3
Indian	1.0	0.4	1.5
Pakistani	0.2	0.1	0.9
Bangladeshi	0.1	0.1	0.3
Chinese	0.2	0.2	0.3
Other Asian	0.3	0.2	0.4
Other	0.5	0.3	0.5

Source: Census of Employment, OPCS

Social development policies and strategies to disperse and 'integrate' new arrivals to the town appear, in fact, according to some commentators from within the black community, to have had the unintended consequence of exacerbating the sense of isolation felt by people from black and ethnic minority backgrounds. This may also have hindered the development of a stronger collective voice among these communities in Swindon. One local authority officer described the implications of this:

> "This Council operated a policy which basically meant that people were dispersed.... I think the main characteristic of the minority communities in Swindon is that they are quite dispersed and there isn't like a geographical focus for communities and also there is no premises. There are no buildings [or] community centres that are particularly sort of catering for the minority communities.... It is certainly something the communities themselves have identified for years as their main drawback, their main disadvantage stems from not having a geographical place from [which] to operate and be a sort of meeting place."

The black and ethnic minority population within Swindon comes from very diverse backgrounds, including Indian, Pakistani, Chinese, Bangladeshi, Black Caribbean and other Asian and black groups, as well a significant Irish born population. Each group is, however, fairly small in numerical terms (see Table 7.6) and may also have little in common with other groups. It has been difficult, therefore, for black and ethnic minority communities in Swindon to have a powerful voice in community affairs. There has tended to be a lack of critical mass and collective purpose and as one representative of an organisation working with black and ethnic minority communities described it, they also have a problem of 'visibility' in policy circles:

> *"But we in Swindon, we don't have the same sort of ... although I don't want to emphasise the numbers game, but the number of black and ethnic minorities here is considerably smaller compared with some of the bigger cities.... I think there was a tendency to perceive that because the numbers were so few, that there wasn't a problem.... In fact in a town like this, I think the problem's exacerbated because of being a visibility factor if you like. Because there isn't the sort of pressure on local services, ie, pressure equated to numbers, there's a tendency I think with policy makers and sort of policy decision makers, those who are responsible for allocating resources, to think that there isn't a problem."*

This problem of visibility has also been described as self-perpetuating in that it takes determined action to demonstrate a need for services which do not currently exist or are not adequately provided. The level of energy required may, however, inhibit demands for particular issues to be addressed, particularly (but not only) in the case of those whose first language is not English. This may lead to a situation in which demand for specialised services ostensibly remains low while the need may actually be quite high among these communities. One example related to the proposed provision of an interpretation service to give people greater access to the Council's services, as one commentator observed:

> *"I think the main issue is because the level of need is low because minority communities are so small, I mean you ... just simply cannot do that in Leicester, you cannot not have interpreters at hand if you are in Leicester. But here, because the issue comes up not that regularly, it comes up rarely maybe, then it takes a much lower sort of priority and it's a sort of circular argument because ... the less people know that you can ask and you will get it without hassle, the less people ask so people don't tend to approach the housing department unless they are desperate, or they won't approach social services unless they're desperate...."*

As the main concentration of black and ethnic minority groups in the county, Swindon is also called upon to play a more regional role in providing services such as translation and specialist advice services to meet the needs of the wider area.

As described earlier, the Council has had a long-standing policy of providing communal buildings and facilities to foster community development. This has tended, however, to focus on more geographically defined communities rather than on other means of affiliation such as race and ethnicity – as noted earlier, Swindon's ethnic minority population tends to be relatively dispersed across the town as a whole. A recent case summarised by d'Ancona highlights one aspect of this:

> Over the last five years the Asian community has been the focus of one of the town's fiercest disputes: where to locate a mosque which Swindon's Asians have long been trying to build. The problem is a familiar one. There is little overt racism in Swindon but few white Swindonians want a minaret in their back yard.
> (d'Ancona, 1996)

A succession of possible sites fell through until finally, in 1995, as d'Ancona explains, "an old school site in central Swindon was found to be acceptable to all, pending the permission of the Department of Environment...". Subsequently, in fact, central government refused permission to build the mosque on the council-owned, town centre site on the grounds that the land had to be sold at its full commercial value rather than allowing the Muslim community to lease or buy the land for a nominal amount, as was the Council's plan. The logic underlying the Department of the Environment's rejection of the site was not fully appreciated by several of those interviewed within the Council given the fact that many other town centre sites are currently available and are not attracting the interest of investors.

In terms of economic position and integration into the labour market and formal economy, there are also considerable differences in terms of race and ethnicity. This replicates patterns in the country as a whole but, again, is perhaps more significant in the context of Swindon as a relatively buoyant local economy and labour market. In Swindon at the time of the 1991 Census, just over 7% of the economically active white population were unemployed compared with almost 10% of the population from black and other minority ethnic groups.

Disabled people: for the first time, the 1991 Census asked whether individuals had 'any long-term illness, health problem or handicap' which limited work or daily activities. This gives some indication of the scale of disability locally, although there are clearly alternative definitions. In 1991, 7% of the population of working age in Swindon reported long-term illness or handicap and nearly 11% of the population as a whole (Table 7.4). Again, however, there was marked variation across the town as a whole. This reflects differences in age profile between different areas. Focusing on those of working age only, however, reduces the effects of age difference. On this basis, between 10% and 12% of those of working age living in Park, Central, Whitworth and Walcot had some form of long-term health problem or handicap. In Freshbrook, Highworth and Toothill, the figure was less than 5%. As this suggests, there is a strong coincidence with patterns of poverty and deprivation described earlier. This emphasises the association between poverty and deprivation on the one hand and the incidence of illness and disability on the other.

Again, perhaps, reflecting the era in which it was written, the *Silver Book*, representing at one level a very enlightened framework for town expansion, offered little for disabled people in its vision for Swindon. Indeed, it observed that that:

> The 370 registered physically handicapped people
> in Swindon at present have three social centres

and a sheltered workshop. There is no reason to
suppose that there will be more than a pro rata
increase in their numbers in the coming years, but
as techniques for assisting the handicapped
improve, more of them will be able to be
gainfully employed, and it is hoped that industry
will be able to engage these people. Also,
handicapped people need better jobs than they
often acquire at present to match their increasing
level of education. There may also be a need to
provide some residential accommodation for
those of the handicapped who can no longer be
looked after by their families. (Swindon Borough
Council et al, 1968, p 116)

In keeping with educational thinking at the time, it also saw the
need to provide 'special school accommodation' for "educationally
sub-normal children in separate Junior and Senior Schools" and, as
the town grew, "small schools for maladjusted children, for
physically handicapped children and for partially hearing children"
(Swindon Borough Council et al, 1968, p 118). The vision was
one of a life of segregation from mainstream society with separate
educational provision, sheltered employment and potentially
separate residential accommodation.

For disabled people, the struggle has perhaps been one of
resisting other people's visions of their position which have
consistently placed them on the margins. As one representative of
disabled people locally put it:

*"I'm not sure that they're actually recognising the
fact that some disabled people have the same skills
... and are quite as capable of doing the job as
anyone else ... Community Development [have]
got the same problem that the rest of Swindon has
got, that it captured from the old days of the
railway when they built the railway village and
the railway hospital ... which was all for looking
after the workers so that the workers had to rely
on the railway. If they left the railway, they
would lose all those benefits. So it was a ...
patronising attitude coming out of it.... I think
Swindon, the history of Swindon is about doing*

> *things for people and it could be to do with the*
> *labour movement, the Labour Party, is also part*
> *of the whole philosophy is that people need help.*"

Since the early 1980s there have been attempts to raise the profile of disability issues on the Council's agenda. These have met with differing levels of success. With 1980 designated nationally as the Year for the Disabled, the Borough appointed an access officer who was to oversee the process of making buildings in Swindon more accessible to disabled people by liaising with architects and planners as new construction took place. While this reflected a degree of commitment on the part of the Council to making buildings fully accessible to disabled people, this has been difficult to achieve in practice and there is some suggestion that it was not a principle which had been wholly incorporated into planning processes thus far.

> *"I think the philosophy of the community*
> *development manager about access, the access*
> *officer was that he had a dual role or several roles*
> *to play, but one of those roles was that he would*
> *train and educate other architects, planners and*
> *building control officers and make them alert to*
> *the needs of disabled people in the way of*
> *access.... Unfortunately, people in those positions*
> *still tend to think of disability as an after-*
> *thought.... It seems, over the years, it's developed*
> *better, but suddenly after they've made the budget*
> *out and someone's complained that they haven't*
> *done this or done that, oh, we haven't got the*
> *money to do it...."*

Thus, a report in 1996 noted that: "The Borough Council provides its services through 70 buildings which are open to the public. Three are fully accessible to disabled people." (*Audit report to the Community Development Committee*, 11 June 1996, p 1). The profile of disability issues has increased to some extent recently. A 'shop mobility' scheme started operating in 1996 providing wheelchairs for use while shopping in the town centre. It is supported by a combination of the Borough Council, local traders, other major businesses in the area, a local equipment dealership and a nominal membership fee from those using the service. In response to a request from the Thamesdown Association for

Disabled People to establish an advisory body or forum to better consider the needs of disabled people, the Council commissioned a report evaluating its current provision of facilities and services for disabled people. A consultation project was set up to determine the best way to organise such a forum in Swindon and consultants recommended that a Coalition of Disabled People should be established in Swindon in line with successful projects running in other local authority areas. This, it was proposed, should be supported by the new unitary authority as "a key representative body of disabled people working in partnership with the Authority". An elected Disabled People's Forum would serve the same type of function that the Race Relations Advisory Panel and the Women's Advisory Panel had provided. Potentially, at least, this indicates the extent to which thinking has changed since the time of the *Silver Book*.

Culture, community and ways of life

This final section looks more generally at culture, community and ways of life in Swindon and how this has changed over recent years. It draws on earlier research carried out locally in the mid-1980s, together with more work undertaken for this book. As might be expected, life in Swindon up to the last war revolved around the railworks. As a long-standing local resident interviewed in 1986 put it: "just everybody used to work in the railway. GWR was Swindon and that was it". The heavily structured work culture and the rhythms of activity in the works permeated the community to which it gave birth (Williams, 1915; Peck, 1983). Both daily life and major social occasions centred on the works. The annual children's fete, which continued up to the Second World War, was attended by 34,000 in 1904. In 1905, the annual holiday week, 'the trip', saw 24,500 people, almost half the population, leave the town on 22 special trains. This dominance declined only slowly in postwar years and the feelings of older residents over the final closure of the works in 1986 reflected the loss of something much more than simply jobs:

> *"From a personal point of view, I think we've lost*
> *our heritage, because I was born when Swindon*
> *was railway and I believe that that was real, and I*

> *think the high tech is plastic. I think it's made*
> *possibly a generation of 50-year-olds feel a bit*
> *useless really ... they were skilled workers ... very*
> *skilled ... I think the suit and briefcase lady is*
> *coming to be.... We've lost our culture, the rail-*
> *way culture was a way of life."*

Identification of the town with rail engineering remained strong
even in the 1980s. Right through from the 19th century to the
1980s, if you worked in the railworks you were talked of as
'inside'. A survey carried out in 1986 (Boddy, 1987), the year the
rail works closed, showed that over half of those interviewed still
associated Swindon closely with railways and rail engineering.
The dominant feelings, however, were regret and nostalgia: *"it's
sad because we're talking about tradition, heritage"*. There was
also, however, a more hard-nosed realism: *"Everyone says it's a
shame about the railway, and it is. But at the end of the day it's
something that had to happen. If it's not making money, it had to
go"*.

As described in Chapter Three, postwar expansion greatly
increased the number and diversity of employers. There was much
less overlap between peoples' work and non-work lives – people
tended to live further from where they worked and to have less in
common in terms of work experience with those living around
them. With the massive in-migration of population from London
and elsewhere described earlier in Chapter Two and Chapter Six,
much of the town was marked by the newness of the population
and the lack, initially at least, of extended social networks. Among
those interviewed in 1986 there was still considerable awareness of
the contrasts between 'Swindonians' and the 'newcomers', particularly Londoners, arriving in the late 1950s and early 1960s:

> *"When the Londoners first came and they didn't*
> *like this and they didn't like that, then I used to*
> *get so uppity about that. I used to think if you*
> *don't like it, go back to where you came from.*
> *Now I know quite a few Londoners. They're quite*
> *nice once you get to know them."*

The feelings were often mutual. As one newcomer from the 1960s
put it: *"We were very much resented when we arrived, 'damned
Londoners taking all our jobs' for a very long time"*. Similarly:

> *"There was a lot of resentment when we first moved down here because regardless of who you were, what you were, you were all classed as Londoners and classed as outsiders. That could be difficult when you first came. I mean, it was like a village, you couldn't call it a town."*

Only about a third of the 1986 population had actually been born locally and a proportion of these would have been children of migrants. Stereotypes of Swindonians and Londoners remained strong, however. Swindonians were described as *"reserved"*, *"slow to accept you"*, but *"fine once you get to know them"*. The 'Londoners' who came in the early postwar years were in turn, seen as different from the *"the new people"*, the more recent newcomers of the 1970s, *"a different kettle of fish ... it's two completely different towns now"*.

> *"Swindonian people were really working class people, and I think that the people that have come from outside tend to be, as I said, a bit up market.... The new people are different from the Londoners who came in the 1950s who were also working class which helped them integrate."*

This influx of in-migrants was perceived to be associated with a loss of community: *"the new people coming don't seem to think of it as a community. They think of their-selves, people nowadays, as long as I'm all right, that's all that matters."* The contrast with the possibly romanticised community of the interwar period focused around the rail works is stark: *"once everybody knew everybody, now nobody knows nobody"*.

This increased privatism and home-centredness typical of many places in later postwar years was emphasised in Swindon's case by the newness, the isolation of young families, differences in background and the dislocation of social and family ties consequent on in-migration. As one account put it:

> Initially, women were likely to be preoccupied with child-rearing ... by and large they are young married people with families. The men go to the factories, have a beer, watch telly; the women bring up the children. On the estates, they are

> still in the introspective stage. (*Financial Times,*
> 27 May 1966)

Continued in-migration through the 1970s and since has reinforced this predominance of individualised lifestyles: "*it's not unfriendly, but everyone keeps themselves very much to themselves*". In the western expansion:

> "... *people are very wary about knocking on your door and saying, 'Hello, I'm your new neighbour, do you want a cup of tea'.... There are a lot of people who live in this street who leave at seven to eight in the morning, travel to work, work, get home seven to eight at night, so you're knackered.*"

As one community leader put it a decade later in 1996: "*how can somebody working 70 hours a week identify with the neighbour-hood where their house is, even if they should want to?*" Referring to the idea of 'community', one local Councillor commented:

> "*People don't recognise the term. It's individuals and it's individuals and their families. Margaret Thatcher had it right when she said the people don't recognise the concept of, or less people understand the concept of community than they did maybe kind of 15, 20 years ago. There is more mobility, people identify with their job and with their family and not with the kind of people next door. They don't even know the people next door, let alone down the road....*"

There is also considerable awareness of pressures of debt, consumerism and the need to keep up appearances:

> "*This is a successful area, so you have got to be successful.... The majority are mortgaged up to the absolute hilt. From the outside you can look at people and think that they're probably doing extremely well, but you don't realise they are probably up to their eyes in debt ... they are so materialistic.*"

In recent years, debt in Swindon has been linked to unsecured debt on credit cards and credit arrangements and housing related debt including negative equity and rent and mortgage arrears. Statistics from the Thamesdown Citizens' Advice Bureau from the late 1980s to the early 1990s indicated a significant rise in the number of debt related enquiries, from 11% in 1988/89 to 45% in 1991/92 (Thamesdown Borough Council, 1994b, p 55). According to an advice worker locally:

> *"There is considerable tension for women around having to work part-time, but having to earn enough to pay the huge mortgages as a result of the 1980s, particularly paying ex-partners' arrears as well.... A lot of that sort of hidden poverty does exist in Swindon, but because of the nice nature, nice looking nature of the estates, particularly in West Swindon, you wouldn't think there was any poverty there at all."*

The town's overall prosperity also meant little to many of the unemployed, for whom poverty was the dominant experience. Nearly two thirds of a sample of 200 unemployed included in the 1986 survey found it hard to make ends meet. Thirty-four per cent found it "very hard" compared with only 3% of those working full time. Over a quarter thought it very unlikely that they would find a job in the next year. As one unemployed 23-year-old saw it:

> *"It sounds pretty daft, but in Swindon at the moment, they seem to be recruiting a lot of people from outside, especially with skills, and bringing them all in, and unemployed who actually lived here virtually all their lives, they are finding it difficult to get work because it's all specialised industry."*

Over 75% of people interviewed in the 1986 survey thought that is was no different being unemployed in Swindon than elsewhere. Some did think that it was easier to find work, and the feeling that people could find work if they really look for it seems to be stronger in Swindon than in many places. On the other hand, attitudes to unemployment were perceived to be different compared with areas more accustomed to high levels of unemployment: *"there are so many unemployed up at home, in Sunderland, that it is almost the norm, it's accepted, that, and I think that in Swindon, it's an unusual thing not to be working".* It would seem that the poverty and feeling of marginalisation can, if anything, be reinforced in an outwardly prosperous locality such as Swindon:

> *"It's claustrophobic, everybody comes into town, and there is not that much to do within the town itself. So people find it quite boring.... It gets fairly depressing because there is sod all to do in the evenings, unless you have money to go out to the pub ... there isn't a community feel. A lot of people in the street you will smile at, and don't get any response back, and others have said this too.... I still think it gets down to the growth of the place and how many new people are coming in."*

Also of considerable significance in terms of social and community structure is the tendency for a significant proportion of higher grade professional, technical and particularly managerial staff who work in Swindon, to live outside of the town itself, in the smaller towns and villages or further afield in Bath and Bristol, towards Oxford or down the M4 Corridor towards Newbury and Reading. As described in Chapter Five, this possibility has been very explicitly part of the attractiveness of Swindon as a location for major employers and their senior staff. Economic development policy has itself stressed the attractions of areas surrounding Swindon in promoting the town to potential inwards investors. The result is that while these more senior and generally better paid staff work in Swindon, their life, in terms of home, community and social networks lies elsewhere.

In this sense, therefore, there is a section of the community and social structure of the town itself which, if not actually missing, is significantly smaller than it would otherwise be. Swindon itself is in a sense a more working class town in terms of who lives in it than would appear from its employment structure. In basic economic terms, the purchasing power of these higher grade groups is to an extent lost to the town. Also missing is the impact of their particular demands and the support they might generate for different forms of leisure and cultural activities. Many of the larger employers do have very conscious strategies of community involvement and support for local initiatives. The broader, everyday, potential contribution of the large numbers of their higher grade employees who live outside of the town to the social and civic life of the town is, however, lost. As a prominent community leader observed:

> *"This is another sort of feature of the place. I always ask chief executives where they live because the more important you are, the further away you live ... but you know, a lot of people, a lot of people live in different places. They travel, they commute long distances, I mean it's said, isn't it, you know, that one of the attractions of Swindon is it's very easy to get out of. That's one of the sort of jokes that people make about this place. But it's certainly true that one of the reasons that a lot of headquarters have relocated here is that people can work here and live in Gloucestershire, Cotswolds, Salisbury...."*

A resident of Highworth, three miles beyond the edge of the town, interviewed in 1986 went to Swindon *"as little as possible.... I suppose one must bring class into this, which I didn't want to do. Highworth is a relatively well off area. From a marketing point of view most people are As, Bs, possibly C1s around here..."*, and a resident of Purton, three miles west of the town, commented: *"I don't have much to do with Swindon at all"*. The increasing dislocation between workplace and residence, and the increasing fragmentation of the social structure, a marked feature of modern living, is thus exaggerated in the case of Swindon.

This has been reinforced by patterns of urban development and economic growth. Campus-style developments favoured by many of the major employers have tended to fragment and to isolate sections of the workforce both geographically and socially. Social amenities and leisure facilities are often provided for employees at the workplace. In a sense, a new series of self-contained 'communities' or 'corporate villages' have been created, self-consciously so in a number of cases. From one day to the next, employees would neither want nor need to go into the town centre nor make use of district facilities locally. Those who commute in from the surrounding towns and villages relate primarily to their place of work with possibly little if any contact with Swindon as a place. The notion of cohesive communities working locally and relating primarily to urban villages and district centres, still true to some extent in the 1950s and 1960s, has been overtaken by more fragmented and complex patterns linking work and home. Additionally, these campus developments contain what might be considered some of the finest examples of architecture, landscaping and artwork in Swindon, but they are very much private spaces which will never be enjoyed by most of Swindon's residents or by visitors to the town. In this sense, the benefits of the town's transformation into a centre for national and global enterprises would appear not to have permeated much beyond the contributions such organisations make to the local economy.

Overall, however, as a place in which to live, work and bring up children, the town's housing, environment, community and leisure facilities have been widely praised. The area as a whole has benefited from low unemployment and an expanding range of job opportunities compared with much of the rest of the country. Those interviewed in 1986 typically described it as: *"the ideal place for the average family with a couple of kids"*, *"We've got an abundance of leisure facilities in Swindon, there are community centres and sporting paradises being thrown up all over."* Sports and leisure facilities were widely thought to be excellent, *"second to none"* even. Planned housing development, together with the integrated provision of community, leisure and retail provision, has not been without flaws, but would generally appear to have avoided many of the problems associated with other New Town style developments or large-scale private housing schemes elsewhere in the country – *"a new town without the new town blues"* as one resident put it. Retail provision was until recently considered to be barely adequate, with much criticism of the town centre:

> *"It's what I would class a utility town. It's just got the basics here, your normal Marks and Spencers, BHS, C&A. It's not big enough ... you would have to go to Bristol or Bath for anything special."*

The situation has clearly improved recently, however, with the expansion of retail parks, refurbishment of the town centre and the opening of the Great Western Designer Outlet Village. As suggested earlier, the scale and effectiveness of social and community provision may well have been a factor in the continued political support over several decades for an almost unbroken succession of Labour Councils committed to planned and managed growth and high quality social and community provision.

The town would therefore appear to have achieved much in terms of environment, social and community amenities and quality of life for the mass of the local population. At another level, the town was often seen as less than exciting. Managers and professionals, many of them as already noted, living beyond the urban areas itself, typically describe the town as: *"soul-less and lacking in social cachet"*, *"a cultural desert"*. Young people and younger single professionals report finding Swindon boring, with little to offer by way of entertainment or excitement. Apart from the many pubs, a legacy of an earlier male-dominated working class culture, evening entertainment is very limited, with Bath, Bristol or Oxford much more attractive options: *"there's not really much left in Swindon if you're not into sport"*.

Swindon found it relatively easy to sell itself to corporate investors interested primarily in economic advantage, including relocation potential, labour supply and communications. Housing, leisure provision and quality of life were major selling points in attracting corporate investors seeking to relocate employees to the town and convincing them that the town could readily provide a local workforce adequate for their future needs. It has suffered, however, from something of an image problem. Much to the annoyance of many locally, it has been the butt of jibes bracketing it with the joke-places such as Neasden, Slough and Scunthorpe. d'Ancona recently summed up this widespread perspective on the town:

> The humorous BBC television programme Room 101 – which identifies people, objects and places so awful and crass they must be consigned to oblivion – includes the town of Swindon in its opening sequence. There could be no better symbol of the general contempt in which this medium-sized Wiltshire town and its 174,000 citizens are held by those who do not live there (and some who do) as a joke town. Even in the 1930s, J.B. Priestley wrote wryly that it was a place 'where you can work but cannot really play'. Six decades later, the mere mention of its name is often enough to provoke laughter.

> 'Swindon slammed again' is a typical headline in
> the local press. (d'Ancona, 1996, p 8)

The *Silver Book* had set out a vision of high quality municipal
provision of facilities.   As well as plans for sports and leisure
facilities, this included the town centre itself, and a new civic
centre intended to: "provide a major focus for cultural activities
rivalled by few towns in England" (Swindon Borough Council et
al, 1968).   This was to include a new central library, art centre,
museum and art gallery and civic hall.   As noted earlier, much has
been achieved in terms of sports and leisure, including the
showpiece facilities of the Oasis and Link centres.   The grander
aspirations for the civic centre in particular, however, failed to
materialise.   The Wyvern Theatre seldom ventures beyond
pantomime and worthy repertory, and is contrasted unfavourably
with Bath, Bristol or Oxford: "*Well, there's the Wyvern Theatre,
but...*".   The new library and other elements of the grand plan
never got off the ground with the site of the proposed new civic
centre still a car park.   At one level, then, the vision of high
quality municipal provision has been at least partially realised but
failed to carry through to the grander showpiece elements
envisaged in the *Silver Book*. In part this reflects the more limited
growth of the town than had been anticipated. The capacity of the
town and its surrounding areas to support provision of cultural
facilities on any grand scale, particularly given competition from
neighbouring centres, was therefore limited.

It also reflected the priorities of the Labour-controlled Council
which tended to see community-based provision for the greater
mass of the local population as more important than grand civic
projects. The social structure referred to earlier is also a factor:

> "*When I talk to the business community ... most
> of the senior and top managers don't live in
> Swindon so their perspective ... people say it's a
> cultural desert – this is another expression that
> crops up in the papers all the time – and that
> really does quite annoy us.... There is a very strong
> infrastructure of arts and voluntary arts, amateur
> dramatics going on in the town.   So it is
> happening at that level – the fact that there isn't a
> royal concert hall or whatever else ... I don't think
> is the key thing....*"

In terms of image, culture and identity, there are clearly, as this quote indicates, different perspectives. Successive Labour-controlled Councils have, as suggested, been concerned with social and community facilities and quality of life for the great mass of the population. Despite radical shifts in the social and economic structure of the town this has been rooted in a conception of Swindon as still in many respects essentially working class in character. Or if it is not, then that at least is the image of Swindon which the more 'socialist' members of the Council might like to represent.

More recent newcomers, new and expanding social groups, managers and business leaders have been more critical of the town's broader image and identity. As noted in Chapter Four, there was increasing debate between the Council, business leaders and others around image and identity, visions for the future, and specific initiatives including higher education provision and formal city status. This has been driven in part by the Council's strategy of consolidation referred to in earlier chapters, a desire to take stock and to resist unbridled expansion and its concern over provision of local infrastructure and amenities. According to one local authority officer:

> "I think the reason why it [the town's image] becomes an issue though is because ... it's been economically so successful, there's still the potential for a lot of money to be made out of Swindon and it's that tension all the time between basically developers seeing potential and the Borough Council and others who've been here for some time, saying 'well hold on, this is where we live, this is not the place you make money out of and go away from'. And that's when this whole development and a sense of place and where do people live and everything else comes into it. I think there's a thought locally that we need to stop and draw breath and allow some time for this sense of place to emerge."

One is clearly entering into the realms of the subjective and speculative in talking about image and identity. The combination of 19th century industrial town and postwar 'New Town' is clearly, however, reflected in the social, cultural and physical structure of the town and has impacted at the level of identity and image. Its history is such that it lacks the symbols and endowments associated with high culture and the deep-rooted heritage of the historic towns and cities with which Wiltshire and the adjoining counties are exceptionally endowed. The latter is strongly associated with the church, pre-industrial commerce and trade and historic patterns of landed capital and large estates. These, in turn, are typically associated with the endowment of religious and educational establishments, historic buildings, culture and the arts and architecture which Swindon lacks.

The obvious exception, although essentially 19th century in origin, is clearly the rail engineering works itself. A recent newspaper article noted that Swindon had:

> Over 300 listed buildings ... either personally designed by Brunel, or from this workshop under his direct supervision, making the town the biggest treasury of his work anywhere.... (Maev Kennedy, 'Diary charts town Brunel built', *The Guardian*, 6 October 1995)

The Royal Commission on the Historic Monuments of England relocated its National Monuments Record from London to Brunel's former 'general offices' built in 1842 and has itself produced an authoritative account charting the architectural legacy of Swindon as a railway town (Cattell and Falconer, 1995). The original workers' housing of the 'railway village' and associated buildings have been conserved. They represent, along with a small railway museum, something of a showpiece. Until recently, however, following the closure and partial demolition of the engineering works itself, the town has been very low key in its presentation of railway heritage. It is again speculation, but right through to its final closure in 1986, the Labour-controlled Council remained committed to rail engineering as a source of employment and economic activity, firmly rooted in the manual working class origins of the town. This may have made it difficult to embrace and to capitalise on the notion of rail engineering as heritage and the stuff of museums with any degree of enthusiasm.

A decade later much had changed. The setting up of the Royal Commission on the Historic Monuments of England in perhaps the grandest of the 19th century buildings on the site itself did much to raise the profile of the architectural legacy of the town as a whole. Much of the rail works on the site as a whole, acquired for development by Tarmac Properties was, as noted, demolished. Many listed buildings, however, remained to be incorporated into future development. Ironically, as noted earlier, it was late 20th century-style 'leisure-shopping' in the form of the Great Western Designer Outlet Village, a successful and imaginative reuse of part of the remaining buildings, which opened up the rail engineering works both to the local population and to an increasingly regional catchment area. The extent to which the thousands of visitors will see beyond the pastiche of designer labels, up-market shop fronts and fast food outlets to the heritage beneath remains open to question. Together with a successful lottery bid in 1997 to support a major railway museum, however, the site as a whole had all the makings of a high profile visitor attraction based around railway and 19th century architectural heritage which would do much for the overall image of the town.

On the other hand, it may be that the town has undersold itself in other respects in terms of image and identity. Economic development and inwards investment has generated a major concentration of modernist and post-modern industrial and commercial architecture, including the outstanding Norman Foster-designed Renault building. Much of the residential development of urban villages from the early 1950s onwards are classic examples of their type, representing high quality urban design and layout. The more recent heritage in terms of architecture and urban design is thus of considerable significance and a potential asset to the town in terms of image and identity. Again, Swindon would rarely be thought of as a centre for the arts, but in fact has accumulated a significant civic collection:

> ... the Swindon Collection has added single (mostly) works by many other important artists, and the collection is still growing. You could even call it the Tate of the south-west, thanks to the Council's prudent decision in 1966 that buying art was a business best left to experts. Since then, Richard Morphet, Keeper of the British Collection at the Tate Gallery, has shaped Swindon's acquisitions policy.... There are occasional mutters from the locals, but the collection now has work by artists as different but highly regarded as Gillian Ayres, Maggi

> Hambling, Tom Phillips, Richard Hamilton and
> Stephen McKenna.... (Patricia Morison, 'Arts:
> the secret virtues of Swindon', *Financial Times*,
> 23 August 1991, p 11)

Few are aware of these wider cultural assets and attractions and
instead associate the town primarily with its historic connection to
the railway:

> An outsider like myself may wonder whether
> those new companies, British and foreign, who
> have transformed Swindon over the last decade,
> realise quite what an opportunity for enlightened
> patronage is sitting on the doorstep. Swindon
> should conjure up more than what I see its
> publicity people referring to as 'railwayana'....
> (Patricia Morison, 'Arts: the secret virtues of
> Swindon', *Financial Times*, 23 August 1991, p
> 11)

There is a danger, perhaps, of an overemphasis on 'heritage' and
railway history. The idea of 'Authentic' history is obviously a
hotly disputed notion. There is clearly, however, a danger of
pastiche and recreations of history which owe more to the theme
park than to the real lives of previous generations. The lessons
which these previous generations have for subsequent times and
the sense of rootedness and identity which they can generate for
the present day population is in danger of being obscured. It has
also to be recognised that rail engineering, while it clearly has its
place, is now of little relevance to major sections of the local
population. Their roots and identity are many and various. The
common experience for many, however, is of Swindon as a rapidly
expanding economy, mushrooming housing developments and a
place increasingly tied in with and driven by national and global
economic forces. The majority of the local population, moreover,
is, in a sense, new to Swindon.

Conclusion

Economic change, population growth and the physical expansion
of Swindon have clearly been reflected in massive shifts in terms of

social and community structure, culture and ways of life. In some respects these mirror the sorts of changes seen more generally, at national level. The pace and scale of change locally, from a community tightly focused around large-scale, traditional manufacturing to a much more fragmented and diverse set of relationships between work, community and locality was, however, very striking.

Early on in particular, the Borough Council established very active strategies of social and community development and the provision of community facilities linked to the process of town expansion and physical development. The Council's role in this respect was seen as integral to the whole process of town expansion and development. This was reinforced in the vision set out in the *Silver Book* proposals and carried through in practice to the development of West Swindon in the 1970s and 1980s. More recently, the capacity of the Council to sustain a model of active community development as part of a strategy of ongoing expansion was increasingly called into question. This, in part, reflected the capacity and resources of the Council itself, as set out in the *A new vision* debate. Given the shifts in terms of social and community structure and ways of life described earlier, the extent to which the traditional, somewhat paternalistic, approach to social and community development remains relevant is itself questionable. The powers and duties inherited by the new Swindon Council, particularly in relation to education and social services, further complicate the issue. A clear vision for social policy and the role of community development, appropriate to the place Swindon has now become, has yet to emerge.

Social integration and the creation of balanced communities was a key objective of social policy in earlier decades. In overall terms, levels of unemployment, and indicators of deprivation and social exclusion locally compare quite favourably with the national picture. It is clear, however, that one of the challenges facing policy for the future is the extent to which there are quite marked levels of social exclusion, poverty and deprivation experienced by some sections of the local population. These are evident in the marked contrasts between residents in different parts of the town. They are reflected as well in the experience of those who are potentially more vulnerable to disadvantage – disabled people, black and other ethnic minority groups, the homeless. In what is an essentially successful local economy it is very clear that not everyone has benefited from that success.

Economic success, physical expansion, population growth and labour market change have also been accompanied by significant shifts in terms of community, identity and ways of life. The sense of community and identity of traditional working class Swindon, focused around the rail works, can easily be romanticised. Culture and ways of life have, however, changed quite dramatically over a relatively short period of time. From a time when those in the rail engineering works were referred to as being 'inside', Swindon rapidly became a town comprised predominantly of outsiders. Development of 'urban villages' attempted to pin down some sense of local identification. Overall, however, the physical and social structure of the town, its patterns of working life and everyday interactions are quite strongly characterised by fragmentation and lack of focus. The tendency for higher level managers and professionals to live outside of Swindon had reinforced this fragmentation. So, too, have the campus-style corporate head-quarters and business parks linked in to national and global corporate structure reinforced this – for most, Swindon is more a location than a place. This, in turn, has contributed to a perceived image problem for the town as a whole. There is a sense that the town functions very well for much of the population in everyday terms, as a place in which to live and work. At another level, however, it seems somehow less than the sum of its parts. This clearly presents a challenge to the idea of Swindon as a 'city for the 21st century'. It may be, however, that Swindon's accelerated economic and physical development does, in fact, demonstrate to us the nature of urban living for the next millennium.

eight

Discussion and conclusions

This final chapter returns to some of the major dimensions of change impacting on urban areas, including globalisation and economic restructuring raised in Chapter One. It then looks at the ways in which policy and action at the local level have combined with processes operating at regional, national and global scales to shape both the scale and form of development in Swindon. This provides the basis for a broader discussion of strategies for managing urban growth and development in the context of the changing planning system and the increasing pressures for growth on the fringes of the South East region driven by London's role as both national capital and global city.

Globalisation and local change

The pace and scale of restructuring evident in Swindon's economy and labour market since the early 1970s provides a starkly exaggerated example of the profound shifts which have trans-formed the make-up of the national economy as a whole and its place in the world economy. Swindon in the late 1960s still looked in many ways like a misplaced outlier of industrial England on the rural fringes of the South East. Manufacturing employment as a share of the total workforce only peaked in 1970, later than nationally. The next two decades, however, saw a major trans-formation in the town's economic structure, with far reaching implications in terms of occupational mix, culture and social change, and the physical structure of the town itself. Economic transformation also provided the basis for continued expansion and physical development of the town through to the end of the century.

The threat of collapse in the core industrial base of the town was an experience common to many localities which proved to be overdependent on, for example, coal, steel or heavy engineering. Many such localities were hit hard by shifts in market demand, technological change and new competitive forces. In the case of Swindon, heavily dependent on rail engineering, changes in terms of transport technology in particular and the switch from rail to road had major consequences. Technological change, competition from overseas producers in an increasingly globalised market place, and the imperative to achieve productivity gains impacted more generally on many of the town's key employers in manufacturing, mechanical and electrical engineering and vehicles.

The pace and scale of growth in service-based activities, however, was equally dramatic, again outpacing national growth rates. Warehousing, order-processing and distribution emerged as key activities locally. So too did financial services and other major office-based activities. As we have seen, a range of major multinationals including Intel, Burmah and later Motorola selected Swindon as a base for European and global headquarters and key administrative functions. Companies such as these represented major drivers of the local economy. Also important in economic and employment terms was the substantial growth of a wide range of secondary or support services. These include services for local business. They also include a wide range of health, education and other welfare services as well as retailing and other personal services for the growing local population – reflecting changing patterns of social expenditure, household consumption and consumer demand.

Equally important has been the rise of 'new wave' manufacturing, based on leading-edge technologies, new materials and new production processes. Much of this has been driven by international inwards investment into the local economy. Multinationals such as Motorola and Raychem, in the information technology and advanced materials sectors respectively, exemplify this. Honda is representative of a wave of reinvestment in the UK-based car industry, again based largely on overseas investment. Established manufacturing companies which survive from the wartime or early postwar economy, such as Plessey and Rover

Group, have undergone an equally radical transformation in terms of product markets, new investment, corporate structure and ownership – in the case of Rover, acquired by BMW, again reflecting overseas investment.

The fundamental transformation of the local economy which took place in the 1970s and 1980s is reflected in the now considerable diversity of its industrial structure. The long-term aim of reducing dependence on a narrow range of manufacturing and engineering employers has in this sense been achieved. This broadly based industrial structure would seem now to provide a strong and relatively stable economic basis for the locality as a whole. The town's economic and employment profile is now much more typical of the successful growth areas of the outer South East than the manufacturing island in the middle of rural Wiltshire, which it represented in earlier years. The local economy is also now tied in much more closely to national and international economic structures and subject, therefore, to boom and slump in line with economic forces operating at this wider scale.

As this suggests, there is a very real sense in which the 'local' economy is now increasingly integrated with and dependent on international corporate structures, finance and investment, product markets and labour markets. The particular combination of attributes offered by Swindon attracted an expanding volume of overseas direct investment throughout the 1970s and 1980s. Direct employment in the main internationally-owned enterprises established locally was around 16,000 in 1997. Local purchasing by these companies and their employees also supports significant additional employment locally. In terms of markets, while the domestic UK market is important, the larger internationally-owned companies are closely tied into the European or wider international markets. This, on the one hand, reduces dependence on narrow domestic UK market demand but, on the other, means that a significant segment of the local economy is now firmly tied in to European and international economic forces.

Overseas ownership also means, by definition, that the local economy and local employment are increasingly dependent on corporate decision making and investment decisions by managers divorced from the locality itself. The dangers of so-called 'branch plant' economies being vulnerable to outside decision making that may bear little relationship to local circumstances have often been raised at national and local levels. There have clearly been cases where this has been an issue, particularly perhaps historically with overseas investment establishing basic manufacturing in the peripheral regions attracted by financial inducements and cheap labour – although the scale and durability, for example, of Japanese and US investment in Scotland and South Wales provides more positive evidence in this respect.

A significant segment of the Swindon economy and employment locally is now subject, directly or indirectly, to overseas control and decision making in the last instance. The evidence in terms of the specific activities located locally, and the logic for their being located in the UK and in Swindon itself suggests, however, that this represents relatively stable, long-term investment. Overseas firms investing locally have generally been in sectors characterised by long-term growth. Swindon has, moreover, tended to attract relatively high order functions rather than simply basic assembly or manufacture where costs of labour and capital investment in plant and machinery tend to dominate locational decisions.

Swindon is not generally, therefore, in competition with more peripheral parts of the country including South Wales and Scotland, able to offer cheaper labour and subsidised investment. Its niche in terms of inwards investment is therefore somewhat different from such areas. As a location it is differentiated quite sharply from those places which have attracted inwards investment into large-scale manufacturing and assembly work, typically in the electronics sector. In terms of geographical distance it is relatively close, for example, to South Wales. In economic and corporate space it is in many respects worlds away. The particular combination of factors and cost structures offered by South Wales compared with Swindon is such that companies such as Sony and most recently Lucky Goldstar investing in large-scale manufacture and assembly work would not see Swindon as a possible location. Swindon cannot compete with South Wales on the basis of labour cost, land values and public sector subsidies.

The reverse is equally true of those employers which have selected Swindon as a location – South Wales has not generally been able to compete with Swindon in terms of access and communications and attractiveness to key technical, professional and managerial groups. The contrast is particularly sharply defined in relation to international inwards investment but it would tend to apply more generally to companies which have selected Swindon as a location. It emphasises as well the extent to which Swindon is essentially an integral part of the economy of the prosperous south of England and the axial growth corridor extending along the M4 from London and Heathrow in terms of labour markets, communications and corporate networks. In this sense it is a satellite economy linked to the functioning of London as both national capital and global city and linked in via London and Heathrow to the global economy and global structures. More generally, corporate strategies will clearly affect investment decisions and employment whatever the structure or geography of ultimate ownership and decision-making structures. Truly 'local' ownership of companies operating locally in Swindon is, as elsewhere, essentially limited to the small business sector. Given this, it is not clear that UK corporations with their headquarters outside of Swindon would be in any way more or less committed to continued investment locally than would those with headquarters overseas.

The increasing internationalisation of the local economy has, however, introduced a significant shift in work organisation and practices (see below). The effect has been to transform work cultures locally and the experience of work for many local employees compared with earlier periods is now markedly different. These changes have impacted in turn on more traditional, established employers such as Rover Group, in part through their direct involvement with Honda. There is also now a small but influential cadre of managers, senior technical and professional staff working locally who have been transferred in by overseas-owned companies. In terms of labour markets as well, such companies have tended to recruit in the international labour market to a greater extent than many UK-owned enterprises. Having said that, the influence locally of this stratum of overseas nationals has generally been limited beyond the boundaries of the workplace, given that many (like more senior staff generally) live outside of Swindon itself.

As outlined in Chapter Two, it has been argued that successful industrial regions are increasingly dominated by more flexible production systems. These, it is argued, are characterised by small batch rather than mass production, by multiskilled workers operating in looser and flatter organisational structures and by localised networks of interdependent producers. In the case of

Swindon, dominant production systems and forms of work organisation have undoubtedly been transformed in a very major way since the early postwar period. This has reflected both technological change as well as shifts in terms of industrial structure locally. Traditional forms of work organisation in the manufacturing and engineering declined as these sectors shrank. Work organisation and practices in those companies which survive have generally been transformed, while inwards investment has been a major source of innovation in this respect. Honda have introduced Japanese forms of work culture and organisation adapted to the UK context. There has also, for example, been major investment and technological innovation together with innovation in terms of work culture and organisation in Rover Group – influenced in part by its collaboration with Honda. US-owned companies such as Raychem and Motorola have, again, brought major shifts in terms of management practice, work culture and employee relations.

Various forms of flexible production systems including small batch production are evident in a range of enterprises and industrial sectors. On the other hand, the expansion of order processing and distribution and of office-based activities has generated major growth in unskilled manual labour and low-grade clerical work in large service sector organisations. Routinised and tightly managed in the interests of efficiency these 'clerical factories' are in some ways closer to the 'Fordist' mass production traditionally associated with the manufacturing sector.

Changes in work organisation and work practices have also impacted on employment practices. Task flexibility, multiskilling and single status employment are evident locally as elsewhere, with examples in the vehicles and electronics sectors. Employers within Swindon have also, however, developed an expanding repertoire of approaches to matching labour input to need across a range of service sector industries including order-processing and distribution and financial services. This reflects the fluctuating nature of demand for labour in a number of such sectors, in part seasonal. Temporary workers have been used as a 'flexible fringe' to cope with such fluctuations – and also represent a pool of tried and tested workers from among whom permanent staff can be recruited as needed. New employment practices have also emerged in response to increasingly competitive labour markets in periods of economic boom with employers, for example, designing new forms of shift system, different forms of 'part-time' work and working hours contracts to tap in to new sources of labour. With a range of employers competing against each other for essentially the same types of labour, these new forms of employment and labour market flexibility have become a systemic feature of the local labour market as a whole.

In a broader sense, there is little evidence of the emergence of flexible production systems, at the local or subregional level. There is little evidence of interlinked networks of local producers or the development of an integrated regional production complex of the type seen as underpinning the growth of dynamic new industrial districts in mainland Europe, North America or parts of the UK, including the M11 and the M4 Corridor itself. Major companies operating in Swindon tend, if anything, to be relatively autonomous and self-contained with respect to each other and to the local economy more generally. There is some local purchasing of business services and support functions although much of this is sourced regionally or nationally. There appears, however, to be little in the way of mutual interdependence in the form of production linkages among local producers, or much in the way of local subcontracting. Honda's network of approved sub-contractors, for example, is essentially national, the handful of local examples being more the exception than the norm. The same is true of other manufacturers such as Motorola or GEC-Plessey. Linkages and networks tend to extend outside of the local area, with internal corporate networks of major importance for many local employers. The local economy as such is characterised by fragmentation and atomisation rather than by networking, integration or collaborative links. In a sense the local economy represents a coincidence of enterprises with common preferences for the particular bundle of attributes offered by Swindon as a location, rather than an economic structure with any great degree of integration or internal coherence at the local or subregional level. This reinforces the argument that it is essentially a satellite to the global economic structures and to London as national capital and global city. It is in many ways, therefore, a counter example to the idea of closely integrated, densely networked, regional production systems as the increasingly dominant models of the geography of production, in recent years.

Local policy and the management of change

The commitment and very prominent role of the local authority in the whole process of Swindon's growth clearly poses the question of the contribution of the Borough Council itself to the town's growth and development, and the extent to which it was able to shape and control the scale and form which this took. The key role of the local authority in the early phases of town expansion in the immediate postwar period is apparent. Commentators then and now point to the key role of the then town clerk, David Murray John, in terms of his vision and his abilities to negotiate on Swindon's behalf.

The political context locally was, however, crucial. There was a high degree of political consensus in favour of expansion and a general level of support for this beyond the Council, including the more prominent trades unions, local business interests and major local employers. This seems to have been rooted in the particular social and political culture focused historically around the rail works. It also seems to have been reinforced by a common per-ception of the threat to local interests generally represented by overdependence on rail engineering and the need for this to be addressed. This broad-based coalition of interests therefore provided the basis for consensual policy making and imple-mentation by a relatively small group of officers and elected members. They had the expertise, capacity – and political support – to negotiate successfully with landowners, the County Council, central government and other relevant interests in order to drive the expansion process forward in the early days of formal town expansion in the 1950s and early 1960s.

This same set of interests also provided the basis for the second major phase of expansion as set out in the *Silver Book* with plans originally for a city of a quarter of million by the mid-1980s. Officers and members of the Borough Council were very actively involved in securing the town's further expansion in the context of the government's strategic planning framework for managing growth pressures in the metropolitan area and the South East region. As noted in Chapter Two, Swindon was not initially identified by central government planners as a focus for expansion. It was the town's enthusiasm compared with opposition to new development elsewhere in Wiltshire, and its track record of managing planned expansion which clearly shifted the policy agenda. This provided the basis for the expansion of the whole of West Swindon and in effect the northern expansion. It also survived the change in political control in 1968 when the Conservatives held power in what was a critical period for the relaunching plans for expansion.

From the immediate postwar period onwards, the Borough Council, actively committed to growth, was able to attract a number of very able officers. As Bassett and Harloe (1990) observed, development became not just another local authority function but lay at the very heart of almost everything the local authority did, dominating its organisational and financial structures, its politics and decision making. It was closer in many respects to a new town development corporation than a conventional model of local government. Also critical was the model of development pursued by the local authority, based on land acquisition as a basis both for controlling the development process and also for generating development gains, both of which could be ploughed back into the expansion process or used to finance community facilities. Initially developed in the context of the early phases of town expansion, the strategy was astutely rolled forwards as the basis for the local authority's prominent role in the western expansion. This model of development and expansion, steered by the local authority, and providing jobs, housing and community facilities at little direct cost to local taxpayers, provided the material basis for continuing support of this overall approach over many years.

Local commitment to growth, the resources and the expertise which the local authority was able to bring to bear on the expansion process were clearly a necessary component of growth both in the early phases of town expansion and for the western expansion. This contrasts with the somewhat analogous experience of towns such as Ashford and Banbury which also considered using the Town Development Act as a basis for planned expansion. In these cases, however, differences in historical development, in terms of social structure and of local political control led to resistance to growth (Harloe, 1975; Stacey et al, 1975; Brown et al, 1972). The contrast between Swindon's enthusiasm for growth was also, as already noted, in clear contrast with opposition to large-scale development in Berkshire, neighbouring authorities in Wiltshire and Oxfordshire and indeed many parts of the outer South East region. The local policy context was clearly an important and necessary factor.

Local commitment to growth was, however, by no means sufficient on its own to ensure Swindon's development and future expansion. The extent to which this could be realised has clearly also been dependent on central government policy and its willingness to support or at least acquiesce in the expansion process. As described earlier, the pace of town expansion was subject to government policy with regard to IDCs. Generally, however, central government has been willing to support Swindon's expansion, both in the earlier postwar period and again in the 1960s, committing itself to major growth and to a key role for Swindon in the expanding economy of the South East (Bassett and Harloe, 1990).

Also important in policy terms was the commitment of major infrastructure investment to the M4 Corridor, confirming Swindon's nodal location on the growth axis running from London to Bristol and South Wales. Hall in particular (1995, pp 29-30) has stressed the importance of such transportation corridors in the patterns of growth which emerged around major metropolitan areas in a range of international contexts in the 1980s. Government decisions to invest in the M4 motorway, to route it immediately to the south of Swindon and to plan for junctions both to the east and to the west of the town were crucial. This both confirmed Swindon's nodal position in the national communications network and also maximised the range of development opportunities locally with ready access to the motorway itself. Here again, the local authority specifically lobbied the Ministry of Transport at the time, to route the M4 alongside the town and this is considered locally to have influenced the Minister's final decision. British Rail's decision to invest in what was at the time the country's first high speed rail service further reinforced Swindon's location at the core of a major, high speed communications corridor and laid the foundation for major expansion in the 1970s and early 1980s.

The policy context and the framework for planned expansion at the local level combined with national level policy were therefore vital in establishing the basis for growth. Without this combination of policy and decision making at both local and national levels, Swindon would not have had the potential to expand and grow in the way it did. In terms of accounting for

Swindon's continued expansion and for the growth and transformation of its economy, however, location, communications,
access to Heathrow and London, the cost and availability of sites
and premises for industrial and office-based activities, the
availability of labour, the attractions of the surrounding rural
areas, villages and small towns together represented a very
powerful set of forces attracting in investment from within the UK
and overseas. It was this *combined with* the policy context set at
local and national levels which has clearly been crucial.

The specific role of the local authority in attracting inwards
investment as such is very hard to determine with any great degree
of certainty. As Bassett and Harloe (1990) argue, it was working
with a powerful tide in its favour. To distinguish the precise role
of the local authority in this overall flow of inwards investment is
therefore problematic. As discussed in Chapter Three, major
employers had generally found the local authority supportive and
accommodating. In a number of important cases it was the ability
of the local authority to offer sites of its own to potential investors
which was the critical factor. External factors and the general
state of the national and international economy have, however,
been crucial in determining the pace of growth and the capacity of
the local authority to realise its policies for growth.

Explicit marketing efforts were stepped up by the local
authority in the mid-1970s following concern over the scale of
local redundancies. Major companies in particular, however, have
relatively sophisticated search procedures and the type of companies likely to come to Swindon would be likely to have it on
their list anyway. Evidence as to the effectiveness of marketing
strategies generally and the extent to which particular places can
gain a competitive edge by such means is fairly inconclusive. One
can probably say that Swindon would at least appear to have
created a marketing profile approaching that of key rivals such as
Milton Keynes, Northampton or Peterborough. It would also
seem to have been effective in responding to inquiries and particularly in dealing with the negotiations required to secure
investors who showed serious interest. Judging by the rapid
decline in inwards investment and relocation nationally, the fall-
off in inquiries in the late 1980s would, however, seem to have
had more to do with the overall economic situation than with the
deliberate cutbacks by the Borough Council in external marketing.

This would suggest that the overall economic situation was much more important than marketing efforts as such.

By the mid-1980s it had, in any case, been recognised that the resources and capacity of the Borough Council to sustain continued expansion had been severely constrained. Its capacity to shape the development process and to manage this in what it saw as the best interests of local people, supporting infrastructure development, securing community facilities and reinvesting development gain had been severely reduced. Financial constraints imposed as central government progressively tightened the screw on local government were a key factor. The Borough Council had fought hard and with considerable ingenuity to maintain expenditure and investment as best it could, exploiting whatever loopholes it could find. By the end of the 1980s, however, it was running out of room for manoeuvre and government cuts and controls started to bite in a serious way. The particular impacts of revenue and capital expenditure controls fundamentally undermined the way in which the authority had funded the development process and town expansion.

At the same time, as *A new vision* noted, the local authority's own land stocks had been largely exhausted. This in itself reduced very significantly its capacity to drive and to shape future expansion. It was in some ways the victim of its own success in promoting town expansion. Private developers increasingly recognised the continuing growth potential of the town and started to take a controlling option or to buy up land well ahead of development on a speculative basis. This in itself drove up land values and priced the Borough Council out of the market. The success of the town in attracting industry and employment and the scale of population growth and population projections fuelled this process.

The private sector increasingly usurped the role previously played by the Borough Council, and increasingly called the tune in terms of the overall development process. The Council not only lacked the financial resources to compete; it also lacked any specific powers which might have advantaged it over the private sector and given it the capacity to secure land on a preferential basis in terms of price or by means of compulsory purchase. The Labour Government's 1976 Community Land Act, which might have provided such a mechanism, was abolished by the incoming Thatcher government before its somewhat dilute powers might have been exploited. So, while the financial constraints and controls imposed on local government in the 1980s clearly had major impacts locally, the development model which the local authority had very successfully pursued in the 1960s and 1970s, was in any case running into problems in the 1980s. It proved to be in effect a limited life project, a model which could not be sustained in the long run given the erosion by market forces of the Borough Council's capacity to play the lead role in the continuing process of expansion.

In this context, *A new vision*, as argued below, to some extent made a virtue out of necessity, facing up to the realities of the situation in which the Borough Council found itself by the mid-1980s. The ruling Labour Group sought as well to harness or reflect what it perceived to be popular concern as to the benefits of further expansion. This position was maintained into the 1990s under the banner of 'consolidation'. The Borough, along with the County Council, had initially held out against the northern sector development, conceding at the last moment in order to secure what it could in terms of what it saw as local benefits. As described in Chapters Five and Six, it later found itself, by an ironic twist of history, opposing the scale of development proposed by the County Council, which in the past had stood in the way of the Borough's own expansion plans on successive occasions. It has also sought to hold the line against the attempts of development interests to prise out additional land allocations for housing and employment uses through structure and local plan process and via planning appeals. With sharply reduced development pressures in the 1990s, the capacity of the Borough to hold out against renewed development pressures and to maintain its opposition to further expansion on any significant scale has yet to be properly put to the test.

The Borough Council had thus shifted its position quite radically in relation to growth and physical expansion by the late 1980s. The local business community and, to an extent, larger employers on the other hand voiced anxieties over consolidation, concerned in part over future labour supply and the capacity of the town to support future business growth. Property and development interests with a more direct stake in the continued expansion have been more strident in their opposition. The small Conservative Group on the Council, moreover, expressed overt support for the northern sector development and have favoured continued expansion of the town more generally. They also argued in the context of local government reorganisation for boundary extension to the west of the Borough. This, however, was strongly opposed by the Labour Group which could have expected little political support from this area. The broad coalition of interests which had supported planned growth and physical expansion in previous decades thus broke apart in the latter part of the 1980s, with significant fissures developing between different interest groups locally.

At the same time, the growth of new agencies, new forms of partnership and joint working have potentially shifted the terrain of power and influence. A broader set of interests including, in particular, the private sector, are now more centrally involved in policy discussion, if not actual policy formulation and implementation. This extends across a range of policy arenas including economic development in particular but also transport policy and specific initiatives including 'City for the 21st Century', Higher Education bids for funding under the KONVER programme for areas hit by defence cuts, or the Single Regeneration Budget. The Chamber of Commerce, which historically drew more support from local small business interests, has enhanced its profile and status more recently, incorporating many of the larger employers as 'corporate members'. Significantly in this respect, the managing director of Intel UK took on the role of chairman of the Chamber in 1997. Wiltshire TEC represents a new locus of power and influence with its board, as elsewhere, drawn predominantly from the private sector and chaired in 1997 by the managing director of Rover Group.

In part these new arrangements obviously reflect the political ideology of successive Conservative administrations at central government level. In part, however, they reflect broader trends nationally towards joint working reflected locally in the recognition on the part of the Borough Council, expressed in *A new vision*, of the need to work with and through others and to rely increasingly on influence and persuasion in pursuit of policy objectives. Employers and other local interests, for their part, have, to an extent, questioned the capacity of the Council to confront the challenges which the town now faces. There is a view in some quarters that elements at least of the Council remain tied to an outmoded view of Swindon, its economic and social make-up. There is perhaps a reluctance to acknowledge the extent to which the town, its labour markets and its major employers are now tied in to dynamic networks, investment flows and processes of change operating at national and international levels. This somewhat parochial, small town perspective, it is argued, has prevented the Council from developing a more forward-looking vision of how it might develop and change in the future. Some in the Labour Group would argue, in turn, that their aim is specifically that of consolidation and of seeking to preserve and extend the benefits enjoyed by the mass of the existing population of the town itself in the face of such processes of change. Others within the Labour Group, however, express a more pragmatic viewpoint in relation, for example, to future expansion or new forms of partnership and joint working around new initiatives.

Lack of real development pressure in recent years in particular has to some extent limited the questions that have been asked of these new structures and the contours of any change in the power structure remain, therefore, fairly ill-defined. Private sector interests would certainly seem to be more actively involved in policy debate at the local level even if their practical influence over policy outcomes remains to be seen. It is less clear that there has been any equivalent opening up of the policy process to voluntary and community sector interests. With the increasing involvement and influence of private sector business interests, structures of governance in the town and the dominant coalition of interests locally would seem to have moved closer to the sort of power structures more typical of US cities. Within the Borough Council itself, Labour consolidated its political control at the time the new unitary authority was set up. There was considerable turnover, however, at senior officer level including a new chief executive, which is likely to have implications for future developments. Major new service areas, including education and social services, were inherited from the County at this time, which again will have significant implications. The extent to which these changes, taken together, represent the basis for any real shift in the terrain of power and influence locally remains to be seen.

Planning and the management of urban growth

While the overall policy framework at local level since the mid-1980s and *A new vision for Thamesdown* has clearly been expressed in terms of consolidation, elected members and officers have been careful to avoid this being interpreted as constraint as such or as Swindon being 'closed for business'. Initially, the Council's overt stance was perhaps in practice closer to constraint. This was tempered somewhat with the onset of recession and concern that the potential at least for inwards investment should not be undermined. The Council has, however, resisted any commitment to further large-scale expansion beyond the development life-span of the northern sector. It has taken a clear stance in planning terms, in the context of both the Local Plan and the new Wiltshire Structure Plan which has brought it into conflict with development interests keen to see the opening up of what would be, in effect, an eastern sector. There has also been conflict with the County Council which has been seen as aiming to force additional development onto Swindon as a means of managing overall growth pressures at County level. This, in turn, reflected national growth projections which see the need to accommodate significantly higher levels of population and household growth at subregional and regional levels. The Borough Council's stance also generated some concern among local employers and the Chamber of Commerce, who saw continued expansion and the attainment of city-status as the key to meeting future labour needs, accommodating expansion, and upgrading the image and facilities of Swindon.

There are clearly concerns locally as to the impacts of continued expansion. These include the extent to which this would absorb resources which might otherwise have been used more directly for the benefit of the existing population – improving social and community facilities accessible to the older housing estates or continued upgrading of the town centre. With unitary status, moreover, responsibility for schools and infrastructure formerly provided by the County will fall directly on the new Swindon Borough Council. Previously, part of the tension between the Borough and County Council related to the implications for County Council spending on schools, education and other infrastructure generated by Swindon's ongoing expansion. With unitary status, these tensions were, in effect, internalised within the Borough itself. The expenditure implications of further expansion would in future fall directly on its own budgets in competition with other services and spending programmes.

There are also very real concerns as to how effectively the local authority could in future use what powers it still retains in terms of the planning system and the financial regime within which local government now operates. As noted earlier, its capacity to control the development process and to ensure the provision of social and community facilities has clearly diminished over the years. The extent to which land ownership gave the authority control over the development process and also generated major financial resources in the form of development gain is now, largely, history.

Policy in the last decade or so, informed by *A new vision*, can perhaps be seen as a largely pragmatic response to the circumstances in which the local authority found itself by the mid-1980s rather than a coherent strategy or guiding vision for the future of Swindon. It is certainly very different from that set out in detail in the *Silver Book*. Politically, as well, this period has seen something of a pragmatic appeal to what have been seen as the 'NIMBY' instincts of the local population opposed to further development – appealing to those already living in the town, rather than attracting in yet more new employers and further waves of in-migration at the cost of increased congestion and the disappearance of yet more green fields.

It is not clear, however, how effective consolidation might be, either as a practical strategy, or indeed as a political strategy for the incumbent Labour Council. There was a modest degree of protest from localised community interests at the time of the northern expansion. Public consultation carried out by the Borough Council convinced it that there was a degree of support for the type of proposals set out in *A new vision*. Traffic congestion has certainly started to become an issue locally. The local paper itself took a populist, anti-growth stance, campaigning to save the 'front garden'. The effectiveness of officially endorsed NIMBYism remains, however, unproven. It has been suggested in some quarters that the Labour Group is more concerned with the potential impact of new development and possibly boundary extension on the overall political profile of the town than with the issue of expansion itself. On the other hand, earlier phases of expansion do not appear to have undermined Labour support and may even have reinforced it in some respects, so if this is the case then there would be little basis for the Labour Group's concerns.

Nor is it clear how far a strategy of consolidation and resistance to further expansion could be sustained in the face of external pressures for growth. The decade following *A new vision* saw economic growth falling away, unemployment rising sharply and a sustained slump in the housing market. Recovery in the late 1980s was short-lived and turned rapidly again into recession. Development pressures along the M4 Corridor, relocation flows and potential inwards investment fell away sharply. So, too, did household migration and demand more generally in the local housing market, particularly for new development. The pace of new housebuilding locally both in the final phases of West Swindon and in the northern sector, was very slow to get off the ground. Population growth fell away rapidly in the 1990s. Reduced demand for new employment land was accommodated within existing estates and planned allocations – much as the Borough Council had in fact envisaged in debates over planning policy. The one major local relocation within the town, Motorola, was accommodated on local authority-owned land in the northern sector. There is a sense, therefore, in which the capacity of local policy in the post-*A new vision* decade to resist pressures for growth has yet to be put to the test.

There is, however, every reason to expect that sustained economic recovery will be reflected in renewed growth pressure along the M4 Corridor in terms both of employment and household migration. Much of this pressure is effectively driven by processes operating at national and indeed global scales. Renewed outward pressure from London and the wider metropolitan area increasingly reflects the capital's role and status as a global city, driven by international and global financial, economic and social processes of change. This is, in turn, increasingly reflected in the rippling-out of development pressures beyond the outer metropolitan area, along the major growth corridors. As Hall (1995) has observed, patterns of decentralisation around global cities, including London, have taken three main forms in particular: manufacturing, warehousing and distribution attracted to cheaper land, motorway access and the availability of semi-skilled and unskilled labour; research and development, high technology and higher order functions drawn to high amenity attractive environments; and office-based and information processing functions drawn to lower office costs and the availability of clerical labour. Swindon, together with the surrounding rural area, villages and small towns, has been able to offer all three of these, together with fast road and rail links with London and access to the world's busiest international airport. The potential for corporate relocation and inwards investment beyond the outer metropolitan area is likely, therefore, to escalate rapidly, with the next economic upswing. So too is the revival of the housing market and renewed demand for housing development driven by a combination of economic and demographic factors including, in particular, migration, but also increased rates of new household formation.

This has already been anticipated in the debate around the forecast need to house an additional 4.4 million households by the year 2016. The key issue relevant to the case of Swindon is how regional shares of this total are to be accommodated in high growth areas like the South East and South West. This is particularly so given the shortage in the M4 Corridor and the South West region more generally of previously developed 'brown field' sites which it was hoped, in line with environmental agendas, would absorb a major share of anticipated growth nationally. This means greater pressure in the South West for new green field housing development. The need to balance housing development and therefore labour supply on the one hand, with economic development and employment opportunities on the other, moreover, places a premium on those localities with the potential successfully to secure and manage integrated development along these lines.

One option for the Borough Council is to attempt to maintain consolidation in the longer term, resisting any further large-scale development. It would need to be able to maintain its stance in the context of the formal planning process including both the new Structure Plan and subsequent Local Plan. It would also then need to be able to hold the line against opportunistic appeals against refusal of planning permission. In this sense it would be reliant both on the planning inquiry process and, subsequently, on the planning appeal system under the Secretary of State for the Environment of the day. It may well be that considerable pressure would be brought on the new unitary local authority to plan to accommodate significantly greater numbers of households. This might also be reflected in turn in pressures to realise the potential which Swindon would continue to offer for employment growth.

It is probably too early to try to anticipate the outcome of this set of forces as a whole. The outcome would depend to a large extent on how successfully Swindon was able to push development pressures onto local areas more willing to accommodate it or less able to resist. This process as a whole would be mediated through the regional and local planning system in, on the present record, a relatively fragmented and non-strategic fashion. If forced into or acquiescing to further expansion on any significant scale, the problems for Swindon would remain as before – that of ensuring adequate control over the development process, together with adequate provision of social and community facilities and services. Diversion of resources from other local priorities would remain an issue.

In overall planning terms, the process is unlikely to be very satisfactory at the local or regional level whether Swindon is able successfully to resist development or not. It reflects the problems of managing what is essentially a nationally driven growth process linked to by the continued expansion of London and the South East as a global city-region, generating strong growth pressures in surrounding areas. In particular, it reflects the problem of trying to manage this process by means of a loosely coupled system of regional planning on the one hand and a fragmented system of structure and local plans, lacking any real element of overall policy coordination at regional or national scales.

This is clearly far from being a market-led system. Most localities in the area up to and immediately beyond the outer metropolitan area are using the statutory planning framework quite effectively in order to resist development. On the other hand, it falls far short of a planning framework able to ensure coordinated development of the outer metropolitan area and beyond. The system as currently structured, lacks any coordinated planning mechanism of the sort represented by the combination of new and expanded towns in the 1950s and strategic planning at regional level of the 1960s. It also lacks effective mechanisms to allow those localities which might wish to accommodate growth – or be forced to do so – to do so effectively and efficiently in financial and planning terms. Certainly up to mid-1997 at least, the debate as to how the 4.4 million new households were to be accommodated had not addressed these issues effectively. Given this, it is difficult to see how towns such as Swindon might be persuaded, voluntarily at least, to contribute effectively to accommodating and managing the growth process.

This may be forced on it via the statutory planning process, in which case it would have to work within any externally imposed framework of expansion as effectively as it could. The new Local Plan following on from the Structure Plan currently under consideration would be a key document. This could be used to establish, in effect, a master plan for designated development areas. The authority would need to use statutory planning agreements to secure contributions from developers in terms of roads, infrastructure and other development costs as best it could. The development market might well be relatively buoyant, providing a favourable context within which to seek to secure gains to benefit the local community via the planning system.

With the local authority inheriting significant landholdings from the County Council when it became a unitary authority, the new Borough Council would itself potentially stand to benefit from development. Given the nature and location of much of this land in the so-called 'front-garden', this would not be uncontroversial either within the Council or locally. With renewed pressure for development, the Council might well, however, see some benefit, albeit reluctantly, in its own direct involvement both for financial reasons but also in terms of the control which direct ownership would give over the development process. There would also be the possibility of ploughing back development gain into infrastructure, social and community provision for the benefit of local residents more generally. Securing permission to apply capital receipts freely for this purpose, within the context of national legislation controlling local government finance, would be essential. While by no means official policy, there were at least some officers of the Council and some senior politicians who were personally of the opinion that development of part at least of the inherited landholdings was likely at some point. There was also some feeling that development to the east of the town was likely to materialise at some point in the future.

Under this scenario, financial receipts from disposal of the Council's own landholdings might be used to secure an element of control in other areas where the local authority does not have any significant interest by virtue of land ownership. The concept of strategic purchase of limited parcels of land, as with the use of 'performance strips' as used in the northern expansion, might

again be used to back up planning agreements under the statutory
planning framework and to give the authority a greater degree of
leverage in development partnerships.

The case of Swindon can be used more generally, to explore
issues raised by the 1996 Housing Green Paper and the debate as
to how projected household growth might be accommodated.
Discussion following pressures for additional land supply in the
1980s, particularly in the South East, led to proposals for new
private sector-led settlements. Proposals emerged for a series of
what were, in effect, free-standing New Towns in the London green
belt and beyond. Initial proposals, led by a consortium of volume
housebuilders, were promoted at that time on the basis that they
provided a way of meeting the need for new housing land in a
limited number of locations, avoiding thereby, the political controversies arising from more piecemeal development. This would
also have generated sufficient development gain to pay for
substantial infrastructure and service requirements. These initiatives
stemmed, therefore, from private sector concerns over land supply
in a politically difficult local context within the South East, rather
than from any overall national strategy as had been the case with the
postwar New Towns. Numerous proposals for new settlements
came forward in the 1980s. All, however, ran into severe opposition
and were rejected by government.

Official policy in PPG3 *Housing* in 1992 suggested a role for
new settlements, but specified that they should be brought forward
through the local plan process and should command local support.
In practice local opposition in many parts of the country is likely
to make elected members at district or county level extremely wary
of supporting new settlement proposals in this way. Government
insistence on a bottom-up process cast doubt, therefore, on
whether the policy as currently set out had any real meaning.
There are also great uncertainties surrounding the implementation
of new settlements led and financed entirely by the private sector.
Local authorities generally are wary of the real commitment of
developers providing the full range of services and infrastructure
needed to achieve the goal of self-sufficiency. Swindon's specific
experience with the northern sector demonstrates in any case, the
extent to which private sector commitment to large-scale development over an extended time period is vulnerable to fluctuations in
the land and housing market. Without substantial public support

and funding there are grave doubts about the private sector's capacity to deliver.

Swindon's earlier experience would suggest that what is required at the national level is a more effective combination of financial and planning mechanisms if localities are to be persuaded to accept large-scale growth. One can speculate as to the form this might take. Financially, the local authority would need to be able both to secure a share of the returns on development and to reinvest this in social and community facilities. This might take the form of a share of the financial surplus generated by the development process. More specifically, it could involve taxation of development gain. The revenue generated would then be ploughed back into the development itself for the benefit of the local community. As with the 1963 Local Government Act, for example, local authorities could be also be granted the capacity to defer the cost of any borrowing used to finance the development process and to pay for this out of subsequent capital receipts.

In planning terms, local authorities should play a key role in providing master plans for large-scale development as was the case in Swindon with the western and northern expansions. Development based on effective partnership between the public and private sector, as has been the case with much of Swindon's past development, would be the expectation. The statutory status of such master plans would, however, need to be established. It is unlikely, however, that planning powers alone would provide an adequate basis for the local authority to control the development process in line with the overall master plan and to ensure provision of infrastructure and of social and community facilities. Planning agreements as set out in the current legislation are insufficient. These could be strengthened. Experience of successive phases of development in Swindon suggests, however, that an element at least of public land ownership is required to ensure adequate local authority control over the development process. This implies the need to provide the basis for local authorities to have the option to buy land for development purposes using, where necessary, powers of compulsory purchase.

National legislation would be required – although as the 1996 Housing Green Paper observes, the 1946 New Towns Act, the 1952 Town Development Act and the legislation providing for UDCs actually remain on the statute book and could, in theory, be resurrected. Given the appropriate legislative framework, individual local authorities would apply for designation as expanded settlements. In contrast with the new towns and, later, UDCs, development would, however, remain under the control of democratically elected local authorities. It would therefore be integrated with the overall policy process and service provision at local level. The scale of development, its coordination in line with national requirements, and general policy guidelines could be established, however, and agreed at regional and national level. This would allow for an element of planning and coordination at national level to secure, for example, the channelling of development pressures into growth corridors based on effective transport links, to generate economies of scale and spatial concentration, and to achieve goals in terms of environmentally sustainable development.

Swindon's experience in recent decades suggests that this would represent a feasible approach at regional and national levels. In terms of Swindon itself, given an effective policy framework along the lines outlined above, it would be possible to see the town as a key growth node within the London–South Wales growth corridor. It could provide an effective basis for planned expansion. It could provide the basis for overall control and coordination of the development process and effective provision of infrastructure, social and community facilities. It would also provide the basis for expansion to a scale which would support uprated cultural and community facilities and fully commensurate with city status.

As suggested above, environmental debates in the 1980s at international, national and local levels have clearly put issues of sustainability on the urban policy agenda. Central to such issues has been the debate over settlement patterns, transportation and energy consumption and pollution. As noted earlier, both Wiltshire County Council and Thamesdown Borough Council used the language of sustainability in an attempt to back their (conflicting) arguments on the appropriate pattern of future growth and housing development across the county. The County saw concentration of housing development in Swindon as the preferred option while the Borough favoured limiting economic growth in Swindon and a more multicentred pattern of future housing development. Added to this there was clearly growing concern through the 1990s in relation to traffic congestion in the town and the increase in road-based commuting in to the town.

The suspicion is, however, that both County and Borough Councils were, to an extent, using the language of sustainability from their different perspectives, simply to resist pressures for housing development in particular.

The wider debate offers no easy answers or resolution of the conflicting arguments. There have been strong arguments for greater containment of town and cities and high density concentration of development on grounds of travel minimisation, use of public transport and thus energy efficiency, minimising pollution and increasing quality of life (Newman and Kenworthy, 1989). Others have questioned the energy efficiency case for compact cities and towns (Gordon and Richardson, 1989). Reviewing the evidence, Breheny argues that even if the case for containment is proven, the forces driving counter-urbanisation and deconcentration from major urban areas and larger towns, are so strong that containment, in practice, stands little chance of success:

> Demographic trends will make resistance difficult because these areas now have strong built-in household growth ... as a result of earlier rounds of in-migration. If resistance is to some degree successful, it is likely to push development pressures to more rural areas still ... rather than back to the large urban areas. (Breheny, 1995, p 423)

Underlying economic trends and industrial relocation are likely to fuel further growth driving on the fringes of the South East. According to research reported in 1991:

> ... there is nothing in recent data to suggest that this underlying cycle will not be repeated some years hence, once regional output returns to previous levels and once slack in the London premises and labour markets has been taken up ... other things being equal, the same effects are likely to emerge, with those patterns discerned in the 60s and 70s as well as in the recent study, continuing to be characterise future movements.... Indeed, there may be increased rationale for that repetition.... Thus a new wave of business growth, with sufficient strength to catch up on

> ground lost in the recent recession, is likely to
> continue to push economic activity out of London
> and over the South East Regional Boundary, in
> Western and Northern directions. There is no
> intrinsic business logic which will cause such
> movement ... to seek more distant solutions.
> (Prism Research, 1991, p 131, quoted in Breheny,
> 1995, p 423)

Breheny concludes from a sustainability perspective that the
general consensus is in favour of the compact city in terms of
energy efficiency and pollution. Given, however, the strength of
decentralisation and counter-urbanisation, even where planning
regimes favour containment, he suggests that: "Perhaps an
acceptance of counter-urbanisation trends is required, but a more
specific channelling of such movements into environmentally
acceptable, but decentralised settlements." (Breheny, 1995, p 429).

On balance, then, the channelling of the forces of
deconcentration into large-scale decentralised settlements might be
appropriate at the regional scale around London and the South
East rather than attempting to maintain strategies of containment.
Such 'channelled containment' or 'managed counter-urbanisation'
might therefore favour the concentration of development into
urban centres such as Swindon, beyond the outer metropolitan
area which might form the core of the desired 'compact city'
model. Such a strategy would work with the overall tide of
counter-urbanisation. It would also, however, allow for an
element of concentration within this overall flow of deconcentration and decentralisation, rather than a more haphazard,
dispersed pattern of settlement. It would capitalise on the
potential of achieving such concentration offered by places such as
Swindon, Milton Keynes or Northampton. While such a strategy
might make sense in sustainability terms at national or regional
levels, it is clearly not a strategy, however, which would secure
much support locally, within Swindon itself, given the current
policy regime.

Finally, as discussed in Chapter Seven, Swindon may illustrate
something of the changing nature of cities and urban living as we
move into the next millennium. Economic success and physical
expansion have been accompanied by major shifts in terms of
community, identity and ways of life. Corporate structures,
economic processes and labour markets locally are increasingly

tied in with wider processes operating at regional, national and international levels. Places like Swindon on the fringes of the South East growth region are increasingly satellites of London as national capital and of the broader global economy. At the same time, as seen in Chapter Seven, images of economic excellence are challenged by significant and possibly increasing polarisation in terms of the economic and social benefits of success.

More generally, both the social and the physical structure of the urban area are quite strongly characterised by the fragmentation and lack of focus which seems, increasingly, to characterise urban life. This is seen in the campus-style corporate headquarters and business parks, heavily networked and tied in with corporate and economic structures at national and international levels, but representing relatively self-contained communities at the local level. The marked tendency for managers and professionals to live beyond the urban area reinforces this sense of fragmentation. Swindon's historical development, moreover, is such that there is little sense of a focus or core to the urban area. As suggested in Chapter 7, this has, perhaps, compounded the perceived image problem of the town as a whole. At one level, places like Swindon suggest something of the nature of urban living in the 21st century. In some respects it is a model for the 'compact city' seen as the ideal form for sustainable urban development. At the same time it demonstrates the fragmentation and lack of focus characteristic according to some accounts of 'post-modern' as opposed to traditional urban development. Locally, the campaign to secure formal city status for Swindon discussed earlier may be important in symbolic terms. It could do something at least in terms of civic pride. More important, however, will be the extent to which the inevitable pressures for growth and expansion can be harnessed effectively and imaginatively to secure the distribution of benefits from that growth together with the physical structures, amenities, infrastructure and image appropriate to what might be, in a very real sense, a 'city for the 21st century'.

Bibliography

Abercrombie, P. (1944) Greater London Plan, London: HMSO.

Ambrose, P. (1986) Whatever happened to planning?, London: Methuen.

Amin, A. (ed) (1994) Post-Fordism: a reader, Oxford: Blackwell.

Amin, A. and Thrift, N. (eds) (1994) Globalisation, institutions and regional development in Europe, Oxford: Oxford University Press.

Anderson, M., Bechhofer, F. and Gershuny, J. (eds) (1994) The social and political economy of the household, Oxford: Oxford University Press.

Atkins, D., Champion, T., Coombes, M., Dorling, D. and Woodward, R. (1996) Urban trends in England: latest evidence from the 1991 Census, London: DoE, HMSO.

Atkinson, J. (1986) Changing working patterns: how companies achieve flexibility to meet new needs, London: National Economic Development Office.

Ball, M. (1980) The Thamesdown area housing and land market: a background report, Unpublished working paper.

Ball, M. (1983) Housing policy and economic power, London: Methuen.

Barlow, Sir M. (1940) Royal Commission on the distribution of the industrial population, Report, London: HMSO (Cmd 6153).

Bassett, K. (1987) Economic development policy and political change in Swindon, Project Working Paper 9, ESRC Changing Urban and Regional System Initiative: Swindon Project (unpublished).

Bassett, K., Boddy, M., Harloe, M. and Lovering, J. (1989) 'Living in the fast lane: economic and social change in Swindon', in P. Cooke, (ed) Localities, London: Unwin Hyman.

Bassett, K. and Harloe, M. (1990) 'Swindon: the rise and decline of a growth coalition', in M. Harloe, C. Pickvance and J. Urry (eds) *Place, policy and politics*, London: Unwin Hyman.

Boddy, M. and Fudge, C. (eds) (1984) *Local socialism?*, London: Macmillan.

Boddy, M. (1987) *Social change and economic life: Swindon case-study*, Summary Report of Survey Findings, Unpublished Report, University of Bristol: SAUS.

Breheny, M. (1992) 'The contradictions of the compact city: a review of sustainable development and urban form', in M. Breheny (ed) *Sustainable development and urban form*, London: Pion, pp 138-59.

Breheny, M. (1993) 'Fragile regional planning', *The Planner*, January, pp 10-12.

Breheny, M. (1995) 'Counter urbanisation and sustainable urban forms', in J. Brotchie, M. Batty, E. Blakely, P. Hall and P. Newton (eds) *Cities in competition: productive and sustainable cities for the 21st century*, Melbourne: Longman Australia, pp 402-29.

Brindley, T., Rydin, Y. and Stoker, G. (1989) *Remaking planning: the politics of urban change in the Thatcher years*, London: Unwin Hyman.

Brown, T., Vile, M. and Whitemore, M. (1972) 'Community studies and decision taking', *British Journal of Political Science*, vol 1, no 2, pp 133-53.

Cambridge Econometrics (1996) *Regional economic prospects*, Cambridge: Cambridge Econometrics.

Castells, M. (1991) *The informational city: information technology, economic restructuring and the urban-regional process*, Oxford: Basil Blackwell.

Castells, M. (1996) *The rise of the network society*, Oxford: Blackwell.

Cattell, J. and Falconer, K. (1995) *Swindon: the legacy of a railway town*, London: HMSO.

Champion, T. (1996) 'Migration to, from and within the United Kingdom', Population Trends, 83, Spring, pp 5-16.

Cullingworth, J.B. (1961) 'Swindon social survey: a second report on the social implications of overspill', *Sociological Review*, (ns), no 9, pp 151-66.

d'Ancona, M. (1996) *The ties that bind us*, London: Social Market Foundation.

Department of the Environment (1994) *Regional Planning Guidance for the South West* (RPG10), London: HMSO.

Department of the Environment (1996) *Household growth: where shall I live?*

Department of the Environment (1997) Wiltshire County Structure Plan 2011, Examination in Public, Report of the Panel, Trowbridge, DoE.

Dickens, P. (1992) *Global shift: the internationalisation of economic activity*, 2nd edn, London: Paul Chapman Publishing.

Dillon, D., Weiss, S. and Hait, P. (1989) 'Supersuburbs', *Planning*, no 55, pp 7-21.

Financial Times (1984) 'Financial Times Survey: Swindon', Friday 9 November.

Financial Times (1990) 'Financial Times Survey: Swindon', Friday 25 May.

Forrest, R. and Murie, A. (1988) *Selling the welfare state: the privatisation of public housing*, London: Routledge

Forrest, R. and Gordon, D. (1993) *People and places: a census atlas of England*, Bristol: SAUS Publications.

Gallie, D., Marsh, C. and Vogler, C. (eds) (1994a) *Social change and the experience of unemployment*, Oxford: Oxford University Press.

Gallie, D., Penn, R. and Rose, M. (eds) (1994b) *Trade unionism in recession*, Oxford: Oxford University Press.

Garreau, J. (1991) *Edge city: life on the new frontier*, New York: Doubleday.

Gordon, D. and Forrest, R. (1995) *People and places 2: social and economic distinctions in England*, Bristol: SAUS Publications.

Gordon, P. and Richardson, H. (1989) 'Gasoline consumption and cities – a reply', *Journal of the American Planning Association*, vol 55, no 3, pp 342-45.

Grahber, G. (ed) (1993) *The embedded firm: on the socioeconomics of industrial networks*, London: Routledge.

Hall, P., Thomas, R., Gracey, H., and Drewett, R. (1973) *The containment of urban England*, London: George Allen and Unwin.

Hall, P., Breheny, M., McQuaid, R. and Hart, D. (1987) *Western sunrise: the genesis and growth of Britain's major high tech corridor*, Hemel Hempstead: Allen and Unwin.

Hall, P. (1995) 'Towards a general urban theory', in J. Brotchie, M. Batty, E. Blakely, P. Hall and P. Newton (eds) *Cities in competition: productive and sustainable cities for the 21st century*, Melbourne: Longman Australia, pp 3-31.

Hall, P., and Newton, P. (eds) *Cities in competition: productive and sustainable cities for the 21st century*, Melbourne, Longman Australia.

Harloe, M. (1975) *Swindon: a town in transition*, London: Heinemann.

Harloe M. (1987a) *Swindon: housing market and housing policies 1963-86, Project working paper 7*, Swindon: ESRC Changing Urban and Regional System (unpublished).

Harloe, M. (1987b) *Swindon: planning, land and property development 1963-86, Project Working Paper 8*, Swindon: ESRC Changing Urban and Regional System (unpublished).

Harloe, M. and Boddy, M. (1988) 'Living in the fast lane', *New Society*, 22 April, pp 15-17.

Harloe, M. and Boddy, M. (1988) 'Swindon: a suitable place for expansion', *Planning Practice and Research*, September, pp 17-20.

Haughton, G. and Hunter, C. (1994) *Sustainable cities*, London: Jessica Kingsley.

Haughton, G., Peck, J. and Strange, I. (1997) 'Turf wars: the battle for control over English local economic development', *Local Government Studies*, vol 23.1, pp 88-106.

Healey, P. (1992) 'The reorganization of state and market in planning', *Urban Studies*, no 29, pp 411-34.

Held, D. (1995) *Democracy and the global order*, Cambridge: Polity Press.

Hepworth, M., Green, A. and Gillespie, A. (1987) 'The spatial division of information labour in Great Britain', *Environment and Planning A*, vol 19, pp 793-806.

Hirst, P. and Thompson, G. (1996) *Globalisation in question*, Cambridge: Polity Press.

Hudson, K. (1967) *An awkward size for a town: a study of Swindon at the 100,000 mark*, London: David and Charles.

Jones Lang Wooton (1990) *50 centres: a guide to office and industrial rent trends in England and Wales*, London: Jones Lang Wooton.

Levin, P. (1976) *Government and the planning process*, London: Allen and Unwin.

Llewellyn-Davies, Weeks and Partners (1966) *A new city*, London: HMSO.

MacEwan Scott, A. (ed) (1994) *Gender segregation and social change*, Oxford: Oxford University Press.

Malpass, P. (1990) *Reshaping housing policy*, London: Routledge.

Merrett, S. (1979) *State housing in Britain*, London: Routledge.

Ministry of Housing and Local Government (1964) *The South-East study, 1961-81*, London: HMSO.

Newman, P. and Kenworthy, J. (1989) 'Gasoline consumption and cities a comparison of US cities with a global survey', *Journal of the American Planning Association*, vol 55, no 1, pp 24-37.

Ohmae, K. (1990) *The borderless world*, London, New York: Collins.

Peck, A.S. (1983) *The Great Western works at Swindon*, Poole: Oxford Publishing Company.

Penn, R., Rose, M. and Rubery, J. (eds) (1994) *Skill and occupational change*, Oxford: Oxford University Press.

Pollert, A. (1988) 'The flexible firm: fixation or fact', *Work, Employment and Society*, vol 2, no 3, pp 281-306.

Rubery, J. and Wilkinson, F. (eds) (1994) *Employer strategy and the labour market*, Oxford: Oxford University Press.

Salt, R. (1992) 'It started in Swindon', *Housing*, May, p 25.

Sayer, A. and Walker, R. (1992) *The new social economy: reworking the division of labour*, Oxford: Blackwell.

Schaffer, F. (1972) *The New Town story*, London: Paladin.

Scott, L. (1942) *Land utilisation in rural areas*.

Scott, A. (1988) 'Flexible production systems and regional development: the rise of new industrial spaces in North America and Western Europe', *International Journal of Urban and Regional Research*, no 12, pp 171-86.

South West Regional Planning Conference (1993).

Stacey, M. (1960) *Tradition and change: a study of Banbury*, London: Oxford University Press.

Stacey, M., Batsone, E., Bell, C. and Murcott, A. (1975) *Power persistence and change: a second study of Banbury*, London: Routledge and Kegan Paul.

Stallings, B. (ed) (1995) *Global change, regional response: the new international context of development*, Cambridge: Cambridge University Press.

Storper, M. and Scott, A. (1989) 'The geographical foundations and social regulation of flexible production complexes', in J. Wolch and M. Dear (eds) *The power of geography: how territory shapes social life*, Winchester, MA: Unwin Hyman.

Swindon Borough Council (1945a) *Planning for Swindon*, Swindon: SBC.

Swindon Borough Council (1945b) *Memorandum on the potentialities of Swindon for industrial development*, Swindon: SBC.

Swindon Borough Council, Wiltshire County Council and the Greater London Council (1968) *Swindon: a study for further expansion*, Swindon: SBC.

Swindon Borough Council (1976) *Budget handbook, 1976/77*, Swindon: SBC.

Thamesdown Borough Council (1983) *An area profile of Park North and Park South*, Swindon: TBC.

Thamesdown Borough Council (1986) *Budget Handbook, 1986/87*, Swindon: TBC.

Thamesdown Borough Council (1984) *A new vision for Thamesdown*, Swindon: TBC.

Thamesdown Borough Council (1991a) *Swindon town centre – retail strategy*, Swindon: TBC.

Thamesdown Borough Council (1991b) *A review of homelessness in Thamesdown – report of survey*, Swindon: TBC.

Thamesdown Borough Council (1993a) *Thamesdown homelessness survey, summary*, Swindon: TBC.

Thamesdown Borough Council (1993b) *Economic development plan, 1993/94*, Swindon: TBC.

Thamesdown Borough Council (1993c) *Annual Budget 1993/94 Commentary*, Swindon: TBC.

Thamesdown Borough Council (1994a) *Thamesdown local plan: deposit draft 1994*, Swindon: TBC.

Thamesdown Borough Council (1994b) *Thamesdown trends 1994b*, Swindon: TBC.

Thamesdown Borough Council (1995a) *Thamesdown local plan: deposit draft 1994*, Public Local Inquiry Statements of Thamesdown Borough Council, Statement C/4/TEM0/LMJ01: Overall Employment Allocations, Swindon: TBC.

Thamesdown Borough Council (1995b) *Thamesdown Local Plan: Deposit draft 1994*, Public Local Inquiry, Statements of Thamesdown Borough Council, Statement C/4/TEMRT/ LMJ00): Employment Land Round Table Topic Paper/ Statement, Swindon: TBC.

Thamesdown Borough Council (1995c) *Thamesdown Local Plan: Deposit draft 1994*, Public Local Inquiry, Statements of Thamesdown Borough Council, C/4/TEM2/MWT, Northern Development Area – Groundwell West Employment Land, Swindon: TBC.

Thamesdown Borough Council (1995d) *Thamesdown Local Plan: Deposit draft 1994*, Public Local Inquiry, Statements of Thamesdown Borough Council, C/4/TEMOM/LMJ31, Employment Omission and TEV55 Areas of Local Landscape

Importance: Land at Marston Farm, South Marston, Swindon: TBC.

Thamesdown Borough Council (1995e) *Thamesdown Local Plan: Deposit draft 1994, Public Local Inquiry*, Statements of Thamesdown Borough Council, C/4/OMTEMO/LMJ35, Employment Omission and TEV55: Land at Highworth Road ('Triangle site'), Swindon: TBC.

Thamesdown Borough Council (1995f) *Economic development plan, 1995/96*, Swindon: TBC.

Thamesdown Borough Council (1996) *Housing strategy statement*, Swindon: TBC.

Thornley, A. (1991) *Urban planning under Thatcherism: the challenge of the market*, London: Routledge.

Uthwatt, Lord Justice (1942) *Report of Expert Committee on Compensation and Betterment*, chaired by Lord Justice Uthwatt, Cmd 6386.

Vincent, L. and Gorbing, R. (1963) *Swindon, a plan for expansion*, Swindon: Swindon Borough Council.

Williams, A. (1915) *Life in a railway factory*, reprinted 1984, Gloucester: Alan Sutton.

Williams, P.(1992) 'Housing', in P. Cloke (ed) *Policy and change in Thatcher's Britain*, Oxford: Pergamon.

Wiltshire County Council (1981) *North East Wiltshire Structure Plan*, WCC.

Wiltshire County Council (1991) *Structure Plan alteration no 2*, Explanatory Memorandum, WCC.

Wiltshire County Council and Thamesdown Borough Council (1992) *Swindon transport study, final report*, WCC and TBC.

Wiltshire County Council (1996) *Wiltshire Structure Plan*, Draft, WCC.

Wiltshire County Council, Swindon Borough Council and Llewelyn-Davies Weeks, Forestier-Walker and Bor (1971) *Swindon: further expansion: report of joint technical team on selection of first area, Toothill*, WCC and SBC, January 1991.

Index

346 *City for the 21st century?*

production systems, 6-7, 309-
10, 311
infrastructure provision, 140-1
and private developers, 187,
189
in northern sector, 194, 195,
197, 198, 200-2, 203, 262-4
in-migration
to Thamesdown, 234 *see also*
overspill
to Wiltshire, *206*, 222-4, *226*
Intel, *62*, 133, *142*
expansion, 61, 63, 66, 73, 75,
77, 87
foreign ownership, 76, *78*, 80,
83, 306
site, 86, 110, 148-9, 158, 159
Intergraph, 73, *78*
internationalisation *see*
globalisation
inwards investment, 37, *55*, 176
international, 4, 306-8
and job growth, 73-5
ISIS Properties, 146

Jarman index (deprivation), 278,
279
Jones Lang Wooton, 85

Kembrey Park Estate, *142*, 145,
150
Kennedy, Maev, 300
Kennett District Council, 194
Kenworthy, J., 329
key workers, 24, 25, 231, 233,
235
Killingworth New Town, 255-6
King Homes, 240
King Sturge, 166
Konver Initiative, 123, 128

Labour Group
and consolidation, 44, 112
control of Council, 22, 36, 38-
9, 298-9

and 'new left', 113-14
in unitary authority, 48, 319
Labour Party, Swindon, 114
labour supply
and employment, 89-96
and flexibility, 7
land acquisition
by Council, 186, 220
postwar, 24, 26-7
problems, 40, 194
land stocks: depletion, 116
Lawns, 24, *185, 270, 271, 274*
poverty levels, *276, 277, 279*
social class, *269, 272*
leisure services *see* community/
leisure
Levin, P., 29
Lewis, John, 47
Liberal Democrats: on Council,
48
Liden Estate, 31, 184-5, *185,*
236, 242
'Limits to Growth' (conference),
44
Link Centre, 298
Lister Petter, 72
Llewelyn-Davies, Weeks and
Partners, 28-9, 32, 33, 35,
182, 185
local authority housing *see*
council housing
Local Government Act (1963),
327
Local Government Act (1992),
47, 214
Local Government (Financial
Provisions) Act (1963), 31
local government reorganisation,
47-9
location, strategic, 2, 29, 34-5,
81-3, 309, 314
on GWR network, 18-19
Londoners *see* overspill
Lovells (builders), 242
Lovering, John, vi-vii